BRITISH AND AMERICAN PLAYWRIGHTS
1750–1920

General editors: Martin Banham and Peter Thomson

**David Garrick and
George Colman the Elder**

OTHER VOLUMES IN THIS SERIES

To be published in 1982:

TOM ROBERTSON edited by William Tydeman
W.S. GILBERT edited by George Rowell
HENRY ARTHUR JONES edited by Russell Jackson

Further volumes will include:

THOMAS MORTON AND GEORGE COLMAN THE
  YOUNGER edited by Barry Sutcliffe
J.R. PLANCHÉ edited by Don Roy
A.W. PINERO edited by Martin Banham
DION BOUCICAULT edited by Peter Thomson
CHARLES READE edited by M. Hammet
TOM TAYLOR edited by Martin Banham
ARTHUR MURPHY AND SAMUEL FOOTE edited by George
  Taylor
H.J. BYRON edited by J.T.L. Davis
WILLIAM GILLETTE edited by Don Wilmeth and Rosemary Cullen
AUGUSTIN DALY edited by Don Wilmeth and Rosemary Cullen

Plays by

David Garrick and
George Colman the Elder

THE LYING VALET
THE JEALOUS WIFE
THE CLANDESTINE MARRIAGE
THE IRISH WIDOW
BON TON

Edited with an introduction and notes by
E.R. Wood

CAMBRIDGE UNIVERSITY PRESS

Cambridge
London   New York   New Rochelle
Melbourne   Sydney

Published by the Press Syndicate of the University of Cambridge
The Pitt Building, Trumpington Street, Cambridge CB2 1RP
32 East 57th Street, New York, NY 10022, USA
296 Beaconsfield Parade, Middle Park, Melbourne 3206, Australia

First published 1982

Printed in Great Britain at
the University Press, Cambridge

Library of Congress catalogue card number: 81-17079

British Library Cataloguing in publication data

Plays by David Garrick and George Colman the
Elder. – (British and American playwrights 1750–1920)
I. Garrick, David II. Colman, George
III. Wood, E.R. IV. Series
822'.5   PR2466

ISBN 0 521 23590 1 hard covers
ISBN 0 521 28057 5 paperback

GENERAL EDITORS' PREFACE

It is the primary aim of this series to make available to the British and American theatre plays which were effective in their own time, and which are good enough to be effective still.

Each volume assembles a number of plays, normally by a single author, scrupulously edited but sparingly annotated. Textual variations are recorded where individual editors have found them either essential or interesting. Introductions give an account of the theatrical context, and locate playwrights and plays within it. Biographical and chronological tables, brief bibliographies, and the complete listing of known plays provide information useful in itself, and which also offers guidance and incentive to further exploration.

Many of the plays published in this series have appeared in modern anthologies. Such representation is scarcely distinguishable from anonymity. We have relished the tendency of individual editors to make claims for the dramatists of whom they write. These are not plays best forgotten. They are plays best remembered. If the series is a contribution to theatre history, that is well and good. If it is a contribution to the continuing life of the theatre, that is well and better.

We have been lucky. The Cambridge University Press has supported the venture beyond our legitimate expectations. Acknowledgement is not, in this case, perfunctory. Sarah Stanton's contribution to the series has been substantial, and it has enhanced our work.

Martin Banham
Peter Thomson

CONTENTS

List of illustrations   page   ix

Introduction   1
Biographical record   30
THE LYING VALET by David Garrick   35
THE JEALOUS WIFE by George Colman the Elder   57
THE CLANDESTINE MARRIAGE by David Garrick and   113
George Colman the Elder
THE IRISH WIDOW by David Garrick   169
BON TON by David Garrick   193

The dramatic works of David Garrick   213
The dramatic works of George Colman the Elder   215
Bibliography   217

ILLUSTRATIONS

1   *The Modern Duel*, engraving by Charles Mosley. A scene in   *page*   3
Garrick's farce, *Miss in her Teens*, Covent Garden, 1747. The
players, L. to R. are Hannah Pritchard (Tag), David Garrick
(Fribble), Jane Hippesley (Miss Biddy) and Henry Woodward
(Captain Flash). Notice the spikes intended to protect actors
from audience, the stage boxes, the chandeliers and the back
scene
(Reproduced by permission of the Trustees of the British
Museum)

2   David Garrick and his wife (Eva Maria Veigel), oil painting by   34
William Hogarth, 1752
(Reproduced by gracious permission of Her Majesty the Queen)

3   George Colman, oil painting by Thomas Gainsborough   56
(Reproduced by permission of the Trustees of the National
Portrait Gallery)

4   *The Marriage Contract*, no. 1 in a series of six paintings by   112
William Hogarth of *Marriage à la Mode*. A satirical picture of
negotiations between a grim, gouty nobleman and a rich
merchant, while the young couple to be married appear
indifferent to each other. The situation and characters gave
Colman his first ideas for *The Clandestine Marriage*
(Reproduced by courtesy of The National Gallery)

5   *a* Wren's Drury Lane. Isometric reconstruction by Richard   168
Leacroft from *The Development of the English Playhouse*
(Reproduced by permission of Eyre Methuen Ltd and
Cornell University Press)
b Wren's drawing of a theatre, presumed to be Drury Lane,
1674
(Reproduced by permission of All Souls College, Oxford)

6   The stage at Covent Garden, 1763, during a riot which   192
interrupted a performance of Arne's *Ataxerxes*. Engraving
by L. Boitard. Notice stage boxes, stage doors, chandeliers
and the scene
(Reproduced by permission of the Trustees of the British
Museum)

7   Garrick reciting his Ode to Shakespeare, engraving by John   212
Lodge. This was a re-enacting on the stage at Drury Lane,
1769, of a celebration in the Shakespeare Jubilee at
Stratford upon Avon earlier in that year
(Reproduced by permission of the Trustees of the British
Museum)

INTRODUCTION

When David Garrick came to London in 1737 there were five theatres, Drury Lane, Covent Garden, Goodman's Fields, Lincoln's Inn and the Little Theatre in the Haymarket. In that year the new Licensing Act gave the Lord Chamberlain power to ban the performance of plays at any playhouse except the first two, the long-established Patent Houses. When Garrick made his London début four years later at Goodman's Fields, the audience who flocked to see him paid, by a legal subterfuge, to hear some music, and the plays were announced as an extra, free of charge. The theatre season ran its normal course, that is, to the end of April, without interference from the Lord Chamberlain; but the managements of Drury Lane and Covent Garden then complained that the law was being circumvented, and Goodman's Fields was closed down. During the next thirty years other theatres tried other evasions of the law. Samuel Foote, for example, invited the public to take tea with him. They paid for the refreshment but enjoyed the theatrical entertainment gratis. Later he obtained a licence to put on plays at the Haymarket for a season after the patent theatres closed for the summer. But with such exceptions, Drury Lane and Covent Garden had a firm monopoly.

When Goodman's Fields was suppressed, many of the players, including Garrick, were taken on at Drury Lane; others at Covent Garden. Although Garrick later acted at Covent Garden, it was at Drury Lane that he spent his greatest years, and it was for Drury Lane that all the plays in this book (except *The Lying Valet*, which first came to life in that historic season at Goodman's Fields) were written.

THE THEATRE

Drury Lane had been built by Wren in 1674 and remained unchanged in essentials until 1775, near the end of Garrick's reign, when the Adam brothers designed a new interior. Garrick had contrived to increase the seating capacity from a little over 1000 at the beginning of his career to twice that number at the end.

The typical eighteenth-century theatre was in three parts: the *scene*, behind the curtain and proscenium arch; the *platform* or fore-stage; and the *house* or auditorium. Behind the scene were dressing rooms, the green room, stores and offices. The scene was a raked area about forty feet wide and fifteen feet deep, with movable settings and a possible up-stage exit. The platform, in front of the curtain, was about the same size as the scene. This was where most of the acting took place, for this was the most brightly lighted part of the theatre. At either side of the platform were stage boxes, ordinarily occupied by the most exalted members of the audience, and the stage doors, the most usual means of entry and exit for the players.

The platform was separated from the house by a small orchestra pit and a row of

1

iron spikes to discourage spectators from invading the acting area. The house may be visualised as an elongated U shape, occupying about half the total length of the theatre building. The pit was an inclined floor rising to about the level of the stage at the back and furnished with rows of backless benches. It was bounded at the rear by a wooden palisade dividing it from a curved line of boxes, each of which could accommodate about twenty people. This line of boxes facing the stage was continued along each side of the house to join the stage boxes on the platform. There was another level of boxes above these, and at the rear a gallery, and an upper gallery usually occupied by servants and footmen who had secured seats below for their employers.

An important part of Garrick's achievement as manager was in the evolution of new possibilities in lighting and setting, influenced by what he had seen in theatres in Italy and France. When he first came to the theatre, stage and house were illuminated by a number of large rings or chandeliers, each containing a dozen candles, suspended over platform and scene. There was also a trough along the front of the platform containing lighted wicks floating in oil, and there were candles in sconces fixed down the sides of the stage boxes. Later there were 'ladders', vertical battens holding candles or oil lamps, fixed at the back of the wing flats at either side of the stage. From 1765 (when Garrick came back from his travels abroad) there was an immense increase in candle-power. Expenditure on candles at the end of Garrick's time was five times the figure at the beginning. Illumination was increased by reflectors on footlights and battens and there were more ladders to light the scene. The chandeliers over the platform had always been a nuisance to spectators in the galleries and upper boxes, glaring in their eyes, and Garrick reduced their numbers or shaded them, while increasing illumination from concealed sconces or battens.

Once the scene was well lighted, there was encouragement to improve the settings and make more use of the space as a playing area. Until then there had always been scenes painted on shutters sliding in grooves on the floor and above, or drop scenes on rollers, providing conventional settings such as a sea-coast, a rural prospect, a street scene, a room in a palace, a bedchamber. It had been possible to play a scene before the exterior of a house, which could then slide open or roll up to reveal an interior into which the actors could walk up stage. Where a scene ended with a general exit, the next scene could follow without any delay; critics complained of the tatty condition of scenery and the negligence of stage hands who left dull clouds from an outdoor scene still hanging in a lady's bedchamber for the next.

Now that the rear of the stage was more brightly lighted there was more need to brighten up the scenery and encouragement to develop its scope. In 1772 Garrick appointed a noted scene designer from Alsace, de Loutherberg, who made great advances. He was interested in new possibilities of lighting his sets, in varying colour and intensity of lights by reflectors and silk screens, and even some directional lighting from lamps on movable pivots. So he was able to produce imaginative effects such as Prospero's cave in atmospheric chiaroscuro. Much money was spent

1. *The Modern Duel*, engraving by Charles Mosley. A scene in Garrick's farce, *Miss in her Teens*, Covent Garden, 1747. The players, L. to R. are Hannah Pritchard (Tag), David Garrick (Fribble), Jane Hippesley (Miss Biddy) and Henry Woodward (Captain Flash). Notice the spikes intended to protect actors from audience, the stage boxes, the chandeliers and the back scene

on lights and scenery, and plays were advertised as having entirely new settings. All this stimulated the public demand for spectacle.

THE AUDIENCE

Readers of theatrical memoirs of the period may gather the impression that all London went to the theatre, from the king and the aristocracy, poets and politicians, lawyers and merchants, to prostitutes and servants (few artisans or labourers, whose working hours precluded theatre-going). Estimates suggest, however, that fewer than two per cent of the city population did so. This limited public had some sense of belonging to a community which included the players. Many of them were there long before the play began. Since the whole house was illuminated throughout the evening, it was easy to see one's friends and acquaintances before and during the play. Players on the stage would greet their friends in the audience, sometimes when their attention should have been on the play in progress.

Performances began at six, but the doors were open for at least an hour before. As there was no reserving of seats or queuing for orderly admission, there was sometimes violent and even dangerous jostling to get in and find a place. The gentry sent their servants to jostle for them and keep their places until they arrived.

Audiences were often boisterous and rowdy. From the upper gallery came a din of catcalls, animal noises, insults and badinage, and often a hail of orange peel and oranges or apples, and, on the worst occasions, bottles. On an evening in 1775 a young lady was injured by a hard lump of cheese weighing half a pound, flung from above, and a German visitor once complained that his hat was so saturated by a liquid which he did not identify that he had to have it cleaned next day at the hatter's. The uproar was not confined to the upper galleries: Boswell among the gentry once entertained the audience at Drury Lane by lowing like a cow.

Before the play opened the platform was swept clean of the rubbish that had been thrown on to it. When the curtain rose, the audience normally fell silent. 'All noise and bombardment ceases,' a German visitor reported, 'and one is bound to admire the quiet attentiveness of such an estimable folk.' The theatre-going public was interested in acting and susceptible to its spell.

But it was not always so! Garrick himself in his play *Lethe* gives a vivid impression of the reaction of the house to a beau asserting his right to a place on the scene or the platform:

> FINE GENTLEMAN: I dress in the evening and go behind the scenes at both playhouses, not, you may imagine, to be diverted with the play, but to intrigue and show myself. I stand upon the stage, talk loud and stare about, which confounds the actors and disturbs the audience; upon which the galleries, who hate the appearance of one of us, begin to hiss and cry 'Off, off!' while I, undaunted, stamp my foot, so – loll with my shoulder, thus, take snuff with my right hand, and smile scornfully – thus. This exasperates the savages, and

they attack with volleys of sucked oranges and half-eaten pippins.

AESOP: And you retire?

FINE GENTLEMAN: Without doubt, if I am sober; for oranges will stain silk, and an apple disfigure a feature.

Insulting the actors was a common recreation, and Tate Wilkinson (*Memoirs*, 1790) says that it came from different parts of the house, 'too often from those places of more fashionable resort'. There were many occasions when serious riot developed and the great Garrick himself was humiliated. One of the worst was in 1755, when he had engaged Noverre, a Swiss choreographer, to present his Chinese Festival. War with France was imminent, and an anti-French section of the audience, wrongly supposing Noverre and his company to be French, noisily expressed their disapproval on the first night, when the king was present. On subsequent nights interruptions grew into violence when the dancers came on. Thomas Davies (*Memoirs of the Life of David Garrick*, 1780) says that the upper-class elements wanted the show to go on and fought the plebeian objectors:

The contest between the boxes and other parts of the house was attended with great distress to the managers, for they knew not which party they could oblige with safety. At last after much mutual abuse and many violent blows and scuffles, the combatants fell upon that which could make no resistance, the materials before them. They demolished the scene, tore up the benches, broke the lustres and [chandeliers] , and did in a short time so much mischief to the inside of the theatre that it could scarce be repaired for several days . . . Mr Garrick thought his life was in danger from the ungovernable rage of the people, who threatened to demolish his house . . . The mob went so far as to break his windows.

Garrick was helpless and abject in face of rioters, but it is a relief to learn that a few days after this riot he stood up to an obstreperous audience with dignity and courage. He came on in the role of Archer (in Farquhar's *The Beaux' Stratagem*) to insults and demands for apology. He advanced to the front of the stage and after talking of the damage he had suffered, both to his property and his reputation, he declared that unless he was allowed to perform that night to the best of his ability, he would never appear on the stage again. The house listened in silence and then burst into universal applause.

Opposition from the public frustrated many of Garrick's attempts to reform stage conditions. It had long been customary to allow members of the audience — not merely beaux and idlers such as were satirised in *Lethe* — to sit or stand on the stage. On big occasions, such as a popular player's benefit night, as many as 200 might be seated on benches built up in a sort of amphitheatre behind the actors, in addition to the usual idlers crowding the side entrances and impeding the actors. Garrick tried to get rid of this nuisance without success until 1762, when he greatly increased the seating capacity of the house. He failed completely to withdraw the customary concessions to late-comers, whereby they were admitted at half-price after the third act of the main play.

His choice of plays and provision of programmes were often influenced by the taste of the public rather than his own. Pantomimes were much more popular than dramas, comedies than tragedies. Farcical afterpieces (which could be enjoyed by the half-price late-comers) were in great demand. A typical evening's programme would include a five-act play, a pantomime or half-length farce, and songs, dances or a pageant. Well-known plays of Shakespeare, much shortened and altered, and many old favourites of the Restoration and later, could be counted on to run for up to a dozen performances in a season. New plays were more of a risk.

During his twenty-nine years as manager of Drury Lane, Garrick gave the public what they wanted but he also widened their horizons. He brought back to the stage many long-neglected plays of Shakespeare and his contemporaries, and introduced 85 new main plays and 150 afterpieces. By one objective standard his achievement is indisputable: he made the theatre pay.

GARRICK AS ACTOR

All ages have had their great actors, but it is reasonable to wonder what we should have thought of them, and especially of their less exalted colleagues. Acting before Garrick's time was harshly described by Aaron Hill (in *The Prompter*, 1731):

> The puffed, round mouth, an empty, vagrant eye, a solemn silliness of strut, a swing-swang slowness in the motion of the arm, and a dry, dull, drawling voice that carries opium in its deadly monotony.

A critic writing in *The Champion* in October 1741 praises Garrick in *Richard III* for what he did not do, thus revealing something about the style of acting that Garrick's example was to reform. He did not 'whine, bellow and grumble'; his mien was 'neither strutting, mincing, stiff nor slouching'; he was attentive to whatever was spoken and never dropped his character when he had finished a speech by either 'looking contemptuously on an inferior performer, unnecessary spitting or suffering his eyes to wander through the whole circle of spectators'.

The new star made a great impression by his vigour, by the intensity of his varying expression and the power in his eyes, by breaking up his speeches with pauses, quickening and slowing of pace, and above all by using his imagination to become 'the very man'. An impression of the old and the new styles together in the same play is given by Richard Cumberland (*Memoirs*, 1807), who saw Garrick and Quin at Covent Garden in 1746:

> With very little variation of cadence, and in deep, full tones, accompanied by a sawing kind of motion which had more of the senate than the stage in it, [Quin] rolled out his heroics with an air of dignified indifference that seemed to disdain the plaudits bestowed upon him; when . . . Garrick . . . young and light, and alive in every muscle and every feature, [came] bounding on to the stage — heavens, what a transition! It seemed as if a whole century had been stepped over in the changing of a single scene.

Charles Macklin, intending to belittle the great actor who had once been his friend and ally, damned him for what was perhaps his greatest virtue — attack:

> Garrick huddled all passions into strut and quickness — bustle was his favourite — Archer, Ranger, Don John, Hamlet, Macbeth, Sir John Brute — all was bustle, bustle, bustle.

As it happens, we have the impressions of a German visitor who saw Garrick in two of these roles. From his account it is clear that bustle was not all: Garrick was infinitely variable.

The first is the drunken Sir John Brute in *The Provoked Wife* by Vanbrugh: after a description of his appearance, his wig awry, his stockings wrinkled, his garters hanging down, it continues:

> In this condition he enters the room where his wife is, and in answer to her anxious inquiries as to what is the matter with him, he, collecting his wits, answers: 'Wife, as well as a fish in the water'. He does not, however, move away from the doorpost, against which he leans as closely as if he wanted to rub his back. Then he again breaks out in coarse talk, and suddenly becomes so wise and merry in his cups that the whole audience bursts into a tumult of applause . . . The way in which with shut eyes, swimming head and pallid cheeks he quarrels with his wife, and uttering a sound where r and l are blended, now appears to abuse her, then to enunciate in thick tones moral precepts, to which he himself forms the most horrible contradiction; his manner, also, of moving his lips, so that one cannot tell whether he is chewing, tasting or speaking; all this as far exceeded my expectations as anything I have seen of the man. If you could but hear him articulate the word 'prerogative' — he never reaches the third syllable without two or three attempts.

The next is a scene in *The Beaux' Stratagem* by Farquhar:

> Garrick played Archer, a gentleman of quality who passes himself off for a servant, and Weston played Scrub, a real tapster at the wretched inn where the former is lodging . . . This scene should be witnessed by anyone who wishes to observe the power of contrast when it is brought out by perfect collaboration . . . Garrick throws himself into a chair with his usual ease of manner, places his right arm on the back of Weston's chair, and leans towards him for a confidential talk. His magnificent livery is thrown back, and coat and man form one line of perfect beauty. Weston sits, as is fitting, in the middle of his chair, though rather far forward, and with a hand on either knee, as motionless as a statue, with his eyes fixed on Garrick. If his face expresses anything, it is an assumption of dignity, at odds with a paralysing sense of the terrible contrast . . . While Garrick sits there at ease with an agreeable carelessness of demeanour, Weston attempts, with back stiff as a poker, to draw himself to the other's height. When Archer with an easy gesture crosses his legs, Scrub tries to do the same, not without some help from his hands, and with eyes all the time either gaping or making furtive comparisons. And when Archer begins to stroke his mag-

nificent silken calves, Weston tries to do the same with his miserable red woollen ones, but thinking better of it, pulls his green apron over them with an abjectness of demeanour arousing pity in every breast.[1]

A detail of Drury Lane history illustrates Garrick's versatility and generosity: on the occasion of the benefit of a young member of the company Garrick let him take over the role of Archer, while he himself played Scrub. The manager was never too grand to play servants, tapsters and yokels.

Although he became famous throughout Europe, Garrick always had jealous detractors and hostile critics at home. When he and Quin were in the same company at Covent Garden in 1746, they usually avoided being in the same plays. When they acted together, Garrick did not always outshine the older man. In *Henry IV* Quin as Falstaff was considered to be better than Garrick as Hotspur, and Garrick soon relinquished the part. He was a failure as Othello, and the butt of Quin's malicious wit. But on the whole the rivals respected each other and after Quin's retirement they were good friends. A more dangerous rival was Spranger Barry. When Garrick's Romeo at Drury Lane coincided with Barry's at Covent Garden, Barry's tall figure and romantic good looks were contrasted with Garrick's small stature (5 feet 4 inches) and expressive but less than handsome face. A woman said that if she had been Juliet she would have wanted Mr Garrick to climb up into her balcony, but she would have jumped down to Mr Barry. Yet such was Garrick's magnetism that in drawing full houses he outlasted Barry.

Apart from a few such rivalries, Garrick was so much the supreme star of England that other men in the company were overshadowed, and some of his admirers and pupils were criticised for imitating his style and speech. (This is hardly surprising, since he used to take beginners through their lines, telling them how each should be spoken.) The women were more free to develop their own genius, though much stimulated by acting with him. So there emerged a succession of outstanding actresses with whom he shared as equals the public's adulation: Peg Woffington, until they parted; Susannah Cibber until her health broke down; Hannah Pritchard and Kitty Clive until they retired. The bright stars of the next generation, Mrs Abington, Mrs Yates, Mrs Barry and Miss Pope, all tended to outshine the men in the company, except, of course, Garrick.

The general level of acting can hardly have approached what is expected of actors today. A play rarely settled down for a run of more than a dozen performances, and at a few hours' notice might be taken off because it was damned, or ill-attended, or because a principal performer was ill — or said she was. There can have been little rehearsal and direction such as we understand it.[2]

COLMAN AS MAN OF THE THEATRE

Colman's association with Drury Lane began as a member of Garrick's circle of friends and admirers, and it was as an amateur, earning his real living as a barrister, that he began writing plays. When Garrick set out in September 1763 for his prolonged continental tour, he left the theatre in the joint care of his partner James Lacy, his brother George, and his friend George Colman. Of the three, Colman was the best suited for choosing and adapting plays, recruiting and encouraging players, and promoting the business of the stage. But he had not yet abandoned the Law, and did not do so until his uncle the Earl of Bath died in 1764, leaving him a modest annuity instead of the fortune he had hoped for. He had always preferred the theatre: now he was free to choose. He needed to work seriously if the theatre was to be his profession. When Garrick returned in 1765 Colman may have felt a diminished role; and it is not surprising that he deserted Drury Lane when the opportunity arose in 1767 to buy a share in the Covent Garden patent. Garrick understood his motives, and was offended only because his friend had been secretive, and because he lured away some of the best Drury Lane actors.

Colman had stipulated to his colleagues that the organisation of plays and players should be in his hands, but he was soon involved in a bitter wrangle with two of his new partners, culminating in a lawsuit. They accused him of arrogating too much power to himself, of bad judgement of plays, of losing money; but he vindicated himself and the court found in his favour. He had set out to make Covent Garden a theatre for straight drama, but he had to modify his policy to suit the public taste for musical and spectacular entertainments. Yet he put on many full-length plays, a high proportion of them by Shakespeare, and several of his own plays, old and new. He early revived *The Jealous Wife* and when he produced *The Clandestine Marriage* his relations with Garrick were still so amicable that he was able to borrow two players from the rival company at Drury Lane. He gave Goldsmith his first hearing in the theatre, first with *The Good Natured Man* and later *She Stoops to Conquer*, both of which had first been offered to Garrick. Goldsmith, though a friend of both managers and a frequenter of the same clubs and coffee-houses, was despairing of ever seeing *She Stoops to Conquer* performed when he wrote to Colman, 'For God's sake take the play and let us make the best of it.' Colman took it, but gloomily, predicting failure; and he was not pleased when it proved a triumph. His judgement had erred — but so had Garrick's!

In the same year he suffered at the hands of a rioting mob a humiliation as deep as any of Garrick's. He had engaged Macklin to play Macbeth, but a faction hostile to this eminent actor refused to hear him. Macklin tried to appease the malcontents, but an apple hit him in the face and then everybody began to throw apples, and Macklin retreated. The mob demanded his dismissal, and insisted that Colman himself should announce it. The wretched manager was dragged on to the stage and abased himself to declare, 'It is our object always to please the public, and happiness to conform to their pleasure when we know what this pleasure is.'

Apart from such troubles, Covent Garden flourished in the seven years of his management, and in 1774 he sold his share at a handsome profit. He then busied himself as a writer and resumed relations with Garrick, writing new plays for Drury Lane.

In 1776 he bought from Samuel Foote his special licence, renewable annually,

for a summer season at the Haymarket, which had been the home of mixed entertainment, from opera to dancing dogs, until the Foote regime. Colman made of it
an important addition to London theatre, recruiting a lively company of players,
engaging new authors such as O'Keefe, Holcroft, Mrs Inchbald and his own son
George the Younger, and presenting many new plays of his own and adaptations of
Shakespeare, Jonson, Beaumont and Fletcher, Voltaire and Beaumarchais. Though
increasingly afflicted by gout, epilepsy, paralysis and eventual insanity, he worked
in the theatre until his son took it over in 1790. His career had amply justified his
choice of profession.

THE PLAYS OF GARRICK AND COLMAN

Neither of the authors claimed originality as a virtue of their plays: indeed, Colman
appeared unnecessarily eager to declare his sources as if needing their authority.
They both exploited well-tried theatrical situations and themes, and easily recog-
nisable comic types. Their plays are typical of their age, and among the best. Why,
then, have they been so long neglected?

Classical comedy is preoccupied with the follies and foibles of a stable society,
and some of these — cuckoldry, marriages of convenience, master—servant relations
— seem less relevant today. Others, such as snobbery, affectation, intolerance
between old and young, country simplicity set against city sophistication, still
persist though in changing guises. The theatre nowadays craves for newness — a
fresh, original viewpoint, a sharper bite, less ultimate reassurance — and the word
'traditional' has become a term of disparagement. Yet human folly is eternal, and
theatre audiences can enjoy recognising in the sillinesses of past ages their equiv-
alents in ours. And traditional stage situations can still make audiences laugh.

The survival of Sheridan seems to prove this. He cultivated the same ground, but
with richer invention and greater felicity than the predecessors from whom he
borrowed freely. He still holds the stage and all his plays are in print, some in
school editions, while Garrick's and Colman's have been more difficult to obtain.
The texts printed here are now available to be appraised and tried out as vehicles
for acting and presentation before audiences. It is in performance that their merits
should be seen.

THE LYING VALET (1741)

This was not Garrick's first writing for the stage: *Lethe* had already been presented
at Drury Lane in April 1740 before its author had made up his mind to be an actor.
The Lying Valet was produced during that sensational season at Goodman's Fields
when all London was talking of the new actor, and the gentry in their coaches,
crowding to see him in *Richard III*, created long traffic jams. Writing to his brother
about his triumphs, and his resolve to forsake the family wine business for a career
on the stage, he added: '*The Valet* takes prodigiously and is approved of by men of

genius, and thought to be the most diverting farce that ever was produced. I believe
you'll find it read pretty well, and in performance 'tis a general roar from beginning
to end. I have got as much reputation in the character as in any other.'

More objective evidence is in the number of nights it was done. It was repeated
nine times in the first fortnight and frequently throughout the season. During
Garrick's management of Drury Lane it was played more than a hundred times
there. The text was published in 1742 and reprinted seven times in Garrick's lifetime as well as being included in collections of his plays. In the next century it
appeared in several drama anthologies in Britain (such as Mrs Inchbald's and
Dibdin's) and more often in America.

The basis of the plot comes from a late seventeenth-century comedy by Motteux,
itself derived from a French play by Hauteroche, but Garrick freely altered and
invented to make it his own. The servant who is sharper-witted than his master, and
the cheeky maid with more sense than the men, are in the Molière tradition, but
here adapted to the qualities of known players. Garrick created the character of
Sharp for himself to play, and continued to play it throughout his acting life.

The other principal part, Kitty Pry, was first taken by Jane Hippesley. Earlier
that year she had been in the company at the Ipswich Theatre, where Garrick, dis-
guised under the name of Mr Lydall, had made his real début on the professional
stage. At Goodman's Fields she played Ophelia to Garrick's Hamlet, and later at
Covent Garden she was the first Miss Biddy in his farce, *Miss in Her Teens*. When
Garrick moved to Drury Lane in 1747 she was one of the players he took with
him.

After the first season of *The Lying Valet* the part of Kitty Pry became the preserve of Kitty Clive, the outstanding comic actress of the age. She was born in
Ireland in 1711, but grew up in the neighbourhood of Drury Lane, where she was
first engaged as a singer with a gift for moving audiences to tears one minute and to
laughter the next. In 1733 she married George Clive, a London barrister from a
Herefordshire family, but they parted soon after the wedding, keeping a discreet
silence about the cause. Her rich personality and comic gifts made a strong
impression on writers like Henry Fielding and Samuel Johnson, and theatre colleagues such as Thomas Davies, Benjamin Victor and Tate Wilkinson. Fielding wrote
of her 'prodigious fund of natural spirit and humour' and declared 'nothing, though
ever so barren, can be flat in her hands' — though he wished she would not attempt
characters out of her range, such as Ophelia. Johnson said that what she did best, she
did better than Garrick — though she could not do half so many things well. Victor
records that in *The Merchant of Venice* she was not Shakespeare's Portia, but in the
trial scene she delighted the house by her brilliant mimicry of well-known barristers.
He wrote, 'If ever there was a true comic genius, Mrs Clive is one . . . She was
always inimitable when she appeared in strongly marked characters of middle and
low life'; and mentioned the 'spirit, roguery and speaking looks of her chambermaids'. Thomas Davies's memoirs contain many enthusiastic tributes to her
qualities; 'She was so formed by nature to represent a variety of laughing, droll,

humorous, affected and absurd creatures', and off the stage 'her conversation was a mixture of uncommon vivacity, droll mirth and honest bluntness'.

In standing up for her rights she was involved in some notorious rows with other members of the company and there is a hint of this aspect in Tate Wilkinson's judgement: 'Mrs Clive was a mixture of combustibles — she was passionate, cross, vulgar, yet sensible, and a very generous woman; and, as a comic actress, of genuine worth — indeed, indeed, she was a diamond of the first water.' Charles Churchill, no easy flatterer, wrote of her in *The Rosciad*:

> In spite of outward blemishes, she shone,
> For humour famed, and humour all her own;
> Easy as if at home the stage she trod,
> Nor sought the critic's praise, nor feared his rod.
> Original in spirit and in ease,
> She pleased by hiding all attempts to please.
> No comic actress ever yet could raise
> On humour's base more merit or more praise.

She had a great capacity for friendship and lived an exemplary private life. Among her society friends was Horace Walpole, who provided a house for her on his Strawberry Hill estate when she retired. With Garrick her relations were always warm, sometimes with affection, sometimes with resentment, but always with mutual appreciation. She quarrelled with him about pay and parts, offended his dignity by making fun of him, played tricks to try to make him laugh on stage, but she admired him deeply — sometimes against her will. Once after a wrangle she watched him from the wings playing Lear; then suddenly broke away, brushing a tear from her cheek. 'Damn him!' she exclaimed, 'I believe he could act a gridiron.' She had acted in his very first play, *Lethe*, and she chose the same play for her fare-well performance in 1769. When Garrick retired she paid warm tribute to him in a letter that deeply touched him:

> I have seen you with your magical hammer in your hand, endeavouring to beat your ideas into the heads of creatures who had none of their own. I have seen you with your lamb-like patience endeavouring to make them comprehend you; and I have seen your lamb turned into a lion. By this your great labour the public was entertained; they thought they all acted very fine — they did not see you pull the wires.

A prominent member of the cast of *The Lying Valet* was Richard Yates, who had the small part of Dick (masquerading as a cook) but who took over Garrick's role of Sharp in some performances, and was to repeat it in later years. Gentleman wrote in 1770, 'His forte we have always thought is old men, yet we admit his Sharp to be inimitable.' In 1741 he was already a well-known actor, and like Miss Hippesley he had acted with 'Mr Lydall' at Ipswich, as had Paget (Judge Guttle) and Mrs Dunstall (Prissy). At Goodman's Fields he starred as Hamlet, with Garrick as Osric. They became close friends.

Mrs Yates (his first wife) was Melissa. She also had been in the company at

Ipswich, playing minor parts, but when Garrick appeared at Goodman's Fields in his epoch-making performance as Richard III, she was the Duchess of York. She died young.

Blakes (Gayless) normally played dashing young blades. He moved on to Drury Lane, where he was Tybalt in Garrick's version of *Romeo and Juliet* and — a big change — Caliban in *The Tempest*. In Garrick's *Lethe* he played a Frenchman, and later, having made a reputation in such parts, he was to be cast as Paris in *The Jealous Wife*.

THE JEALOUS WIFE (1761)

Colman's first play, *Polly Honeycombe*, was presented anonymously at Drury Lane, and at first widely attributed to Garrick, who had merely given some advice. He had a firmer hand in the next, *The Jealous Wife*. In the advertisement to the first edition, Colman acknowledges his obligation to Garrick: 'To his inspection the comedy was submitted in its first rude state, and to . . . his advice in many particulars, relating both to the fable and to characters, I know that I am much indebted for the reception that this piece has met with from the public.'

Garrick was probably most concerned with cutting it to speed up the action. Arthur Murphy (*Life of Garrick*, 1801) says that Colman's next play, *The Musical Lady*, had originally formed part of *The Jealous Wife* 'till Garrick saw it and discarded it as mere surplusage'. When this enjoyable little satire was presented a year later at Drury Lane, Garrick wrote the prologue.

Colman also made a point of acknowledging his debt to Fielding's *Tom Jones*, which he said must be obvious to the most ordinary reader. It is not. Hazlitt, praising *The Jealous Wife* half a century later, said that after seeing it several times he could not imagine what part of the plot was taken from Fielding. 'Colman might have kept his counsel,' he concluded, 'and nobody would have been the wiser.' It might be helpful, though, for an actor preparing to play Charles, to see him as a sort of Tom Jones, a bold wilful youth, prone to drink and fight and get into scrapes, but essentially a good fellow, rather than as a conventional young lover. And Tom Jones's Sophia could be a useful guide to playing Harriot, a girl of spirit who knows which of her three suitors she wants and will choose, even in defiance of her fond but wilful father.

Dr Johnson said of *The Jealous Wife*: 'Though not written with much genius, it was yet so well adapted to the stage, and so well exhibited by the actors, that it was crowded for nearly twenty nights.' Evidently a good piece of theatre rather than a work of literature.

Garrick as Oakly and Hannah Pritchard as his wife were the main attraction. Nowadays Mrs Oakly seems more tiresome than amusing, and Oakly perhaps shows too much forbearance to be effective; other scenes of the play seem livelier than theirs and other characters more rewarding to act. But Thomas Davies recorded:

The scenes of jealousy between Oakly and his wife were worked up with all the warmth of comedy; nor did Mr Garrick ever give stronger proof of his great knowledge of nature than in his making Oakly a character of importance. Mrs Oakly was a finished portrait of a wilful and obstinate woman who pretends to fits of jealousy and love that she may govern her husband with absolute power, and was admirably personated by Mrs Pritchard.

Hannah Pritchard was one of the greatest actresses of the Garrick era. She had never been a beautiful woman, and, at the age of fifty, she had grown very fat. She had always been taller than Garrick, and now, when they were on stage together, the contrast was apt to provoke titters. (Zoffany's picture of them in *Macbeth* verges on the ludicrous.) Her speech was marred by mispronunciations (such as *gownd* for *gown*) but, according to Davies: 'her easy manner of speaking supplied the want of elegant form . . . She had an unaccountable method of charming the ear; she uttered the words, as the great poet advises the actor, smoothly and trippingly on the tongue, and however voluble . . . her part might require her to be, not a syllable of articulation was lost.'

As an actress her range was remarkable. With Garrick she played the great Shakespearian roles in tragedy and comedy. Horace Walpole said that her Beatrice had more spirit and originality than Garrick's Benedick. In more recent comedy she had played such widely different parts as the elegant and sophisticated Millamant in *The Way of the World* and the uncouth virago Tag in Garrick's *Miss in Her Teens* (usually Kitty Clive's part). She retired in 1768 and died a few months later. Churchill's *Rosciad* (1761) mentions *The Jealous Wife* as one of her triumphs:

Oft have I, Pritchard, seen thy wondrous skill,
Confessed thee great, but find thee greater still;
That worth which shone in scattered rays before,
Collected now, breaks forth with double power;
The Jealous Wife! On that thy trophies raise,
Inferior only to the author's praise.

Her daughter played Harriot. She had made her début five years earlier as Juliet, led in by her mother as Lady Capulet — a moving experience for a sentimental audience. Tate Wilkinson said: 'Her features fixed the eye of every beholder — the face was so exquisitely handsome; but the daughter wanted the mother's soul, her feeling, her fire, her whim, her imagination.' Nevertheless, she was thought to be quite good in *The Jealous Wife*. Perhaps she was sparked off by the attentions of John Palmer, who was her lover Charles in the play and who became her husband in real life shortly after.

According to Gentleman, John Palmer 'may be called a handsome figure, but greatly injured by defective carriage. In comedy he has very pleasing talents . . . but he has been pushed rather beyond his mark.' Looking for evidence of the virility and rake-helly impulsiveness necessary for the part of Charles, we find that he played Mercutio in Drury Lane's *Romeo and Juliet* in 1767. In a revival of *The*

Jealous Wife in that year he changed to Sir Harry Beagle. He died the following year at the age of forty. His widow retired from the stage and married a politician.

Kitty Clive as Lady Freelove was able to have fun taking off the affectations of society ladies, at which she was as lively as in her pert chambermaid roles. Major Oakly, the voice of solid common sense in the play, was Richard Yates, Garrick's friend and colleague from twenty years ago. Now sixty years of age, he had recently played Polly Honeycombe's father in Colman's first play. 'The first comedian of the age' (according to Davies), he was a favourite with Drury Lane audiences.

Thomas King (Sir Harry Beagle) had first appeared at Drury Lane in 1748, on the recommendation of Yates, but Garrick was not impressed, and King moved to Bristol and later to Dublin. He came back to Drury Lane ten years later, and soon became Garrick's right-hand man. He played big parts and served as a deputy manager. At the time of *The Jealous Wife* he was thirty-one, a suitable age for Sir Harry. Though a character in one dimension, a broadly comic country baronet, Sir Harry has some of the drollest lines in the play, and the part must have been fun. The following year he played Mask, the leading man, in Colman's *The Musical Lady*, with Yates as his old father.

William O'Brien (Lord Trinket) had joined the company in 1758, and under the tuition of Garrick had made great progress. 'As handsome as Barry and a much more amiable character' was the verdict of a contemporary. His grace and skill in handling a weapon suggested aristocratic birth, but the truth was that he was the son of a fencing-master. He grew in favour with Garrick, and it was for him (on his benefit night in the same season as *The Jealous Wife*) that Garrick exchanged roles in *The Beaux' Stratagem*, playing Scrub to O'Brien's Archer, as already related. But O'Brien's promising career on the stage was cut short by romance. He suddenly eloped with the daughter of the Earl of Ilchester. Her family, unable to accept an actor into their society, arranged for the pair to start a new life in America. After some years they came back, and O'Brien set up as a country gentleman in Dorset. He also tried his hand at writing plays: the first, *The Duel*, produced by Garrick at Drury Lane, failed; but the second, *Cross Purposes*, had some success at Covent Garden under Colman.

John Moody (Terence O'Cutter) had joined Drury Lane in 1759. Garrick had seen him at Portsmouth as the gravedigger in *Hamlet*, and at once offered him an engagement. He was a native of Cork, but denied he was an Irishman. He often played Irish roles, and had here a little gem of a part in that tradition. His stand against the Half-Price Riot in 1762 was more effective and more creditable than Garrick's. Garrick had tried to withdraw the long-established privilege of admission at half-price at the end of the third act; but a powerfully organised riot, culminating in the smashing of chandeliers and tearing up of benches, forced him to capitulate. Moody had forcibly dealt with a rioter he caught setting fire to the scenery. The mob demanded an apology. He tried to laugh this off by saying (in his strongest Irish brogue) he was sorry for having given offence by saving their lives. This enraged the mob more, so that they demanded an apology on his knees. Moody stoutly refused. 'By God, I will not!' he shouted, and strode off the stage. Garrick received him with open arms, saying that he would never have forgiven him if he had yielded. But the rioters were so inflamed that Garrick was cowed into promising that Moody would not appear at Drury Lane again. Moody, undaunted, sought out the chief instigator, a dandified Irishman called Fitzpatrick, offered to fight him and frightened him into writing a letter to Garrick asking for Moody's reinstatement. Moody triumphantly returned to the theatre, but the half-price privilege remained.

The success of *The Jealous Wife* was phenomenal. William Hopkins, the Drury Lane prompter, recorded in his diary that the applause was greater than any play had evoked since *The Suspicious Husband*, fourteen years earlier. It was revived in fifteen more seasons during Garrick's tenure, and held the stage for a century in Britain and America. Mrs Oakly became Sarah Siddons's best comedy role.

The text was published promptly and reprinted the same year. It went into five editions in Colman's lifetime. The first edition contained a letter of dedication to Colman's uncle the Earl of Bath. Colman was still practising the Law, as his uncle had wished, but he was thinking of abandoning this vocation for the theatre, and hoped for his approval. The earl was not placated, however, and Colman lost a fortune.[3]

THE CLANDESTINE MARRIAGE (1766)

The collaboration on *The Clandestine Marriage* probably arose from Garrick's help with *The Jealous Wife.* Its germ was an idea of Colman's, based on the first plate of Hogarth's series of six called *Marriage à la Mode.* This depicts the negotiation of a marriage between a rich business man's daughter and the son of an aristocratic family. 'I had long wished to see those characters on the stage,' Colman wrote to Garrick, 'and mentioned them as proper objects of comedy, before I had the pleasure of your acquaintance.' Garrick transformed the grim and gouty old nobleman into a more engaging and humorous character, a part offering wonderful scope for an actor of his quality, a faded and painted old beau with illusions of romantic youthfulness, Lord Ogleby.

To Colman's original theme of marriage as a financial transaction is added a romantic one, a secret marriage of genuine lovers. The two strands become interwoven when the young bride, turning in desperation to the old nobleman for help, but afraid to explain her situation clearly, causes him to leap to the ridiculous idea that he himself is the object of her secret love. The second theme of true lovers in distress was probably Colman's too.

The collaborators each wrote drafts of the plot, and then completed scenes which they discussed together, and by the time Garrick left in the autumn for a continental tour that was to last two years, they had completed three acts. Garrick wrote from Naples in December 1763: 'I have not yet written a word of *The*

Clandestine Marriage, but I am thinking much about it.' In April 1764, he writes: 'Speed your plough, my dear friend. Have you thought of *The Clandestine Marriage*? I am at it.' Garrick seems eager to drive on: Colman, busy at Drury Lane, seems to have gone off the boil. There is a long hold-up when Garrick is seriously ill. Then he writes: 'Did you receive my letter about our comedy? I shall begin, the first moment I find my comic ideas return to me, to divert myself with scribbling.' But when Garrick came home in April 1765, the work was still to be done. They each did parts of the fourth act, and then came on great problems with the dénouement. Finally, Garrick wrote the brilliant fifth act.

In the early drafts of the work, Garrick had referred to his characters by the names of the players whom he visualised bringing them to life on the stage. Thus Ogleby was called Garrick; Sterling, Yates; Mrs Heidelberg, of course, was Clive; Lovewell was O'Brien. Melvil was then intended for King. It must have been a great advantage, in writing the play, to develop his characters to suit the particular abilities of his players. But now that the play was ready, the situation had changed. O'Brien, now in America, was replaced by William Powell, who had been a great success in playing Garrick's main parts in his absence. But a more serious change was that Garrick himself, for whom Lord Ogleby had been created, had decided after his illness — and perhaps some weariness of the theatre — to take on no new parts. He proposed that King should play Ogleby in his stead. Colman was deeply offended. He had counted on Garrick in the central role to ensure the success of the play. A quarrel resulted, which spread into a querulous dispute about who had written which parts of the play, no doubt exacerbated by trouble-makers passing on to each of them reports of what the other had claimed. All through his career Garrick was inclined to get into quarrels, but also capable of warm generosity in making them up. So in this case he cut through the pettiness: 'I have ever thought of you and loved you as a faithful and affectionate friend,' he wrote to Colman, 'but surely your leaving London so abruptly and leaving complaints of me behind you was not a very becoming instance of your kindness to me. Your suspicions of my behaving in a *manager-like manner* are very unworthy of you. I have never assumed the consequence of a manager to anybody, much less to someone who — I leave your heart to supply the rest . . . ' Reconciliation followed and on Christmas Day 1765, in church, instead of listening to the sermon, Garrick scribbled a Christmas greeting to his friend, including these lines:

> Though wicked gout has come by stealth
> And threats encroachment on my health . . .
> Yet think not, George, my hours are sad —
> Oh no, my heart is more than glad!
> That moment all my cares were gone
> When you and I again were one.
> This gives to Christmas all his cheer,
> And leads me to a happy year.

Although relations were strained a number of times later — notably when Colman joined the management of the rival Covent Garden Theatre, without consulting Garrick — they always recovered the old friendship.

Controversy about the credit for *The Clandestine Marriage* has persisted. Colman's son gave it new twists with stories about what his father had told him. The evidence has been painstakingly sifted by scholars — most thoroughly by Elizabeth Stein and Frederick Bergmann — and leaves no doubt that the main credit should go to Garrick. Lord Ogleby is certainly his creation, being a development of Lord Chalkstone, a character in his early play *Lethe*. So is Mrs Heidelberg, who resembles Mrs Riot in the same play (where the part was also played by Kitty Clive). The lovers are in the sentimental tradition more congenial to Colman, and the satirical picture of the lawyers is surely based on his experience as a barrister on the Oxford Circuit. The last act, a lively example of skilled craftsmanship, is agreed to be Garrick's, very typical in its brisk pace. Twenty-five years on the stage, putting into practice his own positive ideas about acting and about the nature of comedy, had equipped him well for this first venture in creating a full-length play. Unfortunately, his only venture! The break-up of the collaboration may have robbed the English theatre of many great comedies. Colman was a man of letters with a good sense of the theatre; Garrick knew the techniques and traditional situations that worked in the theatre, and both knew their players and their capabilities. The withdrawal of Garrick's influence is supposed to have been a serious loss to Colman's future as a playwright, allowing him to move away from sharp comedy into a more sentimental vein. Certainly neither of them ever again achieved anything to equal *The Clandestine Marriage*.

A study of Garrick's first drafts shows that his revision was directed to shortening speeches or breaking them up with interruptions. As an actor whose guide was nature, he sought to make speech sound natural rather than literary. His dialogue shows a change from the elegant prose of earlier playwrights, still popular in his repertoire, such as Congreve. Only rarely do we find the sparkle of graceful wit, such as Ogleby's line: 'Beauty, madam, is to me a religion, in which I was born and bred a bigot, and hope to die a martyr.'

Garrick once defined what he expected of comedy, in a message to a playwright whose work he found lacking: 'the varying humours of the characters thrown into spirited action and brought into interesting situations, naturally arising from a well-constructed fable or plot'. Thus his characters are to be played as convincing people who evoke laughter by revealing their own follies unaware — not grotesques or butts of cold satire, nor distressed lovers shedding or provoking tears until a happy outcome is contrived. There is, of course, an element of this last in the secret marriage and in the *volte face* at the end which turns Ogleby into a generous benefactor of the lovers. After reading *The Jealous Wife*, one may reasonably attribute this to Colman. But Garrick was never so rigid as to eschew all sentiment; and the spirit of the play as a whole suits his definition of comedy.

Whatever profit or interest may be gained by pursuing analysis of Garrick's or

Colman's hand in the play, the important point is that the collaboration was a brilliant success. Garrick at first concealed his share of the authorship, because, he explained, he had so many enemies among writers on account of his refusing their plays that he sought to avoid the torrent of abuse that their malice would pour upon him. But in a note to the printed play, published a fortnight after its first performance, he could safely claim his share. 'Both the authors beg leave to make their joint acknowledgement for the very favourable reception of *The Clandestine Marriage*.'

The loss of Garrick from the cast proved less crippling than had been feared. Thomas Davies said that when Garrick was in a play 'his genius raised him to that eminence that he was considered by the greatest part of the audience as the only object worthy of attention'. Without this dazzling star the cast formed a well-balanced team. 'It must be granted,' Davies goes on, 'that when the abilities of the performers are nearer upon a level, and the parts of a dramatic piece are disposed with judgement, much rational delight will result to the audience.' Moreover, King, though rather young for the part, proved a success beyond anything expected.

Francis Gentleman, recalling the event four years later, wrote:

> Lord Ogleby is as much a child of laughter as any character on the stage — harmlessly vain, pleasantly odd, commendably generous, a coxcomb not void of sense, a master full of whim, a lover full of false fire, yet a valuable friend, possessed of delicate feelings and nice honour. The peculiarities of this difficult part are supported with eminent abilities by that excellent comedian Mr King, who notwithstanding his chief praise derived from his being a chaste delineator of nature, here strikes out in a watercolour painting of life, a most beautiful and striking caricature conceived with some degree of poetic extravagance, yet so meliorated by his execution that thousands who have never seen such a human being as Lord Ogleby must, amidst loud bursts of laughter, allow — nay, wish — that there may be such a man, whose foibles are so inoffensive.

It was perhaps churlish of Garrick to say later 'but it is not *my* Lord Ogleby'; yet he was underlining an obvious truth about the theatre — that there is no single interpretation of a role: every actor has his own contribution to make.

Next to King the most important player was Kitty Clive. The part of Mrs Heidelberg had been written for her, with an eye and ear for the sort of follies and foibles she would most enjoy taking off. Gentleman, writing after her lamented retirement, began:

> Mrs Heidelberg was lost to the public when Mrs Clive retired . . . The ignorant affectation, volubility of expression and happy disposition of external appearances she was remarkable for, render it difficult to find an equivalent. In many characters she proved herself mistress of a fund of laughter, but was in none more luxuriously droll than in this. Every line of the authors was very becomingly enforced, and many passages were much improved by emphatic illustration.

On the first night, much of the credit for the play's reception went to her personally. Many changes had been made in the text at the last rehearsal, and the players were still uncertain of the altered lines. The audience became critical and restive, but according to a witness, Mrs Clive 'rallied her forces and bustled about in such a style that victory was proclaimed'.

The authors had written the part of Miss Sterling for a close friend of Kitty Clive, who resembled her in temperament and style, the twenty-five-year-old Jane Pope. She had played Polly Honeycombe in Colman's first play, and Sophy in his *Musical Lady*. She had a keen eye for the comic aspects of the rather unpleasant young lady, sharply contrasted with her sentimental sister Fanny. When Kitty Clive retired Pope took over several of her roles, including, many years later, Mrs Heidelberg.

Sterling was played by that old friend of both the authors, Richard Yates. A breach with Garrick was to come, for when Colman left Drury Lane for Covent Garden, Yates and his accomplished second wife went with him. In 1774, however, when Colman sold out at Covent Garden, Garrick persuaded the Yateses to come back to Drury Lane. There, later, under Sheridan's management, he was to play Sir Oliver Surface in *The School for Scandal* (1777). But as he grew old he was overshadowed by the brilliance of his wife.

Fanny Sterling was Mrs Palmer. Gentleman thought she spoke well to head and heart. Her secret husband in the play was William Powell. Powell and Charles Holland (Melvil) can usefully be taken together because they were friends, both pupils of Garrick and apt to imitate his acting, often praised for the same virtues and criticised for the same faults; both died young and within six months of each other.

Powell, like Garrick, was born in Hereford. He went to school in London and was a prosperous clerk until Holland introduced him to Garrick and he rapidly became a rising star at Drury Lane. When Garrick went away on his continental tour, Powell took over many of his parts and was very enthusiastically received. He wrote to Garrick in Paris, expressing gratitude, saying that his infant daughters were taught to remember him in their prayers, adding that Mr Colman was showing him such friendship as he had never experienced except from Garrick himself. Garrick, perhaps not entirely delighted to learn that Powell was filling Drury Lane as full as it had ever been when he himself was playing there, replied a little stiffly, warning him that he needed to work hard to correct the errors that the public might excuse in a young performer. 'You must give to study and an accurate consideration of your characters those hours which young men too often give to their friends and flatterers . . . Study hard, my friend, for seven years, and you may play the rest of your life.'

When Garrick came back, Powell was not in high favour. With Colman, however, he got on well, and, when in 1767 Colman deserted Drury Lane to join the management of Covent Garden, Powell went too, as his partner and principal actor. Garrick's friendship with Colman survived the betrayal, but he never forgave Powell — 'the scoundrel'.

Thomas Davies said that Powell had 'natural gifts for playing lovers and heroes — a strong and manly countenance, a strongly marked and expressive brow, a good ear and voice, and great sensibility'. He thought he lacked humour. His fault was that 'he indulged all his tender feelings to excess — indeed, he had sometimes a propensity to whine and blubber'. Such a tendency may not have been a disadvantage in Lovewell, whose sentimental side can be played for laughs. 'Mr Powell never made a more agreeable figure in comedy,' says Gentleman, 'nor perhaps so good a one, as in this part.'

Charles Holland was 'what we call a good-looking man,' writes Davies, with 'a fine manly voice, used too generously'. He was a favourite with the public. 'He paid great attention to the voice and manner of Garrick, and when under the eye of the master, he was scrupulously exact, but he was too much elated by applause, and too soon thought he was able to walk alone.' In Garrick's absence he had been one of the acting managers at Drury Lane. Later he often deputised for Garrick in his roles, especially after the defection of Powell, when he played Richard III, Hamlet, and Oakly in *The Jealous Wife*; and he was good as Iago. Davies says that Powell and Holland did not read enough or spend enough time among learned or polite men. 'A boisterous laugh and the courage to say anything to anybody supplied the place of humour and pleasantry.' When the Patent theatres were closed for the summer, the two friends jointly managed a season at the Bristol theatre, where they were popular as actors. It was in Bristol in the summer of 1769 that Powell suddenly died of pneumonia following a cold caught at a cricket match. Holland died of smallpox a few months later.

A great strength of *The Clandestine Marriage* was the attention to small parts in the writing and in the performance. 'Betty will never again be performed with merit equal to the lady who with much justice declined the insertion of her name in the [cast list] for so insignificant a character', said Gentleman. The lady was Mrs Abington, an actress of the first rank. But he was surely wrong about the insignificance of the part. She erupts into one of the liveliest opening scenes in English comedy. Exposition is a technical necessity that is sometimes painful and often daunting, but here we take in the situation with enjoyment, and without being conscious of its technical purpose. Betty has also a rewarding part in the last act. Mrs Abington was experienced in the parts of chambermaids, hoydens and country girls, but equally in upper-class coquettes and fine ladies. She was always popular because of her high spirits. She began life as Fanny Barton in 1731, the daughter of a cobbler, and became a flower seller in St James's Park before she tried millinery. At a milliner's she picked up the style of society ladies. She was engaged at Drury Lane, where, finding herself outclassed by actresses like Hannah Pritchard and Kitty Clive, she took singing lessons from an army trumpeter called Abington, whom she briefly married in 1759. Like Mrs Clive, she dropped the husband but kept the name. She left Drury Lane and went to Dublin, where she was a sensation, often in rivalry with Mrs Dancer, the future Mrs Barry. Among her successes was Mrs Oakly in *The Jealous Wife*. She came back to Drury Lane in 1765 at the height of her popularity. Critics praised her elegance, grace, wit, quick intelligence, taste, perfect audibility. Perhaps understandably, she was prickly about the parts she would play. She tried the patience of Garrick, who once concluded a letter about her refusals: 'In short, madam, if you play you are uneasy, and if you do not you are more so.' She was wise to play in *The Clandestine Marriage*, even anonymously: she made a big mistake later by refusing the part of Kate Hardcastle in the first production (by Colman) of *She Stoops to Conquer*. One of her future triumphs was a Letitia Tittup in *Bon Ton*, and a greater one as Sheridan's first Lady Teazle.

Ogleby's servants are especially well conceived, Canton being interestingly contrasted with Brush. Their technical purpose in act II is to prepare the audience for their first sight of Lord Ogleby, which they do with telling comic detail, but they become enjoyable characters in themselves, so that we look forward to their reappearance. The parts were given to very accomplished actors. Brush was played by Palmer and the French-Swiss valet Canton was Baddeley. Robert Baddeley had served as a soldier on the continent, where he had picked up foreign languages. Gentleman praised what he called 'his Swiss dialect'.

The lawyers also come alive in a nice satirical scene. Serjeant Flower was played by James Love, a man of long experience in the theatre as actor, writer and manager. He had known Garrick since his early days at Goodman's Fields, when he had written a comedy based on Richardson's novel *Pamela*, in which Garrick had played. As an actor he had a reputation for Falstaff, but tended to bring Falstaff into every part he played. Gentleman said he was 'a bloody murderer of blank verse', but admitted he was all right as Falstaff. It seems that he later replaced Yates as Sterling in *The Clandestine Marriage*, for Gentleman says uncharitably that it was a pity he ever rose higher than Serjeant Flower — 'the florid, unvarying importance of physiognomy he commonly wears being better adapted to a lumber-headed lawyer than any other character'.

Even the tiny part of Trueman was taken by an old stager, James Aickin, an Irishman, usually a heavy father or worthy steward. Indeed the play was very strongly and felicitously cast. Though it is fun to read, it is pre-eminently an actors' play.

It ran to nineteen performances in its first season, and sixty-eight in the remaining nine years of Garrick's reign. It was frequently revived for great actors to play Lord Ogleby during the nineteenth century. When it was performed in London in 1871, with Samuel Phelps as Ogleby, a critic in *The Times* wrote: 'If forty years ago an habitual playgoer had been asked which was the best-known comedy in the English language, the two celebrated works of Sheridan being set aside, he would probably have named *The Clandestine Marriage* . . . This comedy might be regarded as one of the most genuine classics of the British stage.'

There have been a few memorable revivals in this century. When Donald Wolfit played Ogleby at the Old Vic in 1951, Ivor Brown wrote: 'The crumbling gallant with December in his limbs, who fancies himself to be a lover in the flush of May, might be an ugly figure, a cruel cartoon; it becomes, with Wolfit, an essay in the courtesy of comedy, like a glimpse of a late Autumn garden, frosty but kindly, mellow in all its colours of absurdity.'

The printed text went into three editions in the first six weeks. In the nineteenth century it appeared in numerous volumes in Britain and America, and in German and Italian versions. In Britain it has remained available in the Everyman Library since 1928, and in at least four anthologies published in America.[4]

THE IRISH WIDOW (1772)

Garrick said that he wrote this afterpiece in five days, and it certainly reads more like a working script than a long-matured work. The dialogue, though often vigorous and amusing, could have benefited from polishing and rephrasing in places. The indications of Irish speech are perfunctory, with little enrichment of the language by Irish idiom. Irish players were plentiful in the London theatre, and Garrick could no doubt leave it to them to provide the rich brogue required. The characters' names are hardly realised. Mrs Brady is addressed as 'widow' by every-one, including even her father, though in forthcoming moods he calls her Pat. (Her name, it seems, is Martha.) Her lover calls her 'my sweet widow', and 'thou charm-ing, adorable woman', but never either Martha or Pat. Old Whittle's name is Tom when the mood is friendly, and his old retainer is — perhaps a little confusingly — Mr Thomas. His nephew was Lively Billy before the play opened, and Melancholy William in the first scene, but after the first page his name seems to be forgotten. Bates is Frank when Whittle is Tom, but only briefly. Even allowing for the greater formality of the times, it does seem that Garrick sketched his characters out as stage types, and never eased them into their names.

The characters and situations are in essence taken from theatre stock; a good deal is borrowed from Molière's *Le Mariage Forcé*, with echoes of Ben Jonson's *Epicoene*; and the basic theme — tight-fisted old age versus ardent youth — comes from Latin comedy. Still, the traditional comic elements are given fresh life and individuality, and there are two characters of Garrick's own creation from English life, Old Kecksy and Thomas. The whole is expertly contrived for an immediate purpose, a stage performance by players then available at Drury Lane.

Evidently Garrick felt no inclination to refurbish the text for publication, nor for any of the subsequent editions published in his lifetime.

It was written specially for Mrs Barry, the rising star of the Drury Lane company. Garrick expressed a wish to see her in an Irish part and she wanted to show what she could do. Although she had made her name in Dublin, she was not an Irish girl. She came of well-to-do parents in Bath, where she grew up with a schoolgirl passion for the theatre, and ran away with a mediocre actor called Dancer, whom she married against the strong opposition of her mother. He took her eventually to Dublin, and died there. She had worked as an undistinguished

actress for many years when she came under the influence of Spranger Barry, then
manager of Crow Street Theatre in Dublin. His training made her into one of the
great actresses of the day.

When Barry, Garrick's former rival, came back to Drury Lane in 1767, after nine
years in Ireland, he brought the elegant Mrs Dancer (not yet his wife) with him.
Garrick welcomed them eagerly with an offer of £1500 for their first season. She
and Barry played favourite roles alternating with Garrick and Hannah Pritchard,
and when Mrs Pritchard retired two seasons later, Anne Barry played Cordelia to
Garrick's Lear and Lady Macbeth to his Macbeth. She was brilliant in comedy too,
and when Garrick saw her performance as his Irish widow immediately after a tragic
part, he exclaimed: 'She is the heroine of heroines!'

Lichtenberg, visiting England in 1775, wrote:

> Of all the actresses here, Mrs Barry is in my opinion the greatest, or at least
> the most versatile, being in this respect the only one who could bear com-
> parison with Garrick. She can be trimly laced up like a saucy little waiting
> maid, and trip about as coyly and with such charming self-complacency
> that all the young misses and all the tall servants in the whole house lose
> their hearts to her; or, on the other hand, she can sweep in with a cascade
> of rustling and rippling silk behind her, with an upright carriage and head
> turned as though her vanity impelled her to feast her eyes on the set of her
> train. She is a great beauty, being even by the light of day — so they tell
> me — handsome, and moreover a born actress.

The Irish Widow gave her scope to show her versatility — three characters in one,
including a breeches role. It became one of her famous performances — 'the first
and best and richest-brogued of Widow Bradys' according to Doran — throughout
her long career, which ended only when Sarah Siddons began to outshine her. She
retired in 1798.

The only woman in the cast, she was strongly supported by experienced and able
men. The widow's father, Sir Patrick, was played by John Moody, whom we have
already met as Captain O'Cutter in *The Jealous Wife*. William Parsons (Old Whittle)
specialised in old men, though only in his thirties at this time. He later became a
popular favourite in the Haymarket company under the management of George
Colman, especially appreciated as Justice Shallow in *Henry IV* and the gravedigger
in *Hamlet*.

Robert Baddeley (Bates) was another actor with a reputation for playing old
men. He had played Polonius in the Drury Lane *Hamlet* in 1767 and he was to
create the part of Moses in *The School for Scandal*.

Samuel Cautherley (Nephew) had been employed at Drury Lane to copy out the
actors' parts from the prompt-book, but he had played Charles in a revival of *The
Jealous Wife* in 1767; and Francis Gentleman, though he damned him as 'a tragedy
schoolboy, effeminate and insipid', conceded that he was 'a decent Lovewell' in a
revival of *The Clandestine Marriage*. The colourless nephew in *The Irish Widow* gave
him less scope than the virile hero of *The Jealous Wife*. Soon afterwards Garrick

ticked him off for giving himself airs about the parts he would or would not play. 'You talked to my brother,' he wrote, like a heavy schoolmaster, 'of being *just to yourself* – a foolish, conceited phrase; you had better be careful to be just to other people, and do your duty.' But the young man's aspirations were evidently justified, for he later played Romeo to the famous Mrs Baddeley's Juliet at the new theatre in Richmond, and Hamlet to her Ophelia.

James Dodd, who had the most rewarding male part as Old Kecksy, was only thirty-one. Boaden described him as 'one of the most perfect actors', and Charles Lamb, paying affectionate tribute to his memory many years after his death, recalled his performances in several Sheridan roles, Lord Foppington, Backbite and Bob Acres, and also as Fribble (Garrick's own part in his *Miss in her Teens*) and Aguecheek (in *Twelfth Night*). He was evidently very versatile: in a revival of *The Lying Valet* in 1774 he played Sharp, and he was to play Lord Minikin in *Bon Ton* in the same season.

Thomas Weston (Thomas) was much admired by fellow actors. Garrick thought Weston's Abel Drugger (in *The Alchemist*) better than his own, which was famous. Thomas Davies wrote that he 'threw his audience into loud fits of laughter without discomposing a muscle of his features'. Lichtenberg (whose account of Weston playing Scrub to Garrick's Archer has already been quoted) said he was 'one of the drollest creatures on whom I have ever set eyes. Figure, voice, demeanour and all about him move one to laughter, although he never seems to desire this and himself never laughs.' One wonders whether he was somewhat wasted as Thomas, who is not so particularly laughable. His Christian name may be the source of the otherwise pointless surname of the character in the play.

There were two small speaking parts not mentioned in the cast list of the first performance, an unnamed servant in Whittle's household (in addition to Mr Thomas, who hardly behaves like one), and a black boy called Pompey, who adds tone to the widow's retinue while making a stand for racial discrimination in reverse. (In eighteenth-century society a black servant suggested extravagance and splendour.)

In its first season *The Irish Widow* was performed twenty times. It was published without delay and went into five editions within two years. The first edition contained a letter of dedication to Mrs Barry, in which Garrick modestly disparaged his farce as 'a trifle', but added 'your performance has raised it into some consequence'. He did not think his work worth putting his name to, and signed the letter: 'Your great admirer and humble servant, THE AUTHOR'.

BON TON OR *HIGH LIFE ABOVE STAIRS* (1775)

This afterpiece was first presented at Drury Lane on 18 March 1775, on the occasion of Thomas King's benefit 'as a token of regard for one who during a long engagement was never known, unless confined by real illness, to disappoint the public or distress the manager'.

The alternative title has reference to an earlier play, *High Life below Stairs*, long attributed (wrongly) to Garrick, in which the servants ape the snobbery, extravagance and disreputable manners of their employers. Its production at Drury Lane in 1759, with a strong cast that included Mrs Clive, Mrs Abington, King, O'Brien, Yates, Moody and Palmer, provoked disorder from the footmen in the gallery.

Bon Ton was at first presented anonymously. Garrick had handed over the direction of rehearsals to King, who played Sir John Trotley and spoke the Prologue written by Colman. This explains at length what *Bon Ton* means:

> ... *Bon Ton*'s a constant trade
> Of rout, Festino, ball and masquerade.
> 'Tis plays and puppet shows; 'tis something new!
> 'Tis losing thousands every night at loo! ...
> To visit friends you never wish to see;
> Marriage 'twixt those who never can agree;
> Old dowagers, dressed, painted, patched and curled;
> This is *Bon Ton*, and this we call *the world*!

It is interesting to note the reinvolvement of Colman who, having sold his share of Covent Garden, was no longer a business rival. The play was withdrawn after its first performance, and Garrick, in a note obviously designed to keep the authorship secret from the Drury Lane staff, invited Colman's help in revising it:

> The author of *Bon Ton* presents his best compliments and thanks to Mr Colman for his excellent prologue and would wish to add to the obligations by desiring him to look over the farce and draw his pencil through the parts which his judgement would omit in the next representation. Mr Garrick not being present at the representation, he likewise should be very happy if Mr Colman would show his regard for him and take the trouble which is wanting to make *Bon Ton* palatable. Mr Garrick will do anything at any time to show his attachment to his old friend.

The result was that the original three-act play was cut to two acts, a surgery that recalls Garrick's treatment of *The Jealous Wife*. Garrick evidently thought highly of Colman's opinion. The revised version was presented nine days later with great success.

Bon Ton is satirical comedy rather than farce. It chastises the profligacy of fashionable society, perhaps with more scorn than merriment, by setting it against the old virtues of an honest country gentleman. It shows country folk corrupted by London morals and manners, servants corrupted by the life-style of their employers, and London society corrupted by aping foreigners. For a change, it seems to suggest that the young have something to learn from the old, the present from the past. Then, lest a comedy should become a sermon, the exponent of the old virtues is himself exposed to laughter. Letitia Tittup gives a revealing glimpse of the good life as practised at Trotley Place: 'reading formal books ... going so constantly to church with my elbows stuck to my hips and my toes turned in'. Sir John is splendid in his denunciation of the follies and iniquities of the age, but he goes too far and shows himself too rigid. Like some of his counterparts in our own times, he is obsessed with hair styles. 'I hate innovation', he declares. He thinks that because women's shoulders and legs are delightful objects they should be concealed. In the end he triumphs, not because he convinces anyone, but because he has money to bequeath or withhold.

This enviable role provides marvellous scenes for the actor, passages of robust common sense by which to judge the follies, affectations, fopperies and vices of the times, and highly laughable scenes where the laughter is indulgent rather than malicious. It presents a foretaste of Sheridan's Sir Peter Teazle, which King was also to play in its first production two years later.

Dodd, who had played Kecksy, the coughing cuckold of *The Irish Widow*, was here in a very different character, Lord Minikin, a survival of the Restoration rake, with a well-bred indifference to middle-class standards on marriage, morals and such unfashionable institutions ('minikin' means 'mincing'). He later played another Restoration coxcomb, Lord Foppington in *A Trip to Scarborough*, Sheridan's version of Vanbrugh's *The Relapse.*

Lady Minikin was in the accomplished hands of Jane Pope. She is a sophisticated society lady with attitudes reciprocating her husband's, insincere in love and friend-ship, interested only in fashionable pleasures. It is a character well within the com-pass of Miss Pope.

The real star part went to Mrs Abington. Letitia Tittup is a nasty minx, who has picked up all the worst values of her new milieu, but a fascinating stage character. She expresses herself wittily and pursues her pleasures with spirit; she is sharp and realistic, fun to be with — for a time. The part suited Mrs Abington. Thomas Davies said:

> Her person is formed with great elegance, her address is graceful, her look animated and expressive . . . The tones of her voice are not naturally pleasing to the ear, but her incomparable skill in modulation renders them perfectly agreeable; her articulation is so exact that every syllable she utters is conveyed distinctly, even harmoniously. Congreve's Millamant of past times she has skilfully modelled and adapted to the admired coquette and lovely tyrant of the present day.

Lichtenberg described her:

> showing off her magnificent form with an agreeable suggestion of doing so intentionally . . . She far surpasses all other English actresses in wit . . . In silent parts, or when walking up and down without speaking, she would often, contrary to the habit of players, turn her back on the audience and walk towards the back of the stage. I wish you could have seen the propriety with which she swayed her hips, with each step evincing a desire to aggravate the glances of envy and admiration with which a thousand eyes followed her.

Lichtenberg mentions *Bon Ton* among the plays in which she pleased him most.

Colonel Tivy is another Restoration rake, even less attractive than Lord Minikin.

Because he is a younger son, his main interest in life is to acquire an income. His marital hopes are coldly financial, and when he finds that his fiancée is unlikely to inherit a fortune, he is frozen off. There is still hope that his elder brother may break his neck out hunting. The character is a cold monochrome, easy but unrewarding for an actor of the quality of Brereton, who had played the warm-blooded Squire Russet in *The Jealous Wife*.

Davy, a country bumpkin corrupted by the city, is in a traditional low comedy mould. No doubt Parsons (Whittle in *The Irish Widow*) could spread himself in such a small part. Davies called him 'an actor born to relax the muscles and set mankind a-tittering'.

Jessamy was an eighteenth-century word for a dandy, the type nowadays called a pansy, and still a common butt of comedy. Lamash played this and similar small parts in Sheridan, notably Charles Surface's parasite in *The School for Scandal*. Burton, the Frenchman Mignon, had a similar part, La Varole, in Sheridan's *A Trip to Scarborough*.

Garrick spoke of the excellence of all the actors in *Bon Ton*, which is certainly among his best plays. The dialogue is above his usual standard, having some of the wit and elegance of Congreve, less literary, less charming to read, but more suitable for the theatre. Speeches are trimmed down and broken up to reduce strain on the attention of audiences. It has at least two rich acting roles, the rest offering adequate scope to resourceful players. The satire is incisive and not entirely irrelevant to other ages, including our own. The last act is mainly plot and manipulation, somewhat farcical, but worked out to an unsentimental conclusion.

The text of the revised version (sixteen pages shorter than that originally submitted for the Lord Chamberlain's licence) was published in 1775 and went into three more editions; it was included in several play anthologies within the next fifty years, after which it dropped out except in America. In England it has suffered surprising neglect.

Notes

1   The quotations from Lichtenberg are taken from *Lichtenberg's Visits to England*, trans. Margaret Mare and W.H. Quarrel (Oxford, 1938), by permission of Oxford University Press.

2   For further discussion of this point see K.A. Burnim's *David Garrick, Director* (Pittsburgh, 1961).

3   Hazlitt's lecture *The English Comic Writers of the Last Century* (1818) contains an excellent critical appreciation of *The Jealous Wife*.

4   An excellent critical appreciation of *The Clandestine Marriage* is to be found in Elizabeth Stein's *David Garrick, Dramatist* (New York, 1938).

NOTE ON THE TEXTS

The text of each play is taken from the first published edition, but spelling and punctuation have been modernised and in rare cases where a later reading offers clear advantages it has been used. Some stage directions have been adjusted or expanded. In general there is little significant difference between the first and subsequent editions.

BIOGRAPHICAL RECORD

1717	David Garrick born at Hereford, where his father, Captain Peter Garrick, was on recruiting duty. After baptism in All Saints' Church, leaves his birthplace for a happy childhood in Lichfield, where he is educated at Lichfield Grammar School.
1727	[Accession of George II.]
	Aged ten, Garrick makes first stage appearance when he organises a performance at the Bishop's Palace, Lichfield, of Farquhar's *The Recruiting Officer*. He plays Sergeant Kite.
1732	George Colman born at Florence, where his father was a diplomatic envoy. George II becomes his godfather.
1733	On the death of Colman's father, his uncle, the Earl of Bath, assumes responsibility for his upbringing.
1735	Garrick attends a private school started by Samuel Johnson, a friend of the family nine years older than David. Not a success.
1737	Garrick and Johnson set out for London together, sharing one horse, Garrick to study Law, Johnson to earn his living as writer. [Walpole's Licensing Act gives Lord Chamberlain authority to prohibit performance of any play not licensed by him, and restricts legitimate theatre to Drury Lane and Covent Garden.]
1737–40	Garrick abandons the Law and sets up in the wine trade with his brother Peter. Becomes friendly with Hogarth (artist), Macklin (actor) and Giffard (theatre manager). Involved in acting, at first as an amateur.
1740	Garrick's first play, *Lethe*, performed at Drury Lane.
1741	Garrick makes a sensational (anonymous) appearance as Richard III at Goodman's Fields. He plays Sharp in his own farce, *The Lying Valet*. This season he makes 140 appearances in nineteen different roles.
	George Colman enters Westminster School.
1742	The Garrick triumph at Goodman's Fields leads to its closure, when the two Patent theatres invoke the Licensing Law against it. Garrick is engaged at Drury Lane at record salary. Falls in love with Peg Woffington and lives and acts with her for three years. Their eventual separation ends their very successful stage partnership. [Prime Minister Walpole overthrown by combination of rivals including Lord Bath, Colman's uncle.]
1745	[Jacobite Rebellion.]
	Resulting panic in London ruins theatre business. Garrick volun-

teers for regiment being raised by Earl of Rochford, but when his offer is not accepted he goes to Dublin to manage a lucrative season in partnership with Thomas Sheridan.

1746   Returning from Dublin, Garrick joins Covent Garden, where a strong company includes old friends and rivals. Plays Hotspur to Quin's Falstaff.

1747   Continuing season at Covent Garden, plays Fribble in his own short farce, *Miss in Her Teens*. Buys share in Drury Lane patent and becomes joint manager with James Lacy for next twenty-nine years. Colman, still at Westminster School, appears in school production of Terence's *Phormio*.

1749   Garrick marries Eva Maria Veigel, an Austrian dancer. They settle at 27 Southampton Street, and live happily ever after. (After his death in 1779, she lives on a further forty-one years.)

1751   Rivalry of Drury Lane and Covent Garden at peak in simultaneous productions of *Romeo and Juliet*, Garrick and George Anne Bellamy versus Spranger Barry and Susannah Cibber. Garrick wins by thirteen versus twelve consecutive nights.

1751   Colman leaves Westminster for Christchurch, Oxford. Lord Bath writes to him: 'I look upon you almost like a second son and will never suffer you to want anything . . .'.

1753   The Garricks take Hampton House on the Thames and employ the Adam brothers to rebuild its frontage and Capability Brown to lay out its grounds.

1755   Colman graduates BA and enters Lincoln's Inn to read for the Bar. Lord Bath urges him to work hard and adds: 'I must have no running to playhouses or other places of public diversion . . . I will have you closely watched'.
Fiasco of *The Chinese Festival* (a ballet devised by a French-Swiss, ignorantly thought to be a Frenchman) costs Garrick £4000 in riot damage.

1756   Garrick's *Lilliput*, based on *Gulliver's Travels*, presented at Drury Lane by child actors.

[1756–63   Seven Years' War with France. Chief gains in India and Canada.]

1757   Garrick's farce *The Male Coquette* presented at Drury Lane. Colman called to the Bar and practises on Oxford Circuit, but much drawn to literary and theatrical circles.

1759   Garrick not a success in *Antony and Cleopatra* but very good in his own short comedy, *The Guardian*. Colman actively involved on Garrick's side in controversy about the management of Drury Lane.

1760   [Accession of George III.]

The new king attends Drury Lane to see Garrick in *Richard III.*
Two nights later, at *King John*, he prefers the performance of
Thomas Sheridan as John to that of Garrick as Falconbridge.
Colman's first play, *Polly Honeycombe*, presented at Drury Lane
with a prologue by Garrick.

1761   Colman's *The Jealous Wife* presented at Drury Lane with Garrick
as Oakly. Colman dedicates printed edition to Lord Bath, hoping
(in vain) to mollify his impatience of Colman's preoccupation with
the theatre.

The Rosciad. Colman's schoolfellow Charles Churchill attacks the
acting of the age, but praises Garrick (and Colman).

1762   Half-price Riots do great damage at Drury Lane and disgust Garrick.
Colman's *The Musical Lady* performed with prologue by Garrick.
A son (George Colman the Younger) is born to Sarah Ford, a
minor actress living with Colman despite disapproval of Lord Bath.

1763   The Garricks leave for two-year continental tour. Colman shares
management of Drury Lane with Lacy and Garrick's younger
brother George. William Powell takes on main roles of Garrick.
Colman puts on his own adaptation of *A Midsummer Night's
Dream* – a failure. His comedy *The Deuce is In Him* does better.

1764   Lord Bath ('the richest man in England') dies, leaving Colman a
modest annuity instead of the expected fortune, which he
bequeaths to his brother General Pulteney.

1765   Colman's translation of Terence establishes his reputation as a
scholar.

Garrick returns from abroad considering retirement, but enjoys
great reception as Benedick in royal command performance of
Much Ado.

Garrick's decision not to play Lord Ogleby in *The Clandestine
Marriage* (a Garrick–Colman collaboration) provokes quarrel with
Colman.

1766   *The Clandestine Marriage* presented at Drury Lane with strong cast.
Colman builds a villa at Richmond, where Sir Joshua Reynolds is
his neighbour.

1767   Colman's *The English Merchant* presented at Drury Lane. Colman
buys a share in Covent Garden Theatre. Resulting estrangement
with Garrick, who resents his desertion. But the old friendship is
renewed. Colman marries his mistress, Sarah Ford, in defiance of
General Pulteney, from whom he still hopes to inherit the fortune
left by Lord Bath. The general dies, leaving the fortune to a niece.

1768   Colman makes success of Covent Garden. In two seasons he presents forty-six full-length plays, including fourteen by Shakespeare.

1769   Fiasco of Stratford Jubilee, Garrick's celebration of Shakespeare, ruined by rain and ridicule. He recoups his losses by popular show, *The Jubilee*, at Drury Lane. Colman puts on at Covent Garden *Man and Wife* or *The Shakespeare Jubilee*.

1771   Accidental death of Sarah Colman through some confusion of medicine bottles. Colman threatened with epilepsy.

1772   Garrick's *The Irish Widow* performed at Drury Lane.

1773   Ugly riots against Macklin at Covent Garden humiliate Colman.

1774   Colman sells share of Covent Garden and resumes literary work.

1775   Garrick's *Bon Ton* or *High Life above Stairs* performed at Drury Lane.

Extensive rebuilding at Drury Lane (interior) designed by Adam brothers. Garrick reopens with his own *The Theatrical Candidates*.

[1775–83   American War of Independence.]

1776   Colman's adaptation of Jonson's *Epicœne*, offered to Garrick, fails at Drury Lane. His new comedy, *The Spleen* or *Islington Spa*, does better. Garrick writes a prologue to it, in which he announces his retirement. (He has sold his share in Drury Lane to Richard Brinsley Sheridan.) Moving farewell to the theatre. Colman takes over from Foote management of Haymarket Theatre and its special licence to put on a summer season of plays when the two Patent theatres are closed. He makes a great success of it, building a strong company putting on new plays and revivals of Elizabethans.

1777   Garrick, summoned to Windsor to entertain the Royal Family, gets a cool reception. But despite failing health, he enjoys a full social life; he attends first night of Sheridan's *The School for Scandal* at Drury Lane and a revival of *The Merchant of Venice* at the Haymarket, and visits aristocratic and literary friends.

1779   Death of Garrick. Magnificent funeral at Westminster Abbey; pall bearers include a duke and two earls. Sheridan, Gibbon and Colman share one of the fifty mourning coaches.

1783   Colman publishes translation of Horace. Revives *The Clandestine Marriage* at Haymarket. Writes prologue to his son's first play, *Two in One*; but tries to force him to follow career in Law and renounce the theatre and a proposed marriage to a minor actress (thus repeating behaviour of Earl of Bath to him a generation earlier). Young George elopes to Gretna Green.

1785 onwards   Colman troubled by illness and insanity (with some lucid intervals). Young George gradually takes over management of Haymarket.

[1789   French Revolution.]

1790   Young George takes over completely.

1794   Death of George Colman the Elder.

2. David Garrick and his wife (Eva Maria Veigel), oil painting by William Hogarth, 1752

THE LYING VALET

by David Garrick

First performed at Goodman's Fields Theatre,
30 November 1741, with the following cast:

GAYLESS	Mr Blakes
SHARP (the Lying Valet)	Mr Garrick
JUSTICE GUTTLE	Mr Paget
BEAU TRIPPIT	Mr Peterson
MELISSA	Mrs Yates
KITTY PRY	Miss Hippesley
MRS GADABOUT	Mrs Bambridge
MRS TRIPPIT	Miss Medina
PRISSY	Mrs Dunstall

ACT I

SCENE 1.   GAYLESS's *lodgings. Enter* GAYLESS *and* SHARP.

SHARP: How, sir! Shall you be married tomorrow? Eh, I'm afraid you joke with your poor humble servant.

GAY: I tell thee, Sharp, last night Melissa consented, and fixed tomorrow for the happy day.

SHARP: 'Twas well she did, sir, or it might have been a dreadful one for us in our present condition: all your money spent; your movables sold; your honour almost ruined, and your humble servant almost starved; we could not possibly have stood it two days longer. But if this young lady will marry you and relieve us, o' my conscience, I'll turn friend to the sex, rail no more at matrimony, but curse the whores, and think of a wife myself.

GAY: And yet, Sharp, when I think how I have imposed upon her, I am almost resolved to throw myself at her feet, tell her the real situation of my affairs, ask her pardon, and implore her pity.

SHARP: After marriage, with all my heart, sir; but don't let your conscience and honour so far get the better of your poverty and good sense, as to rely on so great uncertainties as a fine lady's mercy and good nature.

GAY: I know her generous temper, and am almost persuaded to rely upon it: what, because I am poor, shall I abandon my honour?

SHARP: Yes, you must, sir, or abandon me: so pray, discharge one of us; for eat I must, and speedily too: and you know very well that that honour of yours will neither introduce you to a great man's table, nor get me credit for a single beefsteak.

GAY: What can I do?

SHARP: Nothing while honour sticks in your throat: do gulp, master, and down with it.

GAY: Prithee leave me to my thoughts.

SHARP: Leave you! No, not in such bad company, I'll assure you! Why, you must certainly be a very great philosopher, sir, to moralise and declaim so charmingly, as you do, about honour and conscience, when your doors are beset with bailiffs, and not one single guinea in your pocket to bribe the villains.

GAY: Don't be witty, and give your advice, sirrah!

SHARP: Do you be wise, and take it, sir. But to be serious, you certainly have spent your fortune, and outlived your credit, as your pockets and my belly can testify: your father has disowned you; all your friends forsook you, except myself, who am starving with you. Now, sir, if you marry this young lady, who as yet, thank heaven, knows nothing of your misfortunes, and by that means procure a better fortune than that you squandered away, make a good husband, and turn economist, you still may be happy, may still be Sir William's heir, and the lady too no loser by the bargain; there's reason and argument, sir.

GAY: 'Twas with that prospect I first made love to her; and though my fortune has been ill spent, I have, at least, purchased discretion with it.

SHARP: Pray then convince me of that, sir, and make no more objections to the marriage. You see I am reduced to my waistcoat already; and when necessity has undressed me from top to toe, she must begin with you; and then we shall be forced to keep house and die by inches. Look you, sir, if you won't resolve to take my advice, while you have one coat to your back, I must e'en take to my heels while I have strength to run, and something to cover me: so, sir, wishing you much comfort and consolation with your bare conscience, I am your most obedient and half-starved friend and servant (*going*).

GAY: Hold, Sharp, you won't leave me?

SHARP: I must eat, sir; by my honour and appetite I must!

GAY: Well then, I am resolved to favour the cheat, and as I shall quite change my former course of life, happy may be the consequences; at least of this I am sure —

SHARP: That you can't be worse than you are at present. (*a knocking without*)

GAY: Who's there?

SHARP: Some of your former good friends, who favoured you with money at fifty per cent, and helped you to spend it; and are now become daily mementoes to you of the folly of trusting rogues, following whores, and laughing at my advice.

GAY: Cease your impertinence! To the door! If they are duns, tell 'em my marriage is now certainly fixed, and persuade 'em still to forbear a few days longer, and keep my circumstances a secret for their sakes as well as my own.

SHARP: Oh, never fear it, sir: they still have so much friendship for you, not to desire your ruin to their own disadvantage.

GAY: And do you hear, Sharp, if it should be anybody from Melissa, say I am not at home, lest the bad appearance we make here should make 'em suspect something to our disadvantage.

SHARP: I'll obey you, sir; but I am afraid they will easily discover the consumptive situation of our affairs by my chopfallen countenance. (*Exit.*)

GAY: These very rascals who are now continually dunning and persecuting me were the very persons who led me to my ruin, partook of my prosperity, and professed the greatest friendship.

SHARP: (*without*) Upon my word, Mrs Kitty, my master's not at home.

KITTY: (*without*) Look'ee, Sharp, I must and will see him!

GAY: Ha, what do I hear? Melissa's maid! What has brought her here? My poverty has made her my enemy too — she is certainly come with no good intent — no friendship there, without fees. She's coming up stairs! What must I do? I'll get into this closet and listen. (*Exit.*)

(*Enter* SHARP *and* KITTY.)

KITTY: I must know where he is, and will know too, Mr Impertinence!

SHARP: (*aside*) Not of me you won't. — He's not within, I tell you, Mrs Kitty; I don't know myself: do you think I can conjure?

---

keep house: stay indoors.

Mrs Kitty: *Mrs* (abbreviation of *mistress*) was formerly applied as a courtesy title to women whether married or single. Eighteenth-century usage was in flux, *Mrs* being commonly applied to unmarried servants, older ladies, and in the theatre to actresses of high standing. As to pronunciation, the *Oxford English Dictionary* lacks evidence for dating the change from *mistress* to *missis*, but shows that by 1828 *missis* was normal.

KITTY: But I know you will lie abominably; therefore don't trifle with me. I come from my mistress Melissa. You know, I suppose, what's to be done tomorrow morning?

SHARP: Ay, and tomorrow night too, girl!

KITTY: (*aside*) Not if I can help it. — But come, where is your master? For see him I must.

SHARP: Pray, Mrs Kitty, what's your opinion of this match between my master and your mistress?

KITTY: Why, I have no opinion of it at all; and yet most of our wants will be relieved by it too: for instance now, your master will get a fortune; that's what I'm afraid he wants; my mistress will get a husband; that's what she has wanted for some time; you will have the pleasure of my conversation, and I an opportunity of breaking your head for your impertinence.

SHARP: Madam, I'm your most humble servant! But I'll tell you what, Mrs Kitty, I am positively against the match; for, was I a man of my master's fortune —

KITTY: You'd marry if you could and mend it. Ha, ha, ha! Pray, Sharp, where does your master's estate lie?

GAY: (*aside*) Oh, the devil! What a question was there!

SHARP: Lie, lie! Why it lies — faith, I can't name any particular place, it lies in so many: his effects are divided, some here, some there; his steward hardly knows himself.

KITTY: Scattered, scattered, I suppose. But hark'ee, Sharp, what's become of your furniture? You seem to be a little bare here at present.

GAY: (*aside*) What, has she found out that too?

SHARP: Why, you must know, as soon as the wedding was fixed, my master ordered me to remove his goods into a friend's house, to make room for a ball which he designs to give here the day after the marriage.

KITTY: The luckiest thing in the world! For my mistress designs to have a ball and entertainment here tonight before the marriage; and that's my business with your master.

SHARP: (*aside*) The devil it is!

KITTY: She'll not have it public; she designs to invite only eight or ten couple of friends.

SHARP: No more?

KITTY: No more: and she ordered me to desire your master not to make a great entertainment.

SHARP: Oh, never fear —

KITTY: Ten or a dozen little nice things, with some fruit, I believe, will be enough in all conscience.

SHARP: (*aside*) Oh, curse your conscience!

KITTY: And what do you think I have done of my own head.

SHARP: What?

KITTY: I have invited all my Lord Stately's servants to come and see you, and have a dance in the kitchen: won't your master be surprised!

SHARP: Much so indeed!

KITTY: Well, be quick and find out your master, and make what haste you can with your preparations: you have no time to lose. — Prithee, Sharp, what's the matter with you? I have not seen you for some time, and you seem to look a little thin.

SHARP: (*aside*) Oh, my unfortunate face! — I'm in pure good health, thank you, Mrs Kitty; and I'll assure you, I have a very good stomach, never better in all my life, and I am as full of vigour, hussy! (*Offers to kiss her.*)

KITTY: What, with that face! well, bye, bye (*going*). Oh, Sharp, what ill-looking fellows are those, were standing about your door when I came in? They want your master too, I suppose?

SHARP: Hum! Yes, they are waiting for him. They are some of his tenants out of the country that want to pay him some money.

KITTY: Tenants! What, do you let his tenants stand in the street?

SHARP: They choose it; as they seldom come to town, they are willing to see as much of it as they can, when they do; they are raw, ignorant, honest people.

KITTY: Well, I must run home, farewell! But do you hear? Get something substantial for us in the kitchen — a ham, a turkey, or what you will — we'll be very merry; and, be sure to remove the tables and chairs away there too, that we may have room to dance: I can't bear to be confined in my French dances; tal, lal, lal (*dancing*). Well, adieu! Without any compliment, I shall die if I don't see you soon. (*Exit.*)

SHARP: And without any compliment, I pray heaven you may!

　　　　　(*Enter GAYLESS. They look for some time sorrowful at each other.*)

GAY: Oh, Sharp!

SHARP: Oh, master!

GAY: We are certainly undone!

SHARP: That's no news to me.

GAY: Eight or ten couple of dancers — ten or a dozen little nice dishes, with some fruit — my Lord Stately's servants, ham and turkey!

SHARP: Say no more! The very sound creates an appetite: and I am sure of late I have had no occasion for whetters and provocatives.

GAY: Cursed misfortune! What can we do?

SHARP: Hang ourselves; I see no other remedy; except you have a receipt to give a ball and a supper without meat or music.

GAY: Melissa has certainly heard of my bad circumstances, and has invented this scheme to distress me, and break off the match.

SHARP: I don't believe it, sir; begging your pardon.

GAY: No? Why did her maid then make so strict an enquiry into my fortune and affairs?

SHARP: For two very substantial reasons: the first, to satisfy a curiosity, natural to her as a woman; the second, to have the pleasure of my conversation, very natural to her as a woman of taste and understanding.

GAY: Prithee be more serious: is not our all at stake?

SHARP: Yes, sir: and yet that all of ours is of so little consequence, that a man with a very small share of philosophy may part from it without much pain or uneasiness. However, sir, I'll convince you in half an hour, that Mrs Melissa knows nothing of your circumstances, and I'll tell you what too, sir, she shan't be here tonight, and yet you shall marry her tomorrow morning.

GAY: How, how, dear Sharp!

SHARP: 'Tis here, here, sir! warm, warm, and delays will cool it; therefore I'll away to her, and do you be as merry as love and poverty will permit you.

> Would you succeed, a faithful friend depute,
> Whose head can plan, and front can execute.

I am the man, and I hope you neither dispute my friendship or qualification.

GAY: Indeed I don't. Prithee be gone.

SHARP: I fly. (*Exeunt.*)

SCENE 2.   MELISSA's *lodgings. Enter* MELISSA *and* KITTY.

MEL: You surprise me, Kitty! The master not at home! The man in confusion! No furniture in the house! And ill-looking fellows about the doors! 'Tis all a riddle.

KITTY: But very easy to be explained.

MEL: Prithee explain it then, nor keep me longer in suspense.

KITTY: The affair is this, madam: Mr Gayless is over head and ears in debt; you are over head and ears in love; you'll marry him tomorrow, the next day, your whole fortune goes to his creditors, and you and your children are to live comfortably upon the remainder.

MEL: I cannot think him base.

KITTY: But I know they are all base — you are very young, and very ignorant of the sex; I am young too, but have more experience: you never was in love before; I have been in love with an hundred, and tried 'em all; and know 'em to be a parcel of barbarous, perjured, deluding, bewitching devils.

MEL: The low wretches you have had to do with may answer the character you give 'em; but Mr Gayless —

KITTY: Is a man, madam.

MEL: I hope so, Kitty, or I would have nothing to do with him.

KITTY: With all my heart — I have given you my sentiments upon the occasion, and shall leave you to your own inclinations.

MEL: Oh, madam, I am much obliged to you for your great condescension, ha, ha, ha! However, I have so great a regard for your opinion, that had I certain proofs of his villainy —

KITTY: Of his poverty you may have a hundred: I am sure I have had none to the contrary.

MEL: (*aside*) Oh, there the shoe pinches.

KITTY: Nay, so far from giving me the usual perquisites of my place, he has not so much as kept me in temper with little endearing civilities; and one might reasonably expect when a man is deficient in one way, that he should make it up in another. (*knocking without*)

MEL: See who's at the door. (*Exit* KITTY.) — I must be cautious how I hearken too much to this girl; her bad opinion of Mr Gayless seems to arise from his disregard of her. (*Enter* SHARP *and* KITTY.) So, Sharp; have you found your master? Will things be ready for the ball and entertainment?

SHARP: To your wishes, madam. I have just now bespoke the music and supper, and wait now for your ladyship's further commands.

MEL: My compliments to your master, and let him know I and my company will be with him by six; we design to drink tea, and play at cards, before we dance.

KITTY: (aside) So shall I and my company, Mr Sharp.

SHARP: Mighty well, madam!

MEL: Prithee, Sharp, what makes you come without your coat? 'Tis too cool to go
    so airy, sure.

KITTY: Mr Sharp, madam, is of a very hot constitution, ha, ha, ha!

SHARP: If it had been ever so cool I have had enough to warm me since I came
    from home, I'm sure; but no matter for that (sighing).

MEL: What d'ye mean?

SHARP: Pray don't ask me, madam; I beseech you don't: let us change the subject.

KITTY: Insist upon knowing it, madam. (aside) My curiosity must be satisfied, or I
    shall burst.

MEL: I do insist upon knowing. On pain of my displeasure, tell me!

SHARP: If my master should know − I must not tell you, madam, indeed.

MEL: I promise you, upon my honour, he never shall.

SHARP: (indicating KITTY) But can your ladyship insure secrecy from that
    quarter?

KITTY: Yes, Mr Jackanapes, for anything you can say.

MEL: I'll engage for her.

SHARP: Why then, in short, madam − I cannot tell you.

MEL: Don't trifle with me.

SHARP: Then since you will have it, madam, − I lost my coat in defence of your
    reputation.

MEL: In defence of my reputation!

SHARP: I will assure you, madam, I've suffered very much in defence of it; which
    is more than I would have done for my own.

MEL: Prithee explain.

SHARP: In short, madam, you was seen, about a month ago, to make a visit to my
    master alone.

MEL: Alone! My servant was with me.

SHARP: What, Mrs Kitty? So much the worse; for she was looked upon as my
    property; and I was brought in guilty as well as you and my master.

KITTY: What, your property, jackanapes!

MEL: What is all this?

SHARP: Why, madam, as I came out but now to make preparations for you and
    your company tonight, Mrs Pryabout, the attorney's wife at next door, calls
    to me: 'Hark'ee fellow!' says she, 'Do you and your modest master know that
    my husband shall indict your house, at the next parish meeting, for a
    nuisance?'

MEL: A nuisance!

SHARP: I said so: 'A nuisance! I believe none in the neighbourhood live with more
    decency and regularity than I and my master,' as is really the case. 'Decency
    and regularity!' cries she, with a sneer, 'why, sirrah, does not my window look
    into your master's bed chamber? And did not he bring in a certain lady, such
    a day?' − describing you, madam. 'And did not I see − '

MEL: See! Oh scandalous! What?

SHARP: Modesty requires my silence.

MEL: Did not you contradict her?

SHARP: Contradict her! Why, I told her I was sure she lied: 'For, zounds!' said I —
for I could not help swearing — 'I am so well convinced of the lady's and my
master's prudence, that, I am sure, had they a mind to amuse themselves they
would certainly have drawn the window-curtains.'

MEL: What, did you say nothing else? Did not you convince her of her error and
impertinence?

SHARP: She swore to such things, that I could do nothing but swear and call
names: upon which out bolts her husband upon me, with a fine taper crab in
his hand and fell upon me with such violence, that, being half delirious, I
made a full confession.

MEL: A full confession! What did you confess?

SHARP: That my master loved fornication; that you had no aversion to it; that Mrs
Kitty was a bawd, and your humble servant a pimp.

KITTY: A bawd! a bawd! Do I look like a bawd, madam?

SHARP: And so, madam, in the scuffle, my coat was torn to pieces as well as your
reputation.

MEL: And so you joined to make me infamous!

SHARP: For heaven's sake, madam, what could I do? His proofs fell so thick upon
me, as witness my head (*showing his head plastered*), that I would have given
up all the maidenheads in the kingdom, rather than have my brains beat to a
jelly.

MEL: Very well! But I'll be revenged! And did not you tell your master this?

SHARP: Tell him! No, madam; had I told him, his love is so violent for you, that he
would certainly have murdered half the attorneys in town by this time.

MEL: Very well! But I'm resolved not to go to your master's tonight.

SHARP: (*aside*) Heavens and my impudence be praised.

KITTY: Why not, madam? If you are not guilty, face your accusers.

SHARP: (*aside*) Oh, the devil! Ruined again! To be sure, face 'em by all means,
madam — they can but be abusive, and break the windows a little: besides,
madam, I have thought of a way to make this affair quite diverting to you — I
have a fine blunderbuss charged with half a hundred slugs, and my master has
a delicate large Swiss broad sword; and between us, madam, we shall so
pepper and slice 'em, that you will die with laughing.

MEL: What, at murder?

KITTY: Don't fear, madam, there will be no murder if Sharp's concerned.

SHARP: Murder, madam! 'Tis self-defence; besides, in these sort of skirmishes,
there are never more than two or three killed: for, supposing they bring the
whole body of militia upon us, down but with a brace of them, and away fly
the rest of the covey.

MEL: Persuade me never so much, I won't go; that's my resolution.

KITTY: Why then, I'll tell you what, madam; since you are resolved not to go to
the supper, suppose the supper was to come to you: 'tis great pity such great
preparations as Mr Sharp has made should be thrown away.

---

taper crab: crab-apple stick.

SHARP: So it is, as you say, Mistress Kitty. But I can immediately run back and un-
bespeak what I have ordered; 'tis soon done.

MEL: But then what excuse can I send to your master? He'll be very uneasy at my
not coming.

SHARP: Oh terribly so! But I have it — I'll tell him you are very much out of order
— that you were suddenly taken with the vapours or qualms; or what you
please, madam.

MEL: I'll leave it to you, Sharp, to make my apology; and there's half a guinea for
you to help your invention.

SHARP: (aside) Half a guinea! — 'Tis so long since I had anything to do with
money, that I scarcely know the current coin of my own country. Oh Sharp,
what talents hast thou! To secure thy master; deceive his mistress; out-lie her
chambermaid; and yet be paid for thy honesty? But my joy will discover me.
— Madam, you have eternally fixed Timothy Sharp your most obedient
humble servant! [aside] Oh, the delights of impudence and a good understanding! (Exit.)

KITTY: Ha, ha, ha! Was there ever such a lying varlet? With his slugs and his broad
swords; his attorneys and broken heads, and nonsense! Well, madam, are you
satisfied now? Do you want more proofs?

MEL: Of your modesty I do: but I find, you are resolved to give me none.

KITTY: Madam?

MEL: I see through your little mean artifice: you are endeavouring to lessen Mr
Gayless in my opinion, because he has not paid you for services he had no
occasion for.

KITTY: Pay me, madam! I am sure I have very little occasion to be angry with Mr
Gayless for not paying me, when, I believe, 'tis his general practice.

MEL: 'Tis false! He's a gentleman and a man of honour, and you are —

KITTY: (curtsying) Not in love, I thank heaven!

MEL: You are a fool.

KITTY: I have been in love; but I am much wiser now.

MEL: Hold your tongue, impertinence!

KITTY: (aside) That's the severest thing she has said yet.

MEL: Leave me.

KITTY: Oh this love, this love is the devil! (Exit.)

MEL: We discover our weaknesses to our servants, make them our confidants, put
'em upon an equality with us, and so they become our advisers — Sharp's
behaviour, though I seemed to disregard it, makes me tremble with apprehensions; and though I have pretended to be angry with Kitty for her advice,
I think it of too much consequence to be neglected.

(Enter KITTY.)

KITTY: May I speak, madam?

MEL: Don't be a fool. What do you want?

KITTY: There is a servant just come out of the country says he belongs to Sir
William Gayless, and has got a letter for you from his master, upon very
urgent business.

MEL: Sir William Gayless! What can this mean? Where is the man?

KITTY: In the little parlour, madam.

MEL: I'll go to him — my heart flutters strangely. (*Exit.*)

KITTY: O woman, woman, foolish woman! She'll certainly have this Gayless: nay, were she as well convinced of his poverty as I am, she'd have him. A strong dose of love is worse than one of ratafia; when it once gets into our heads, it trips up our heels, and then good night to discretion. Here is she going to throw away fifteen thousand pounds; upon what? Faith, little better than nothing — he's a man, and that's all — and heaven knows mere man is but small consolation.

> Be this advice pursued by each fond maid,
> Ne'er slight the substance for an empty shade:
> Rich, weighty sparks alone should please and charm ye:
> For should spouse cool, his gold will always warm ye.

ACT II

SCENE.   GAYLESS's *lodgings. Enter* GAYLESS *and* SHARP.

GAY: Prithee be serious, Sharp. Hast thou really succeeded?

SHARP: To our wishes, sir. In short, I have managed the business with such skill and dexterity, that neither your circumstances nor my veracity are suspected.

GAY: But how hast thou excused me from the ball and entertainment?

SHARP: Beyond expectation, sir. But in that particular I was obliged to have recourse to truth, and declare the real situation of your affairs. I told her we had so long disused ourselves to dressing either dinners or suppers, that I was afraid we should be but awkward in our preparations. In short, sir, at that instant a cursed gnawing seized my stomach, that I could not help telling her that both you and myself seldom make a good meal nowadays once in a quarter of a year.

GAY: Hell and confusion! Have you betrayed me, villain? Did you not tell me this moment, she did not in the least suspect my circumstances?

SHARP: No more she did, sir, till I told her.

GAY: Very well; and was this your skill and dexterity?

SHARP: I was going to tell you; but you won't hear reason; my melancholy face and piteous narration had such an effect upon her generous bowels, that she freely forgives all that's past.

GAY: Does she, Sharp?

SHARP: Yes; and desires never to see your face again; and, as a farther consideration for so doing, she has sent you half a guinea. (*Shows the money.*)

GAY: What do you mean?

SHARP: To spend it, spend it, sir; and regale.

GAY: Villain, you have undone me!

SHARP: What, by bringing you money, when you are not worth a farthing in the whole world? Well, well, then to make you happy again, I'll keep it myself; and wish somebody would take it in their head to load me with such misfortunes. (*Puts up the money.*)

---

ratafia: spirits or cordial.

GAY: Do you laugh at me, rascal!

SHARP: Who deserves more to be laughed at! Ha, ha, ha! Never for the future, sir, dispute the success of my negotiations, when even you, who know me so well, can't help swallowing my hook. Why, sir, I could have played with you backwards and forwards at the end of my line, till I had put your senses into such a fermentation, that you should not have known in an hour's time, whether you was a fish or a man.

GAY: Why, what is all this you have been telling me?

SHARP: A downright lie from beginning to end.

GAY: And have you really excused me to her?

SHARP: No, sir; but I have got this half guinea to make her excuses to you; and, instead of a confederacy between you and me to deceive her, she thinks she has brought me over to put the deceit upon you.

GAY: Thou excellent fellow!

SHARP: Don't lose time, but slip out of the house immediately; the back way, I believe, will be the safest for you, and to her as fast as you can; pretend vast surprise and concern, that her indisposition has debarred you the pleasure of her company here tonight: you need know no more, away!

GAY: But what shall we do, Sharp? Here's her maid again.

SHARP: The devil she is — I wish I could poison her; for I'm sure, while she lives, I can never prosper.

                              (*Enter* KITTY.)

KITTY: Your door was open, so I did not stand upon ceremony.

GAY: I am sorry to hear your mistress is taken so suddenly.

KITTY: Vapours, vapours only, sir, a few matrimonial omens, that's all; but I suppose Mr Sharp has made her excuses.

GAY: And tells me I can't have the pleasure of her company, tonight. I had made a small preparation; but 'tis no matter: Sharp shall go to the rest of the company; and let 'em know 'tis put off.

KITTY: Not for the world, sir; my mistress was sensible you must have provided for her, and the rest of the company; so is she resolved, though she can't, the other ladies and gentlemen shall partake of your entertainment; she's very good-natured.

SHARP: I had better run, and let 'em know 'tis deferred (*going*).

KITTY: (*stopping him*) I have been with 'em already, and told 'em my mistress insists upon their coming, and they have all promised to be here; so, pray, don't be under any apprehensions, that your preparations will be thrown away.

GAY: But as I can't have her company, Mrs Kitty, 'twill be a greater pleasure to me, and a greater compliment to her, to defer our mirth; besides I can't enjoy anything at present, and she not partake of it.

KITTY: Oh, no, to be sure; but what can I do? My mistress will have it so, and Mrs Gadabout and the rest of the company will be here in a few minutes; there are two or three coachfuls of 'em.

SHARP: (*aside*) Then my master must be ruined in spite of my parts.

GAY: (*aside to* SHARP) 'Tis all over, Sharp.

SHARP: I know it, sir.

GAY: I shall go distracted; what shall I do?

SHARP: Why, sir, as our rooms are a little out of furniture at present, take 'em into the captain's that lodges here, and set 'em down to cards; if he should come in the meantime, I'll excuse you to him.

KITTY: (*aside*) I have disconcerted their affairs, I find; I'll have some sport with 'em. – Pray, Mr Gayless, don't order too many things; they only make you a friendly visit; the more ceremony, you know, the less welcome. Pray, sir, let me entreat you not to be profuse. If I can be of service, pray command me; my mistress has sent me on purpose; while Mr Sharp is doing the business without doors, I may be employed within. (*to* SHARP) If you'll lend me the keys of your sideboard I'll dispose of your plate to the best advantage. (*knocking*)

SHARP: Thank you, Mrs Kitty; but it is disposed of already. (*knocking at the door*)

KITTY: Bless me, the company's come! I'll go to the door and conduct 'em into your presence. (*Exit.*)

SHARP: If you'd conduct 'em into a horse-pond, and wait of 'em there yourself, we should be more obliged to you.

GAY: I can never support this!

SHARP: Rouse your spirits and put on an air of gaiety, and I don't despair of bringing you off yet.

GAY: Your words have done it effectually.

> (*Enter* KITTY *with* MRS GADABOUT, *her* DAUGHTER *and*
> NIECE, MR GUTTLE, MR TRIPPIT *and* MRS TRIPPIT.)

GAD: Ah, my dear Mr Gayless! (*Kisses him.*)

GAY: My dear widow! (*Kisses her.*)

GAD: We are come to give you joy, Mr Gayless.

SHARP: (*aside*) You never was more mistaken in your life.

GAD: I have brought some company here, I believe, is not so well known to you, and I protest I have been all about the town to get the little I have – Prissy, my dear – Mr Gayless, my daughter.

GAY: And as handsome as her mother. You must have a husband shortly, my dear.

PRIS: I'll assure you I don't despair, sir.

GAD: My niece, too.

GAY: I know by her eyes she belongs to you, widow.

GAD: Mr Guttle, sir, Mr Gayless; Mr Gayless, Justice Guttle.

GAY: (*aside*) Oh, destruction! One of the quorum.

GUT: Hem, though I had not the honour of any personal knowledge of you, yet at the instigation of Mrs Gadabout I have, without any previous acquaintance with you, throwed aside all ceremony to let you know that I joy to hear the solemnisation of your nuptials is so near at hand.

GAY: Sir, though I cannot answer you with the same elocution, however, sir, I thank you with the same sincerity.

---

quorum: bench of justices.

GAD: Mr and Mrs Trippit, sir, the properest lady in the world for your purpose, for she'll dance for four and twenty hours together.

TRIP: My dear Charles, I am very angry with you, faith; so near marriage and not let me know; 'twas barbarous. You thought, I suppose, I should rally you upon it; but dear Mrs Trippit here has long ago eradicated all my anti-matrimonial principles.

MRS TRIP: I eradicate! Fie, Mr Trippit, don't be so obscene.

KITTY: Pray, ladies, walk into the next room; Mr Sharp can't lay his cloth till you are set down to cards.

GAD: One thing I had quite forgot; Mr Gayless, my nephew who you never saw will be in town from France presently, so I left word to send him here immediately to make one.

GAY: You do me honour, madam.

SHARP: Do the ladies choose cards or the supper first?

GAY: (*aside*) Supper! What does the fellow mean?

GUT: Oh, the supper by all means, for I have eat nothing to signify since dinner.

SHARP: (*aside*) Nor I, since last Monday was a fortnight.

GAY: Pray, ladies, walk into the next room: Sharp, get things ready for supper, and call the music.

SHARP: Well said, master.

GAY: Without ceremony, ladies.

(Exeunt ladies and GAYLESS.)

KITTY: (*aside*) I'll to my mistress, and let her know everything is ready for her appearance. (*Exit.*)

GUT: Pray Mr What's-your-name, don't be long with supper; but hark'ee, what can I do in the meantime? Suppose you get me a pipe and some good wine; I'll try to divert myself that way till supper's ready.

SHARP: Or suppose, sir, you was to take a nap till then; there's a very easy couch in that closet.

GUT: The best thing in the world. I'll take your advice, but be sure to wake me when supper is ready. (*Exit.*)

SHARP: Pray heav'n you may not wake till then! What a fine situation my master is in at present! I have promised him my assistance, but his affairs are in so desperate a way, that I am afraid 'tis out of all my skill to recover 'em. Well, fools have fortune, says an old proverb, and a very true one it is, for my master and I are two of the most unfortunate mortals in the creation.

(Enter GAYLESS.)

GAY: Well, Sharp, I have set 'em down to cards, and now what have you to propose?

SHARP: I have one scheme left which in all probability may succeed. The good citizen, overloaded with his last meal, is taking a nap in that closet, in order to get him an appetite for yours. Suppose, sir, we should make him treat us.

GAY: I don't understand you.

SHARP: I'll pick his pocket, and provide us a supper with the booty.

GAY: Monstrous! For without considering the villainy of it, the danger of waking him makes it impracticable!

SHARP: If he wakes, I'll smother him, and lay his death to indigestion — a very common death among the justices.

GAY: Prithee be serious, we have no time to lose. Can you invent nothing to drive 'em out of the house?

SHARP: I can fire it.

GAY: Shame and confusion so perplex me, I cannot give myself a moment's thought.

SHARP: I have it; did not Mrs Gadabout say her nephew would be here?

GAY: She did.

SHARP: Say no more, but in to your company; if I don't send 'em out of the house for the night, I'll at least frighten their stomachs away; and if this stratagem fails, I'll relinquish politics, and think my understanding no better than my neighbours'.

GAY: How shall I reward thee, Sharp?

SHARP: By your silence and obedience; away to your company, sir. (*Exit GAYLESS.*) Now, dear madam Fortune, for once, open your eyes, and behold a poor unfortunate man of parts addressing you; now is your time to convince your foes you are not that blind whimsical whore they take you for; but let 'em see by your assisting me, that men of sense, as well as fools, are sometimes entitled to your favour and protection. So much for prayer, now for a great noise and a lie. (*Goes aside and cries out.*) Help, help, master; help, gentlemen, ladies; murder, fire, brimstone; help, help, help!

> (*Enter GAYLESS, TRIPPET and the ladies, with cards in their hands, and SHARP enters running, and meets them.*)

GAY: What's the matter?

SHARP: Matter, sir! If you don't run this minute with that gentleman, this lady's nephew will be murdered; I am sure 'twas he; he was set upon at the corner of the street, by four; he has killed two, and if you don't make haste, he'll be either murdered or took to prison.

GAD: For heaven's sake, gentlemen, run to his assistance. (*aside*) How I tremble for Melissa; this frolic of hers may be fatal.

GAY: Draw, sir, and follow me.

> (*Exeunt GAYLESS and GADABOUT.*)

TRIP: Not I; I don't care to run myself into needless quarrels; I have suffered too much formerly by flying into passions; besides I have pawned my honour to Mrs Trippit, never to draw my sword again; and in her present condition, to break my word might have fatal consequences.

SHARP: Pray, sir, don't excuse yourself; the young gentleman may be murdered by this time.

TRIP: Then my assistance will be of no service to him; however — I'll go to oblige you, and look on at a distance.

MRS TRIP: I shall certainly faint, Mr Trippit, if you draw.

> (*Enter GUTTLE, disordered, as from sleep.*)

GUT: What noise and confusion is this?

SHARP: Sir, there's a man murdered in the street.

GUT: Is that all — zounds, I was afraid you had throwed the supper down — a plague of your noise! I shan't recover my stomach this half hour.

> (*Enter GAYLESS and GADABOUT, with MELISSA in boy's clothes, dressed in the French manner.*)

GAD: Well, but my dear Jemmy, you are not hurt, sure?

MEL: A little with riding post only.

GAD: Mr Sharp alarmed us all with an account of your being set upon by four men; that you had killed two, and was attacking the other when he came away, and when we met you at the door, we were running to your rescue.

MEL: I had a small encounter with half a dozen villains; but finding me resolute, they were wise enough to take to their heels; I believe I scratched some of 'em (*laying her hand to her sword*).

SHARP: (*aside*) His vanity has saved my credit. I have a thought come into my head may prove to our advantage, provided monsieur's ignorance bears any proportion to his impudence.

GAD: Now my fright's over, let me introduce you, my dear, to Mr Gayless. Sir, this is my nephew.

GAY: (*saluting her*) Sir, I shall be proud of your friendship.

MEL: I don't doubt but we shall be better acquainted in a little time.

GUT: Pray, sir, what news in France?

MEL: Faith, sir, very little that I know of in the political way; I had no time to spend among the politicians. I was —

GAY: Among the ladies, I suppose.

MEL: Too much, indeed. Faith, I have not philosophy enough to resist their solicitations; (*to* GAYLESS *aside*) you take me.

GAY: (*aside to* SHARP) Yes, to be a most incorrigible fop; 'sdeath, this puppy's impertinence is an addition to my misery.

MEL: (*aside to* GADABOUT) Poor Gayless, what shifts is he reduced to? I cannot bear to see him much longer in this condition; I shall discover myself.

GAD: Not before the end of the play; besides, the more his pains now, the greater his pleasure when relieved from it.

TRIP: Shall we return to our cards? I have a *sans prendre* here, and must insist you play it out.

LADIES: With all my heart.

MEL: *Allons donc.*

(*As the company goes out,* SHARP *pulls* MELISSA *by the sleeve.*)

SHARP: Sir, sir, shall I beg leave to speak with you? Pray, did you find a bank-note in your way hither?

MEL: What, between here and Dover do you mean?

SHARP: No, sir, within twenty or thirty yards of this house.

MEL: You are drunk, fellow.

SHARP: I am undone, sir; but not drunk, I'll assure you.

MEL: What is all this?

SHARP: I'll tell you, sir; a little while ago my master sent me out to change a note of twenty pounds; but I, unfortunately hearing a noise in the street of 'damme, sir', and clashing of swords, and 'rascal', and 'murder', I runs up to the place, and saw four men upon one; and having heard you was a mettlesome young gentleman, I immediately concluded it must be you; so ran back

---

sans prendre: winning hand of cards.

to call my master, and when I went to look for the note to change it, I found it gone, either stole or lost; and if I don't get the money immediately, I shall certainly be turned out of my place, and lose my character.

MEL: (*aside*) I shall laugh in his face. — Oh, I'll speak to your master about it, and he will forgive you at my intercession.

SHARP: Ah, sir! You don't know my master.

MEL: I'm very little acquainted with him; but I have heard he's a very good-natured man.

SHARP: I have heard so too, but I have felt it otherwise; he has so much good nature, that, if I could compound for one broken head a day, I should think myself very well off.

MEL: Are you serious, friend?

SHARP: Look'ee, sir, I take you for a man of honour; there is something in your face that is generous, open, and masculine; you don't look like a foppish, effeminate tell-tale; so I'll venture to trust you. See here, sir — (*Shows his head.*) these are the effects of my master's good nature.

MEL: (*aside*) Matchless impudence! — Why do you live with him then after such usage?

SHARP: He's worth a great deal of money, and when he's drunk, which is commonly once a day, he's very free, and will give me anything; but I design to leave him when he's married, for all that.

MEL: Is he going to be married then?

SHARP: Tomorrow, sir, and between you and I, he'll meet with his match, both for humour and something else too.

MEL: What, she drinks too?

SHARP: Damnably, sir; but mum. You must know this entertainment was designed for madam tonight; but she got so very gay after dinner, that she could not walk out of her own house; so her maid, who was half gone too, came here with an excuse, that Mrs Melissa had got the vapours, and so she had indeed violently; here, here, sir (*pointing to his head*).

MEL: (*aside*) This is scarcely to be borne. — Melissa! I have heard of her; they say she's very whimsical.

SHARP: A very woman, and it please your honour, and between you and I, none of the mildest or wisest of her sex — but to return, sir, to the twenty pounds.

MEL: I am surprised you who have got so much money in his service, should be at a loss for twenty pounds, to save your bones at this juncture.

SHARP: I have put all my money out at interest; I never keep above five pounds by me; and if your honour would lend me the other fifteen, and take my note for it — (*knocking*)

MEL: Somebody's at the door.

SHARP: I can give very good security. (*knocking*)

MEL: Don't let the people wait, Mr —

SHARP: Ten pounds will do. (*knocking*)

MEL: *Allez-vous-en!*

SHARP: Five, sir. (*knocking*)

MEL: *Je ne puis pas.*

SHARP: (*aside*) '*Je ne puis pas.*' I find we shan't understand one another. I do but

lose time; and, if I had any thought, I might have known young fops return
from their travels generally with as little money as improvement. (*Exit.*)

MEL: Ha, ha, ha, what lies doth this fellow invent, and what rogueries does he com-
mit for his master's service? There never sure was a more faithful servant to
his master, or a greater rogue to the rest of mankind; but here he comes again;
the plot thickens; I'll in and observe Gayless. (*Exit.*)

> (*Enter* SHARP *before several persons with dishes in their hands, and
> a* COOK, *drunk.*)

SHARP: (*aside*) Fortune, I thank thee: the most lucky accident! – This way,
gentlemen, this way.

COOK: I am afraid I have mistook the house. Is this Mr Treatwell's?

SHARP: The same, the same: what, don't you know me?

COOK: Know you! Are you sure there was a supper bespoke here?

SHARP: Yes: upon my honour, Mr Cook, the company is in the next room, and
must have gone without, had not you brought it. I'll draw in a table. I see you
have brought a cloth with you; but you need not have done that, for we have
a very good stock of linen – (*aside*) at the pawnbroker's. (*Exit, and returns
immediately, drawing in a table.*) Come, come my boys, be quick. The
company began to be very uneasy; but I knew my old friend Lick-spit here
would not fail us.

COOK: Lick-spit! I am no friend of yours; so I desire less familiarity: Lick-spit too!

> (*Enter* GAYLESS, *and stares.*)

GAY: What is all this?

SHARP: (*aside to* GAYLESS) Sir, if the sight of the supper is offensive, I can easily
have it removed.

GAY: Prithee explain thyself, Sharp.

SHARP: Some of our neighbours, I suppose, have bespoke this supper; but the cook
has drank away his memory, forgot the house, and brought it here; however,
sir, if you dislike it, I'll tell him of his mistake, and send him about his business.

GAY: Hold, hold, necessity obliges me against my inclination to favour the cheat,
and feast at my neighbour's expense.

COOK: Hark you, friend, is that your master?

SHARP: Ay, and the best master in the world.

COOK: I'll speak to him then. Sir, I have, according to your commands, dressed as
genteel a supper as my art and your price would admit of.

SHARP: (*aside to* GAYLESS) Good again, sir, 'tis paid for.

GAY: I don't in the least question your abilities, Mr Cook, and I am obliged to you
for your care.

COOK: Sir, you are a gentleman, and if you would but look over the bill and
approve it (*Pulls out a bill.*) you will over and above return the obligation.

SHARP: (*aside*) Oh, the devil!

GAY: (*looking on a bill*) Very well, I'll send my man to pay you tomorrow.

COOK: I'll spare him that trouble, and take it with me, sir – I never work but for
ready money.

GAY: Hah?

SHARP: (*aside*) Then you won't have our custom. – My master is busy now,
friend; do you think he won't pay you?

COOK: No matter what I think; either my meat or my money.

SHARP: 'Twill be very ill-convenient for him to pay you tonight.

COOK: Then I'm afraid it will be ill-convenient to pay me tomorrow, so d'ye hear —
   (*Enter* MELISSA.)

GAY: Prithee be advised! 'Sdeath, I shall be discovered! (*Takes the* COOK *aside*.)

MEL: (*to* SHARP) What's the matter?

SHARP: The cook has not quite answered my master's expectations about the
   supper, sir, and he's a little angry at him, that's all.

MEL: Come, come, Mr Gayless, don't be uneasy; a bachelor cannot be supposed to
   have things in the utmost regularity; we don't expect it.

COOK: But I do expect it, and will have it.

MEL: What does that drunken fool say?

COOK: That I will have my money, and I won't stay till tomorrow — and, and —

SHARP: (*Runs and stops his mouth*) Hold, hold, what are you doing? Are you
   mad?

MEL: What do you stop the man's breath for?

SHARP: Sir, he was going to call you names. — Don't be abusive, cook; the gentleman is a man of honour, and said nothing to you; pray be pacified; you are in
   liquor.

COOK: I will have my —

SHARP: (*holding, still*) Why, I tell you, fool, you mistake the gentleman; he is a
   friend of my master's, and has not said a word to you. — Pray, good sir, go
   into the next room. The fellow's drunk, and takes you for another. — You'll
   repent this when you are sober, friend. — Pray, sir, don't stay to hear his
   impertinence.

GAY: Pray, sir, walk in — he's below your anger.

MEL: Damn the rascal! What does he mean by affronting me! Let the scoundrel go;
   I'll polish his brutality, I warrant you: here's the best reformer of manners in
   the universe. (*Draws her sword.*) Let him go, I say.

SHARP: So, so you have done finely, now. — Get away as fast as you can: he's the
   most courageous mettlesome man in all England. Why, if his passion was up
   he could eat you. — Make your escape, you fool!

COOK: I won't. Eat me! He'll find me damned hard of digestion though —

SHARP: Prithee come here; let me speak with you. (*They walk aside.*)
   (*Enter* KITTY.)

KITTY: Gad's me, is supper on the table already? Sir, pray defer it for a few
   moments; my mistress is much better, and will be here immediately.

GAY: Will she indeed! Bless me — I did not expect — but however — Sharp?

KITTY: (*aside to* MELISSA) What success, madam?

MEL: As we could wish, girl — but he is in such pain and perplexity I can't hold it
   out much longer.

KITTY: Ay, that not holding out is the ruin of half our sex.

SHARP: I have pacified the cook, and if you can but borrow twenty pieces of that
   young prig, all may go well yet; you may succeed though I could not:
   remember what I told you — about it straight, sir —

GAY: (*to* MELISSA) Sir, sir, I beg to speak a word with you; my servant, sir, tells
   me that he has had the misfortune, sir, to lose a note of mine of twenty

pounds, which I sent him to receive — and the bankers' shops being shut up, and having very little cash by me, I should be much obliged to you if you would favour me with twenty pieces till tomorrow.

MEL: Oh, sir, with all my heart (*taking out her purse*), and as I have a small favour to beg of you, sir, the obligation will be mutual.

GAY: How may I oblige you, sir?

MEL: You are to be married, I hear, to Melissa.

GAY: Tomorrow, sir.

MEL: Then you'll oblige me, sir, by never seeing her again.

GAY: Do you call this a small favour, sir!

MEL: A mere trifle, sir — breaking of contracts, suing for divorces, committing adultery, and such like, are all reckoned trifles nowadays; and smart young fellows, like you and myself, Gayless, should never be out of fashion.

GAY: But pray, sir, how are you concerned in this affair!

MAL: Oh, sir, you must know I have a very great regard for Melissa, and, indeed, she for me; and, by the by, I have a most despicable opinion of you; for *entre nous*, I take you, Charles, to be a very great scoundrel.

GAY: Sir!

MEL: Nay, don't look fierce, sir! and give yourself airs — damme, sir, I shall be through your body else in the snapping of a finger.

GAY: I'll be as quick as you, villain! (*Draws and makes at* MELISSA.)

KITTY: Hold, hold, murder! You'll kill my mistress — the young gentleman, I mean.

GAY: Ah! Her mistress! (*Drops his sword.*)

SHARP: How! Melissa! Nay, then drive away cart. All's over now.
         (*Enter all the company laughing.*)

GAD: What, Mr Gayless, engaging with Melissa before your time. Ah, ah, ah!

KITTY: (*to* SHARP) Your humble servant, good Mr Politician. — This is, gentlemen and ladies, the most celebrated and ingenious Timothy Sharp, schemer general, and redoubted squire to the most renowned and fortunate adventurer Charles Gayless, knight of the woeful countenance: ha, ha, ha! Oh, that dismal face and more dismal head of yours. (*Strikes* SHARP *upon the head.*)

SHARP: 'Tis cruel in you to disturb a man in his last agonies.

MEL: Now, Mr Gayless! What, not a word! You are sensible I can be no stranger to your misfortunes, and I might reasonably expect an excuse for your ill treatment of me.

GAY: No, madam, silence is my only refuge; for to endeavour to vindicate my crimes would show a greater want of virtue than even the commission of 'em.

MEL: Oh, Gayless! 'Twas poor to impose upon a woman, and one that loved you too.

GAY: Oh, most unpardonable; but my necessities —

SHARP: And mine, madam, were not to be matched, I'm sure, o' this side starving.

MEL: (*aside*) His tears have softened me at once. — Your necessities, Mr Gayless, with such real contrition, are too powerful motives not to affect the breast

---

Drive away cart: the cart in which convicted villains were driven to execution. (First edn has *care*.)

already prejudiced in your favour — you have suffered too much already for your extravagance; and as I take part in your sufferings, 'tis easing myself to relieve you: know, therefore, all that's past I freely forgive.

GAY: You cannot mean it, sure: I am lost in wonder.

MEL: Prepare yourself for more wonder — you have another friend in masquerade here: Mr Cook, pray throw aside your drunkenness, and make your sober appearance. Don't you know that face, sir?

COOK: Ay, master, what, have you forgot your friend Dick, as you used to call me?

GAY: More wonder indeed! Don't you live with my father?

MEL: Just after your hopeful servant there had left me, comes this man from Sir William with a letter to me; upon which (being by that wholly convinced of your necessitous condition) I invented by the help of Kitty and Mrs Gadabout, this little plot, in which your friend Dick there has acted miracles, resolving to tease you a little, that you might have a greater relish for a happy turn in your affairs. Now, sir, read that letter, and complete your joy.

GAY: (*reads*) 'Madam, I am father to the unfortunate young man, who, I hear by a friend of mine (that by my desire, has been a continual spy upon him) is making his addresses to you: if he is so happy as to make himself agreeable to you (whose character I am charmed with) I shall own him with joy for my son, and forget his former follies. I am,

Madam,

Your most humble servant,

William Gayless.

P.S. I will be soon in town myself to congratulate his reformation and marriage.' Oh, Melissa, this is too much; thus let me show my thanks and gratitude (*kneeling; she raises him*) for here 'tis only due.

SHARP: A reprieve! a reprieve! a reprieve!

KITTY: (*to* GAYLESS) I have been, sir, a most bitter enemy to you; but since you are likely to be a little more conversant with cash than you have been, I am now, with the greatest sincerity, your most obedient friend and humble servant. And I hope, sir, all former enmity will be forgotten.

GAY: Oh, Mrs Pry, I have been too much indulged with forgiveness myself not to forgive lesser offences in other people.

SHARP: Well then, madam, since my master has vouchsafed pardon to your handmaid Kitty, I hope you'll not deny it to his footman Timothy.

MEL: Pardon! For what?

SHARP: Only for telling you about ten thousand lies, madam, and, among the rest, insinuating that your ladyship would —

MEL: I understand you; and can forgive anything, Sharp, that was designed for the service of your master; and if Pry and you will follow our example, I'll give her a small fortune as a reward for both your fidelities.

SHARP: I fancy, madam, 'twould be better to halve the small fortune between us, and keep us both single: for as we shall live in the same house, in all probability we may taste the comforts of matrimony, and not be troubled with its inconveniences. What say you, Kitty?

KITTY: Do you hear, Sharp, before you talk of the comforts of matrimony, taste the comforts of a good dinner, and recover your flesh a little; do, puppy.

SHARP: The devil backs her, that's certain; and I am no match for her at any weapon.

MEL: And now, Mr Gayless, to show I have not provided for you by halves, let the music prepare themselves, and, with the approbation of the company, we'll have a dance.

ALL: By all means, a dance.

GUT: By all means a dance — after supper though —

SHARP: Oh, pray, sir, have supper first, or, I'm sure, I shan't live till the dance is finished.

GAY: Behold, Melissa, as sincere a convert as ever truth and beauty made. The wild impetuous sallies of my youth are now blown over, and a most pleasing calm of perfect happiness succeeds.

> Thus Aetna's flames the verdant earth consume,
> But milder heat makes drooping nature bloom:
> So virtuous love affords us springing joy,
> Whilst vicious passions, as they burn, destroy.

3. George Colman, oil painting by Thomas Gainsborough

THE JEALOUS WIFE

by George Colman the Elder

First performed at the Theatre Royal, Drury Lane,
12 February 1761, with the following cast:

OAKLY	Mr Garrick
MAJOR OAKLY	Mr Yates
CHARLES	Mr Palmer
RUSSET	Mr Burton
SIR HARRY BEAGLE	Mr King
LORD TRINKET	Mr O'Brien
CAPTAIN O'CUTTER	Mr Moody
PARIS	Mr Blakes
WILLIAM	Mr Ackman
JOHN	Mr Castle
TOM	Mr Clough
SERVANT TO LADY FREELOVE	Mr Fox
MRS OAKLY	Mrs Pritchard
LADY FREELOVE	Mrs Clive
HARRIOT	Miss Pritchard
TOILET	Mrs Johnston
CHAMBERMAID	Mrs Simpson

ACT I

A room in OAKLY's *house. Noise heard within.*

MRS OAK: (*within*) Don't tell me! I know it is so. It's monstrous, and I will not bear it.

OAK: (*within*) But, my dear!

MRS OAK: (*within*) Nay, nay, *etc.* (*squabbling within*)

        (*Enter* MRS OAKLY, *with a letter,* OAKLY *following.*)

MRS OAK: Say what you will, Mr Oakly, you shall never persuade me but this is some filthy intrigue of yours.

OAK: I can assure you, my love —

MRS OAK: Your love! Don't I know your — Tell me, I say, this instant, every circumstance relating to this letter.

OAK: How can I tell you, when you will not so much as let me see it?

MRS OAK: Look you, Mr Oakly, this usage is not to be borne. You take a pleasure in abusing my tenderness and soft disposition. To be perpetually running over the whole town, nay, the whole kingdom too, in pursuit of your amours! Did not I discover that you were great with Mademoiselle, my own woman? Did not you contract a shameful familiarity with Mrs Freeman? Did not I detect your intrigue with Lady Wealthy? Were not you —

OAK: Ooons, madam, the Grand Turk himself has not half so many mistresses! You throw me out of all patience. Do I know anybody but our common friends? Am I visited by anybody that does not visit you? Do I ever go out, unless you go with me? And am I not as constantly by your side as if I was tied to your apron strings?

MRS OAK: Go, go, you are a false man. Have not I found you out a thousand times? And have I not this moment a letter in my hand, which convinces me of your baseness? Let me know the whole affair, or I will —

OAK: Let you know! Let me know what you would have of me. You stop my letter before it comes to my hands, and then expect that I should know the contents of it.

MRS OAK: Heaven be praised! I stopped it. I suspected some of these doings for some time past. But the letter informs me who she is, and I'll be revenged on her sufficiently. Oh, you base man, you!

OAK: I beg, my dear, that you would moderate your passion! Show me the letter, and I'll convince you of my innocence.

MRS OAK: Innocence! abominable! innocence! But I am not to be made such a fool. I am convinced of your perfidy, and very sure that —

OAK: 'Sdeath and fire! Your passion hurries you out of your senses. Will you hear me?

MRS OAK: No, you are a base man, and I will not hear you.

OAK: Why then, my dear, since you will neither talk reasonably yourself, nor listen to reason from me, I shall take my leave till you are in a better humour. So, your servant! (*going*)

MRS OAK: Ay, go, you cruel man! Go to your mistresses, and leave your poor wife to her miseries. How unfortunate a woman am I! I could die with vexation (*throwing herself into a chair*).

OAK: There it is. Now dare not I stir a step further. If I offer to go, she is in one of her fits in an instant. Never, sure, was woman at once of so violent and so delicate a constitution! What shall I say to soothe her? — Nay, never make thyself so uneasy, my dear. Come, come, you know I love you. Nay, nay, you shall be convinced.

MRS OAK: I know you hate me; and that your unkindness and barbarity will be the death of me (*whining*).

OAK: Do not vex yourself at this rate. I love you most passionately. Indeed I do. This must be some mistake.

MRS OAK: Oh, I am an unhappy woman! (*weeping*)

OAK: Dry up thy tears, my love, and be comforted! You will find that I am not to blame in this matter. Come, let me see this letter. Nay, you shall not deny me (*taking the letter*).

MRS OAK: There! take it! You know the hand, I am sure.

OAK: (*reading*) 'To Charles Oakly, Esq.' — Hand! 'Tis a clerk-like hand, indeed! A good round text! and was certainly never penned by a fair lady.

MRS OAK: Ay, laugh at me, do!

OAK: Forgive me, my love, I did not mean to laugh at thee. But what says the letter? — (*reading*)
'Daughter eloped — You must be privy to it — scandalous — dishonourable — satisfaction — revenge' — um, um, um — 'injured father,
Henry Russet.'

MRS OAK: (*rising*) Well, sir, you see I have detected you. Tell me this instant where she is concealed.

OAK: (*to himself*) So, so, so! — This hurts me — I am shocked.

MRS OAK: What! Are you confounded with your guilt? Have I caught you at last?

OAK: (*to himself*) Oh that wicked Charles! To decoy a young lady from her parents in the country! The profligacy of the young fellows of this age is abominable.

MRS OAK: (*half aside and musing*) Charles! — Let me see! — Charles! — No! impossible! This is all a trick.

OAK: (*to himself*) He has certainly ruined this poor lady.

MRS OAK: Art! art! all art! There's a sudden turn now! You have a ready wit for intrigue, I find.

OAK: (*to himself*) Such an abandoned action! I wish I had never had the care of him.

MRS OAK: Mighty fine, Mr Oakly! — Go on, sir, go on! I see what you mean. Your assurance provokes me beyond your very falsehood itself. So you imagine, sir, that this affected concern, this flimsy pretence about Charles, is to bring you off. Matchless confidence! But I am armed against everything. I am prepared for all your dark schemes. I am aware of all your low stratagems.

OAK: See there now! Was ever anything so provoking? To persevere in your ridiculous — For heaven's sake, my dear, don't distract me. When you see my mind thus agitated and uneasy, that a young fellow, whom his dying father, my own brother, committed to my care, should be guilty of such enormous wickedness; I say, when you are witness of my distress on this occasion, how can you be weak enough, and cruel enough to —

MRS OAK: Prodigiously well, sir! You do it very well. Nay, keep it up, carry it on, there's nothing like going through with it. Oh you artful creature! But, sir, I am not to be so easily satisfied. I do not believe a syllable of all this. Give me the letter. (*snatching the letter*) You shall sorely repent this vile business, for I am resolved that I will know the bottom of it. (*Exit.*)

OAK: (*alone*) This is beyond all patience. Provoking woman. Her absurd suspicions interpret everything the wrong way. She delights to make me wretched, because she sees I am attached to her; and converts my tenderness and affection into the instruments of my own torture. But this ungracious boy! In how many troubles will he involve his own and this lady's family! I never imagined that he was of such abandoned principles. – Oh, here he comes!

(*Enter* MAJOR OAKLY *and* CHARLES.)

CHAR: Good-morrow, sir!

MAJ: Good-morrow, brother, good-morrow! What! you have been at the old work, I find. I heard you – ding-dong! i'faith! She has rung a noble peal in your ears. But how now? Why, sure, you've had a remarkable warm bout on't. You seem more ruffled than usual.

OAK: I am indeed, brother! thanks to that young gentleman there. Have a care, Charles! You may be called to a severe account for this. The honour of a family, sir, is no such light matter.

CHAR: Sir!

MAJ: Heyday! What, has a curtain-lecture produced a lecture of morality? What is all this?

OAK: To a profligate mind, perhaps, these things may appear agreeable in the beginning. But don't you tremble at the consequences?

CHAR: I see, sir, that you are displeased with me, but I am quite at a loss how to guess at the occasion.

OAK: Tell me, sir! where is Miss Harriot Russet?

CHAR: Miss Harriot Russet! Sir, explain.

OAK: Have not you decoyed her from her father?

CHAR: I! decoyed her! decoyed my Harriot! I would sooner die than do her the least injury. What can this mean?

MAJ: I believe the young dog has been at her, after all.

OAK: I was in hopes, Charles, you had better principles. But there is a letter just come from her father –

CHAR: A letter! What letter? Dear sir, give it me. Some intelligence of my Harriot, major! The letter, sir, the letter this moment, for heaven's sake!

OAK: If this warmth, Charles, tends to prove your innocence –

CHAR: Dear sir, excuse me. I'll prove anything. Let me but see this letter, and I'll –

OAK: Let you see it? I could hardly get a sight of it myself. Mrs Oakly has it.

CHAR: Has she got it? Major, I'll be with you again directly. (*Exit hastily.*)

MAJ: Heyday! The devil's in the boy! What a fiery set of people! By my troth, I think the whole family is made up of nothing but combustibles.

OAK: I like this emotion. It looks well. It may serve, too, to convince my wife of the folly of her suspicions. Would to heaven I could quiet them forever!

MAJ: Why, pray now, my dear naughty brother, what heinous offence have you committed this morning? What new cause of suspicion? You have been asking one of the maids to mend your ruffle, I suppose; or have been hanging your head out of the window, when a pretty young woman has passed by; or —

OAK: How can you trifle with my distresses, major? Did not I tell you it was about a letter?

MAJ: A letter! hum! a suspicious circumstance, to be sure! What, and the seal a true-lover's knot now, ha? or an heart transfixed with darts; or possibly the wax bore the industrious impression of a thimble; or perhaps, the folds were lovingly connected by a wafer, pricked with a pin, and the direction written in a vile scrawl, and not a word spelled as it should be. Ha, ha, ha!

OAK: Pooh, brother! whatever it was, the letter, you find, was for Charles, not for me. This outrageous jealousy is the devil.

MAJ: Mere matrimonial blessings and domestic comfort, brother! Jealousy is a certain sign of love.

OAK: Love! It is this very love that has made us both so miserable. Her love for me has confined me to my house, like a state prisoner, without the liberty of seeing my friends, or the use of pen, ink, and paper; while my love for her has made such a fool of me, that I have never had the spirit to contradict her.

MAJ: Ay, ay, there you've hit it: Mrs Oakly would make an excellent wife, if you did but know how to manage her.

OAK: You are a rare fellow, indeed, to talk of managing a wife. A debauched bachelor, a rattle-brained rioting fellow, who have picked up your commonplace notions of women in bagnios, taverns, and the camp; whose most refined commerce with the sex has been in order to delude country girls at your quarters, or to besiege the virtue of abigails, milliners, or mantuamakers' prentices.

MAJ: So much the better! So much the better! Women are all alike in the main, brother; high or low, married or single, quality or no quality. I have found them so, from a duchess down to a milkmaid.

OAK: Your savage notions are ridiculous. What do you know of a husband's feelings? You, who comprise all your qualities in your *honour*, as you call it! Dead to all sentiments of delicacy, and incapable of any but the grossest attachments to women! This is your boasted refinement, your thorough knowledge of the world! While, with regard to women, one poor train of thinking, one narrow set of ideas, like the uniform of the regiment, serves the whole corps.

MAJ: Very fine, brother! there's commonplace for you, with a vengeance. Henceforth, expect no quarter from me. I tell you again and again, I know the sex better than you do. They all love to give themselves airs, and to have power. Every woman is a tyrant at the bottom. But they could never make a fool of me. No, no! No woman should ever domineer over me, let her be mistress or wife.

OAK: Single men can be no judges in these cases. They must happen in all families.

---

wafer: thin disc of dried paste used for fixing papers together.
bagnios: brothels.
abigails: maids.

But when things are driven to extremities – to see a woman in uneasiness – a woman one loves too – one's wife – who can withstand it? You neither speak nor think like a man that has loved, and been married, major.

MAJ: I wish I could hear a married man speak my language. I'm a bachelor, it's true; but I am no bad judge of your case, for all that. I know yours and Mrs Oakly's disposition to a hair. She is all impetuosity and fire; a very magazine of touchwood and gunpowder. You are hot enough too upon occasion, but then it's over in an instant. In comes love and conjugal affection, as you call it; that is, mere folly and weakness; and you draw off your forces, just when you should pursue the attack, and follow your advantage. Have at her with spirit, and the day's your own, brother!

OAK: I tell you, brother, you mistake the matter. Sulkiness, fits, tears! These, and such as these, are the things which make a feeling man uneasy. Her passion and violence have not half such an effect on me.

MAJ: Why, then, you may be sure, she'll play that upon you which she finds does most execution. But you must be proof against everything. If she's furious, set passion against passion; if you find her at her tricks, play off art against art, and foil her at her own weapons. That's your game, brother!

OAK: Why, what would you have me do?

MAJ: Do as you please for one month, whether she like it or not; and I'll answer for it, she will consent you shall do as you please all her life after.

OAK: This is fine talking. You do not consider the difficulty that –

MAJ: You must overcome all difficulties. Assert your right boldly, man! Give your own orders to servants, and see they observe them; read your own letters, and never let her have a sight of them; make your own appointments, and never be persuaded to break them; see what company you like; go out when you please; return when you please; and don't suffer yourself to be called to account where you have been. In short, do but show yourself a man of spirit, leave off whining about love and tenderness, and nonsense, and the business is done, brother!

OAK: I believe you're in the right, major! I see you're in the right. I'll do't, I'll certainly do't. But then it hurts me to the soul, to think what uneasiness I shall give her. The first opening of my design will throw her into fits, and the pursuit of it, perhaps, may be fatal.

MAJ: Fits! ha, ha, ha! Fits! I'll engage to cure her of her fits. Nobody understands hysterical cases better than I do. Besides, my sister's symptoms are not very dangerous. Did you ever hear of her falling into a fit, when you were not by? Was she ever found in convulsions in her closet? No, no! These fits, the more care you take of them, the more you will increase the distemper. Let them alone, and they will wear themselves out, I warrant you.

OAK: True; very true; you're certainly in the right. I'll follow your advice. Where do you dine today? I'll order the coach, and go with you.

MAJ: Oh brave! Keep up this spirit, and you're made forever.

OAK: You shall see now, major! Who's there? (*Enter* SERVANT.) Order the coach directly. I shall dine out today.

SERV: The coach, sir? Now, sir?

OAK: Ay, now, immediately.

SERV: Now, sir? The – the – coach, sir? That is – my mistress –

OAK: Sirrah, do as you're bid. Bid them put to this instant.

SERV: Ye – yes, sir; yes, sir. (*Exit.*)

OAK: Well, where shall we dine?

MAJ: At the St Alban's, or where you will. This is excellent, if you do but hold it.

OAK: I will have my own way, I am determined.

MAJ: That's right.

OAK: I am steel.

MAJ: Bravo!

OAK: Adamant.

MAJ: Bravissimo!

OAK: Just what you'd have me.

MAJ: Why, that's well said. But *will* you do it?

OAK: I will.

MAJ: You won't.

OAK: I will. I'll be a fool to her no longer. But hark ye, major! My hat and sword lie in my study. I'll go and steal them out, while she is busy talking with Charles.

MAJ: Steal them! For shame! Prithee take them boldly, call for them, make them bring them to you here, and go out with spirit, in the face of your whole family!

OAK: No, no; you are wrong. Let her rave after I am gone, and when I return, you know, I shall exert myself with more propriety, after this open affront to her authority.

MAJ: Well, take your own way.

OAK: Ay, ay; let me manage it, let me manage it. (*Exit.*)

MAJ: (*alone*) Manage it! Ay, to be sure, you're a rare manager! It is dangerous, they say, to meddle between man and wife. I am no great favourite of Mrs Oakly's already; and in a week's time I expect to have the door shut in my teeth. (*Enter* CHARLES.) How now, Charles, what news?

CHAR: Ruined and undone! She's gone, uncle! My Harriot's lost forever!

MAJ: Gone off with a man? I thought so; they are all alike.

CHAR: Oh, no! Fled to avoid that hateful match with Sir Harry Beagle.

MAJ: Faith, a girl of spirit! Joy, Charles! I give you joy! She is your own, my boy! A fool and a great estate! Devilish strong temptations!

CHAR: A wretch! I was sure she would never think of him.

MAJ: No, to be sure! Commend me to your modesty! Refuse five thousand a year, and a baronet, for pretty Mr Charles Oakly! It is true, indeed, that the looby has not a single idea in his head, besides a hound, a hunter, a five-barred gate, and a horse-race; but then he's rich, and that will qualify his absurdities. Money is a wonderful improver of the understanding. But whence comes all this intelligence?

CHAR: In an angry letter from her father. How miserable I am! If I had not offended my Harriot, much offended her, by that foolish riot and drinking at your house in the country, she would certainly at such a time have taken refuge in my arms.

MAJ: A very agreeable refuge for a young lady, to be sure, and extremely decent!

CHAR: I am all uneasiness. Did not she tell me that she trembled at the thoughts of having trusted her affections with a man of such a wild disposition? What a heap of extravagancies was I guilty of!

MAJ: Extravagancies with a witness! Ah, you silly young dog, you would ruin yourself with her father, in spite of all I could do. There you sat, as drunk as a lord, telling the old gentleman the whole affair, and swearing you would drive Sir Harry Beagle out of the country, though I kept winking and nodding, pulling you by the sleeve, and kicking your shins under the table, in hopes of stopping you; but all to no purpose.

CHAR: What distress may she be in at this instant! alone and defenceless! Where, where can she be?

MAJ: What relations or friends has she in town?

CHAR: Relations! Let me see: faith, I have it. If she is in town, ten to one but she is at her aunt's, Lady Freelove's. I'll go thither immediately.

MAJ: Lady Freelove's! Hold, hold, Charles! Do you know her ladyship?

CHAR: Not much; but I'll break through all forms, to get to my Harriot.

MAJ: I do know her ladyship.

CHAR: Well, and what do you know of her?

MAJ: Oh, nothing! Her ladyship is a woman of the world, that's all. She'll introduce Harriot to the best company.

CHAR: What do you mean?

MAJ: Yes, yes, I would trust a wife, or a daughter, or a mistress, with Lady Freelove, to be sure! I tell you what, Charles! you're a good boy, but you don't know the world. Women are fifty times oftener ruined by their acquaintance with each other than by their attachment to men. One thorough-paced lady will train up a thousand novices. That Lady Freelove is an arrant — By the by, did not she, last summer, make formal proposals to Harriot's father from Lord Trinket?

CHAR: Yes; but they were received with the utmost contempt. The old gentleman, it seems, hates a lord, and he told her so in plain terms.

MAJ: Such an aversion to the nobility may not run in the blood. The girl, I warrant you, has no objection. However, if she's there, watch her narrowly, Charles! Lady Freelove is as mischievous as a monkey, and as cunning too. Have a care of her; I say, have a care of her.

CHAR: If she's there, I'll have her out of the house within this half hour, or set fire to it.

MAJ: Nay, now you're too violent. Stay a moment, and we'll consider what's best to be done.

(*Re-enter* OAKLY.)

OAK: Come, is the coach ready? Let us be gone. Does Charles go with us?

CHAR: I go with you! What can I do? I am so vexed and distracted, and so many thoughts crowd in upon me, I don't know what way to turn myself.

MRS OAK: (*within*) The coach! Dines out! Where is your master?

OAK: Zounds, brother, here she is!

(*Enter* MRS OAKLY.)

MRS OAK: Pray, Mr Oakly, what is the matter you cannot dine at home today?

OAK: Don't be uneasy, my dear! I have a little business to settle with my brother;

so I am only just going to dinner with him and Charles to the tavern.

MRS OAK: Why cannot you settle your business here as well as at a tavern? But it is some of your *ladies'* business, I suppose, and so you must get rid of my company. This is chiefly your fault, Major Oakly.

MAJ: (*coolly*) Lord, sister, what signifies it, whether a man dines at home or abroad?

MRS OAK: It signifies a great deal, sir! And I don't choose —

MAJ: Pooh! Let him go, my dear sister, let him go! He will be ten times better company when he comes back. I tell you what, sister: you sit at home till you are quite tired of one another, and then you grow cross, and fall out. If you would but part a little now and then, you might meet again in good humour.

MRS OAK: I beg, Major Oakly, that you would trouble yourself about your own affairs; and let me tell you, sir, that I —

OAK: Nay, do not put thyself into a passion with the major, my dear! It is not his fault; and I shall come back to thee very soon.

MRS OAK: Come back! Why need you go out? I know well enough when you mean to deceive me; for then there is always a pretence of dining with Sir John, or my lord, or somebody; but when you tell me that you are going to a tavern, it's such a barefaced affront —

OAK: This is so strange now! Why, my dear, I shall only just —

MRS OAK: Only just go after the lady in the letter, I suppose.

OAK: Well, well, I won't go then. Will that convince you? I'll stay with you, my dear. Will that satisfy you?

MAJ: (*aside to* OAKLY) For shame! hold out, if you are a man.

OAK: She has been so much vexed this morning already, I must humour her a little now.

MAJ: Fie, fie! Go out, or you're undone.

OAK: You see it's impossible.

(*aside between* OAKLY *and the* MAJOR)

(*to* MRS OAKLY) I'll dine at home with thee, my love.

MRS OAK: Ay, ay, pray do, sir! Dine at a tavern indeed! (*going*)

OAK: (*returning*) You may depend on me another time, major.

MAJ: Steel! adamant! ah!

MRS OAK: (*returning*) Mr Oakly!

OAK: Oh, my dear!

(*Exeunt. Manent* MAJOR OAKLY *and* CHARLES)

MAJ: Ha, ha, ha! There's the picture of resolution. There goes a philosopher for you! Ha, Charles!

CHAR: Oh, uncle! I have no spirits to laugh now.

MAJ: So! I have a fine time on't, between you and my brother. Will you meet me to dinner at the St Alban's, by four? We'll drink her health, and think of this affair.

CHAR: Don't depend on me: I shall be running all over the town in pursuit of my Harriot. I have been considering what you have said; but at all events I'll go directly to Lady Freelove's. If I find her not there, which way I shall direct myself, heaven knows.

MAJ: Hark ye, Charles! If you meet with her, you may be at a loss. Bring her to my house: I have a snug room, and —

CHAR: Pooh! Prithee, uncle, don't trifle with me now.

MAJ: Well, seriously then, my house is at your service.

CHAR: I thank you. But I must be gone.

MAJ: Ay, ay, bring her to my house, and we'll settle the whole affair for you. You
    shall clap her into a post-chaise, take the chaplain of our regiment along with
    you, wheel her down to Scotland, and when you come back, send to settle
    her fortune with her father. That's the modern art of making love, Charles!
    (*Exeunt.*)

ACT II

SCENE 1.   *A room in the Bull and Gate Inn. Enter* SIR HARRY BEAGLE *and*
TOM.

SIR H: Ten guineas a mare, and a crown the man; hey, Tom?

TOM: Yes, sir.

SIR H: And are you sure, Tom, that there is no f'aw in his blood?

TOM: He's as good a thing, sir, and as little beholden to the ground, as ever went
    over the turf upon four legs. Why, here's his whole pedigree, your honour.

SIR H: Is it attested?

TOM: Very well attested: it is signed by Jack Spur, and my Lord Startall (*giving the
    pedigree*).

SIR H: Let me see. (*reading*)

    'Tom-come-tickle-me was got out of the famous Tantwivy mare, by Sir Aaron
    Driver's chestnut horse White Stockings. White Stockings, his dam, was got by
    Lord Hedge's South Barb, full sister to the Proserpine filly, and his sire Tom
    Jones; his grandam was the Irish Duchess, and his grandsire 'Squire Sportly's
    Trajan; his great-grandam, and great-great-grandam, were Newmarket Peggy
    and Black Moll; and his great-grandsire, and great-great-grandsire, were Sir
    Ralph Whip's Regulus, and the famous Prince Anamaboo.

                               his
                         John X Spur,
                          mark.
                       Startall'

TOM: All fine horses, and won everything! A foal out of your honour's Bald-faced
    Venus, by this horse, would beat the world.

SIR H: Well then, we'll think on't. But pox on't, Tom, I have certainly knocked up
    my little roan gelding, in this damned wild-goose chase of threescore miles an
    end.

TOM: He's deadly blown, to be sure, your honour; and I am afraid we are upon a
    wrong scent after all. Madam Harriot certainly took across the country,
    instead of coming on to London.

SIR H: No, no, we traced her all the way up. But d'ye hear, Tom, look out among
    the stables and repositories here in town, for a smart road nag, and a strong
    horse to carry a portmanteau.

TOM: Sir Roger Turf's horses are to be sold: I'll see if there's ever a tight thing
    there. But I suppose, sir, you would have one somewhat stronger than Snip:
    I do not think he's quite enough of a horse for your honour.

SIR H: Not enough of a horse! Snip's a powerful gelding, master of two stone more than my weight. If Snip stands sound, I would not take a hundred guineas for him. Poor Snip! Go into the stable, Tom; see they give him a warm mash, and look at his heels and his eyes. But where's Mr Russet all this while?

TOM: I left the squire at breakfast on a cold pigeon-pie, and enquiring after Madam Harriot in the kitchen. I'll let him know your honour would be glad to see him here.

SIR H: Ay, do. But hark ye, Tom, be sure you take care of Snip.

TOM: I'll warrant, your honour.

SIR H: I'll be down in the stables myself by and by.

                    (*Exit* TOM.)

SIR H: (*alone*) Let me see — Out of the famous Tantwivy by White Stockings; White Stockings, his dam, full sister to the Proserpine filly, and his sire — Pox on't, how unlucky it is, that this damned accident should happen in the Newmarket week! Ten to one I lose my match with Lord Choakjade, by not riding myself; and I shall have no opportunity to hedge my bets neither. What a damned piece of work have I made on't! I have knocked up poor Snip, shall lose my match, and as to Harriot, why, the odds are that I lose my match there too. A skittish young tit! If I once get her tight in hand, I'll make her wince for it. Her estate joined to my own, I would have the finest stud and the noblest kennel in the whole country. But here comes her father, puffing and blowing like a broken-winded horse up hill.

                    (*Enter* RUSSET.)

RUS: Well, Sir Harry, have you heard anything of her?

SIR H: Yes, I have been asking Tom about her, and he says you may have her for five hundred guineas.

RUS: Five hundred guineas! How d'ye mean? Where is she? Which way did she take?

SIR H: Why, first she went to Epsom, then to Lincoln, then to Nottingham, and now she is at York.

RUS: Impossible! She could not go over half the ground in the time. What the devil are you talking of?

SIR H: Of the mare you were just now saying you wanted to buy.

RUS: The devil take the mare! Who would think of her, when I am mad about an affair of so much more consequence?

SIR H: You seemed mad about her a little while ago. She's a fine mare; a thing of shape and blood.

RUS: Damn her blood! Harriot! my dear provoking Harriot! Where can she be? Have you got any intelligence of her?

SIR H: No, faith, not I. We seem to be quite thrown out here. But, however, I have ordered Tom to try if he can hear anything of her among the ostlers.

RUS: Why don't you enquire after her yourself? Why don't you run up and down the whole town after her? T'other young rascal knows where she is, I warrant you. What a plague it is to have a daughter! When one loves her to distraction, and has toiled and laboured to make her happy, the ungrateful slut will sooner go to hell her own way. But she *shall* have him: I will make her happy, if I break her heart for it. A provoking gipsy! to run away, and torment her poor father, that dotes on her! I'll never see her face again. Sir Harry, how can we get any intelligence of her? Why don't you speak? Why don't you tell me? Zounds, you seem as indifferent as if you did not care a farthing about her!

SIR H: Indifferent! You may well call me indifferent. This damned chase after her will cost me a thousand. If it had not been for her, I would not have been off the course this week, to have saved the lives of my whole family. I'll hold you six to two that —

RUS: Zounds, hold your tongue, or talk more to the purpose! I swear, she is too good for you: you don't deserve such a wife. A fine, dear, sweet, lovely, charming girl! She'll break my heart. How shall I find her out? Do, prithee, Sir Harry, my dear honest friend, consider how we may discover where she is fled to.

SIR H: Suppose you put an advertisement into the newspapers, describing her marks, her age, her height, and where she strayed from. I recovered a bay mare once by that method.

RUS: Advertise her! What! describe my daughter, and expose her in the public papers, with a reward for bringing her home, like horses, stolen or strayed! — Recovered a bay mare! — The devil's in the fellow! He thinks of nothing but racers, and bay mares, and stallions. 'Sdeath! I wish your —

SIR H: I wish Harriot was fairly pounded. It would save us both a great deal of trouble.

RUS: Which way shall I turn myself? I am half distracted. If I go to that young dog's house, he has certainly conveyed her somewhere out of my reach. If she does not send to me today, I'll give her up forever. Perhaps, though, she may have met with some accident, and has nobody to assist her. No, she is certainly with that young rascal. I wish she was dead, and I was dead. I'll blow young Oakly's brains out.

(*Enter* TOM.)

SIR H: Well Tom, how is poor Snip?

TOM: A little better, sir, after his warm mash. But Lady, the pointing bitch that followed you all the way, is deadly foot-sore.

RUS: Damn Snip and Lady! Have you heard anything of Harriot?

TOM: Why, I came on purpose to let my master and your honour know, that John Ostler says as how just such a lady, as I told him Madam Harriot was, came here in a four-wheel chaise, and was fetched away soon after by a fine lady in a chariot.

RUS: Did she come alone?

TOM: Quite alone — only a servant-maid, please your honour.

RUS: And what part of the town did they go to?

TOM: John Ostler says as how they bid the coachman to drive to Grosvenor Square.

SIR H: Soho, puss! yoicks!

RUS: She is certainly gone to that young rogue. He has got his aunt to fetch her from hence. Or else she is with her own aunt, Lady Freelove. They both live

---

pounded: shut (like a stray animal) in a pound.

in that part of the town. I'll go to his house; and, in the meanwhile, Sir Harry, you shall step to Lady Freelove's. We'll find her, I warrant you. I'll teach my young mistress to be gadding. She shall marry you tonight. Come along, Sir Harry, come along! We won't lose a minute. Come along!

SIR H: Soho! hark forward! wind 'em and cross 'em! hark forward! yoicks! (*Exeunt.*)

SCENE 2.   *Scene changes to* OAKLY's.

MRS OAK: (*alone*) After all, that letter was certainly intended for my husband. I see plain enough they are all in a plot against me: my husband intriguing, the major working him up to affront me, Charles owning his letters, and so playing into each other's hands. They think me a fool, I find; but I'll be too much for them yet. I have desired to speak with Mr Oakly, and expect him here immediately. His temper is naturally open, and if he thinks my anger abated, and my suspicions laid asleep, he will certainly betray himself by his behaviour. I'll assume an air of good humour, pretend to believe the fine story they have trumped up, throw him off his guard, and so draw the secret out of him. Here he comes. How hard it is to dissemble one's anger! Oh, I could rate him soundly! But I'll keep down my indignation at present, though it chokes me. (*Enter* OAKLY.) Oh, my dear! I am very glad to see you. Pray sit down. (*They sit.*) I longed to see you. (*mildly*) It seemed an age till I had an opportunity of talking over the silly affair that happened this morning.

OAK: Why, really, my dear –

MRS OAK: Nay, don't look so grave now. Come, it's all over. Charles and you have cleared up matters. I am satisfied.

OAK: Indeed! I rejoice to hear it. You make me happy beyond my expectation. This disposition will insure our felicity. Do but lay aside your cruel, unjust suspicion, and we should never have the least difference.

MRS OAK: Indeed I begin to think so. I'll endeavour to get the better of it. And really sometimes it is very ridiculous. My uneasiness this morning, for instance! ha, ha, ha! Was not I very angry with you? ha, ha, ha! (*affecting a laugh*)

OAK: Don't mention it. Let us both forget it. Your present cheerfulness makes amends for everything.

MRS OAK: I am apt to be too violent: (*fondly*) I love you too well to be quite easy about you. Well; no matter. What is become of Charles?

OAK: Poor fellow! He is on the wing, rambling all over the town in pursuit of this young lady.

MRS OAK: Where is he gone, pray?

OAK: First of all, I believe, to some of her relations.

MRS OAK: Relations! Who are they? Where do they live?

OAK: There is an aunt of hers lives just in the neighbourhood – Lady Freelove.

MRS OAK: Lady Freelove! Oho! Gone to Lady Freelove, is he? And do you think he will hear anything of her?

OAK: I don't know; but I hope so, with all my soul.

MRS OAK: Hope! with all your soul! (*alarmed*) Do you hope so?

OAK: Hope so! Ye–yes. (*surprised*) Why, don't you hope so?

MRS OAK: Well! Yes, (*recovering*) Oh, ay, to be sure. I hope it of all things. You know, my dear, it must give me great satisfaction, as well as yourself, to see Charles well settled.

OAK: I should think so; and really I don't know where he can be settled so well. She is a most deserving young woman, I assure you.

MRS OAK: You are well acquainted with her then?

OAK: To be sure, my dear; after seeing her so often last summer at the major's house in the country, and at her father's.

MRS OAK: So often!

OAK: Oh, ay, very often — Charles took care of that — almost every day.

MRS OAK: Indeed! But, pray — a — a — a — I say, — a — a (*confused*)

OAK: What do you say, my dear?

MRS OAK: I say — a — a — (*stammering*) Is she handsome?

OAK: Prodigiously handsome indeed.

MRS OAK: Prodigiously handsome! And is she reckoned a sensible girl?

OAK: A very sensible, modest, agreeable young lady as ever I knew. You would be extremely fond of her, I am sure. You can't imagine how happy I was in her company. Poor Charles. She soon made a conquest of him, and no wonder. She has so many elegant accomplishments! Such an infinite fund of cheerfulness, and good humour! Why, she's the darling of the whole country.

MRS OAK: Lord! you seem quite in raptures about her.

OAK: Raptures! not at all. I was only telling you the young lady's character. I thought you would be glad to find that Charles had made so sensible a choice, and was so likely to be happy.

MRS OAK: Oh, Charles! True, as you say, Charles will be mighty happy.

OAK: Don't you think so?

MRS OAK: I am convinced of it. Poor Charles! I am much concerned for him. He must be very uneasy about her. I was thinking whether we could be of any service to him in this affair.

OAK: Were you, my love? That is very good of you. Why, to be sure, we must endeavour to assist him. Let me see! How can we manage it? Gad! I have hit it! The luckiest thought! and it will be of great service to Charles.

MRS OAK: (*eagerly*) Well, what is it? (*mildly*) You know I would do anything to serve Charles, and oblige you.

OAK: That is so kind! Lord, my dear, if you would but always consider things in this proper light, and continue this amiable temper, we should be the happiest people —

MRS OAK: I believe so. But what's your proposal?

OAK: I am sure you'll like it. Charles, you know, may perhaps be so lucky as to meet with this lady.

MRS OAK: True.

OAK: Now I was thinking, that he might, with your leave, my dear —

MRS OAK: Well?

OAK: Bring her home here —

MRS OAK: How!

OAK: Yes, bring her home here, my dear! It will make poor Charles's mind quite easy; and you may take her under your protection, till her father comes to town.

MRS OAK: Amazing! This is even beyond my expectation.

OAK: Why, what —

MRS OAK: Was there ever such assurance! Take her under my protection! What! Would you keep her under my nose?

OAK: Nay, I never conceived — I thought you would have approved —

MRS OAK: What! Make me your convenient woman? No place but my own house to serve your purposes?

OAK: Lord, this is the strangest misapprehension! I am quite astonished.

MRS OAK: Astonished! Yes, confused, detected, betrayed by your vain confidence of imposing on me. Why, sure you imagine me an idiot, a driveller. Charles, indeed! Yes, Charles is a fine excuse for you. The letter this morning, the letter, Mr Oakly!

OAK: The letter! Why, sure that —

MRS OAK: Is sufficiently explained. You have made it very clear to me. Now I am convinced. I have no doubt of your perfidy. But I thank you for some hints you have given me, and you may be sure I shall make use of them. Nor will I rest till I have full conviction, and overwhelm you with the strongest proofs of your baseness towards me.

OAK: Nay, but —

MRS OAK: Go, go! I have no doubt of your falsehood. Away! (*Exit.*)

OAK: (*alone*) Was there ever anything like this? Such unaccountable behaviour! Angry I don't know why! Jealous of I know not what! Pretending to be satisfied merely to draw me in, and then creating imaginary proofs out of an innocent conversation! Hints! hints I have given her! What can she mean? (*Enter* TOILET *crossing the stage.*) Toilet! Where are you going?

TOIL: To order the porter to let in no company to my lady today. She won't see a single soul, sir. (*Exit.*)

OAK: What an unhappy woman! Now will she sit all day, feeding on her suspicions, till she has convinced herself of the truth of them. (*Enter* JOHN *crossing the stage.*) Well, sir, what's your business?

JOHN: Going to order the chariot, sir. My lady's going out immediately. (*Exit.*)

OAK: Going out! What is all this? But every way she makes me miserable. Wild and ungovernable as the sea or the wind! Made up of storms and tempests! I can't bear it; and, one way or other, I will put an end to it. (*Exit.*)

SCENE 3.   LADY FREELOVE's. Enter LADY FREELOVE with a card. SERVANT following.

LADY F: (*reading as she enters*) 'And will take the liberty of waiting on her ladyship *en cavalier*, as he comes from the *manège*.' Does anybody wait that brought this card?

SERV: Lord Trinket's servant is in the hall, madam.

LADY F: My compliments, and I shall be glad to see his lordship. Where is Miss Russet?

SERV: In her own chamber, madam.

---

manège: training horses.

LADY F: What is she doing?

SERV: Writing, I believe, madam.

LADY F: Oh, ridiculous! (*aside*) Scribbling to that Oakly, I suppose. Let her know I should be glad of her company here. (*Exit* SERVANT.) (*alone*) It is a mighty troublesome thing to manage a simple girl, that knows nothing of the world. Harriot, like all other girls, is foolishly fond of this young fellow of her own choosing; her first love; that is to say, the first man that is particularly civil, and the first air of consequence which a young lady gives herself. Poor silly soul! But Oakly must not have her, positively. A match with Lord Trinket will add to the dignity of the family. I must bring her into it. I will throw her into his way as often as possible, and leave him to make his party good as fast as he can. But here comes the girl. (*Enter* HARRIOT.) Well, Harriot, still in the pouts? Nay, prithee, my dear little runaway girl, be more cheerful! Your everlasting melancholy puts one into the vapours.

HAR: Dear madam, excuse me. How can I be cheerful in my present situation? I know my father's temper so well, that I am sure this step of mine must almost distract him. I sometimes wish that I had remained in the country, let what would have been the consequence.

LADY F: Why, it is a naughty child, that's certain; but it need not be so uneasy about papa, as you know that I wrote by last night's post to acquaint him that his little lost sheep was safe, and that you are ready to obey his commands in every particular, except marrying that oaf, Sir Harry Beagle. Lord! Lord! What a difference there is between a country and town education! Why, a London lass would have jumped out of a window into a gallant's arms, and, without thinking of her father, unless it were to have drawn a few bills on him, been an hundred miles off in nine or ten hours, and perhaps out of the kingdom in twenty-four.

HAR: I fear I have already been too precipitate. I tremble for the consequences.

LADY F: I swear, child, you are a downright prude. Your way of talking gives me the spleen; so full of affection, and duty, and virtue, it's just like a funeral sermon. And, yet, pretty soul! it can love. Well, I wonder at your taste; a sneaking simple gentleman! without a title! and when, to my knowledge, you might have a man of quality tomorrow.

HAR: Perhaps so. Your ladyship must excuse me, but many a man of quality would make me miserable.

LADY F: Indeed, my dear, these antediluvian notions will never do nowadays; and, at the same time too, those little wicked eyes of yours speak a very different language. Indeed you have fine eyes, child; and they have made fine work with Lord Trinket.

HAR: (*contemptuously*) Lord Trinket!

LADY F: Yes, Lord Trinket. You know it as well as I do; and yet, you ill-natured thing, you will not vouchsafe him a single smile. But you must give the poor soul a little encouragement; prithee do.

HAR: Indeed I can't, madam; for of all mankind Lord Trinket is my aversion.

LADY F: Aversion! Lord, child, who ever heard of aversions in the country? Besides, Lord Trinket is counted a well-bred, sensible, young fellow; and the women all think him handsome.

HAR: Yes, he is just polite enough to be able to be very unmannerly with a great deal of good breeding, is just handsome enough to make him most excessively vain of his person, and has just reflection enough to finish him for a coxcomb; qualifications which are all very common among those whom your ladyship calls men of quality.

LADY F: A satirist, too! Indeed, my dear, this affectation fits very awkwardly upon you. There will be a superiority in the behaviour of persons of fashion.

HAR: A superiority, indeed! for his lordship always behaves with so much insolent familiarity that I should almost imagine he was soliciting me for other favours, rather than to pass my whole life with him.

LADY F: Innocent freedoms, child, which every fine woman expects to be taken with her, as an acknowledgement of her beauty.

HAR: They are freedoms which, I think, no innocent woman can allow.

LADY F: Romantic to the last degree! Why, you are in the country still, Harriot!
        (*Enter* SERVANT.)

SERV: My Lord Trinket, madam. (*Exit.*)

LADY F: I swear now I have a good mind to tell him all you have said. (*Enter* LORD TRINKET, *in boots, etc. as from the riding-house.*) Your lordship's most obedient humble servant.

LORD T: Your ladyship does me too much honour. Here I am, *en bottine*, as you see; just come from the *manège*. Miss Russet, I am your slave. I declare it makes me quite happy to find you together. 'Pon honour, ma'am (*to* HARRIOT), I begin to conceive great hopes of you: and as for you, Lady Freelove, I cannot sufficiently commend your assiduity with your fair pupil. She was before possessed of every grace that Nature could bestow on her, and nobody is so well qualified as your ladyship, to give her the *bon ton.*

HAR: Compliment and contempt all in a breath! My lord, I am obliged to you. But, waiving my acknowledgements, give me leave to ask your lordship, whether Nature and the *bon ton* (as you call it) are so different, that we must give up one in order to obtain the other?

LORD T: Totally opposite, madam. The chief aim of the *bon ton* is to render persons of family different from the vulgar, for whom indeed Nature serves very well. For this reason it has, at various times, been ungenteel to see, to hear, to walk, to be in good health, and to have twenty other horrible perfections of Nature. Nature indeed may do very well sometimes. It made *you*, for instance, and it then made something very lovely; and if you suffer us of quality to give you the *ton*, you would be absolutely divine. But now – me – madam – me – Nature never made such a thing as me.

HAR: Why, indeed, I think your lordship has very few obligations to her.

LORD T: Then you really think it's all my own? I declare now that is a mighty genteel compliment. Nay, if you begin to flatter already, you improve apace. 'Pon honour, Lady Freelove, I believe we shall make something of her at last.

LADY F: No doubt on't. It is in your lordship's power to make her a complete woman of fashion at once.

LORD T: Hum! Why, ay –

HAR: Your lordship must excuse me. I am of a very tasteless disposition. I shall never bear to be carried out of Nature.

LADY F: You are out of Nature now, Harriot! I am sure no woman but yourself
     ever objected to being carried among persons of quality. Would you believe
     it, my lord? here has she been a whole week in town, and would never suffer
     me to introduce her to a rout, an assembly, a concert, or even to court, or to
     the opera; nay, would hardly so much as mix with a living soul that has
     visited me.

LORD T: No wonder, madam, you do not adopt the manners of persons of fashion,
     when you will not even honour them with your company. Were you to make
     one in our little *coteries*, we should soon make you sick of the boors and
     bumpkins of the horrid country. By the by, I met a monster at the riding-
     house this morning, who gave me some intelligence that will surprise you,
     concerning your family.

HAR: What intelligence?

LADY F: Who was this monster, as your lordship calls him? A curiosity, I dare say.

LORD T: This monster, madam, was formerly my head groom, and had the care of
     all my running horses; but growing most abominably surly and extravagant,
     as you know all those fellows do, I turned him off; and ever since my brother
     Slouch Trinket has had the care of my stud, rides all my principal matches
     himself, and —

HAR: Dear my lord, don't talk of your groom and your brother, but tell me the
     news. Do you know anything of my father?

LORD T: Your father, madam, is now in town. This fellow, you must know, is now
     groom to Sir Harry Beagle, your sweet rural swain, and informed me, that his
     master and your father were running all over the town in quest of you; and
     that he himself had orders to enquire after you; for which reason, I suppose,
     he came to the riding-house stables to look after a horse, thinking it, to be
     sure, a very likely place to meet you. Your father perhaps is gone to see you
     at the Tower, or Westminster Abbey, which is all the idea he has of London;
     and your faithful lover is probably cheapening a hunter, and drinking strong
     beer, at the Horse and Jockey in Smithfield.

LADY F: The whole set admirably disposed of!

HAR: Did not your lordship inform him where I was?

LORD T: Not I, 'pon honour, madam. That I left to their own ingenuity to
     discover.

LADY F: And pray, my lord, where in this town have this polite company
     bestowed themselves?

LORD T: They lodge, madam, of all places in the world, at the Bull and Gate Inn in
     Holborn.

LADY F: Ha, ha, ha! the Bull and Gate! Incomparable! What, have they brought
     any hay or cattle to town?

LORD T: Very well, Lady Freelove, very well, indeed! There they are, like so many
     graziers; and there, it seems, they have learnt that this lady is certainly in
     London.

HAR: Do, dear madam, send a card directly to my father, informing him where I

---

cheapening: bargaining over price.

am, and that your ladyship would be glad to see him here. For my part, I dare
not venture into his presence, till you have in some measure pacified him;
but, for heaven's sake, desire him not to bring that wretched fellow along
with him.

LORD T: (*aside*) Wretched fellow! Oho! *courage*, milor Trinket!

LADY F: I'll send immediately. Who's there?

           (*Enter* SERVANT.)

SERV: (*aside to* LADY FREELOVE) Sir Harry Beagle is below, madam.

LADY F: (*aside to* SERVANT) I am not at home. Have they let him in?

SERV: Yes, madam.

LADY F: How abominably unlucky this is! Well, then show him into my dressing
room. I will come to him there.

           (*Exit* SERVANT.)

LORD T: Lady Freelove! no engagement, I hope. We won't part with you, 'pon
honour.

LADY F: The worst engagement in the world; a pair of musty old prudes! Lady
Formal and Miss Prate.

LORD T: Oh, the bedlams! as nauseous as ipecacuanha, 'pon honour.

LADY F: Lud! lud! what shall I do with them? Why do these foolish women come
troubling me now? I must wait on them in the dressing room; and you must
excuse the card, Harriot, till they are gone. I'll dispatch them as soon as I can;
but heaven knows when I shall get rid of them, for they are both everlasting
gossips; though the words come from her ladyship one by one, like drops
from a still, while the other tiresome woman overwhelms us with a flood of
impertinence. Harriot, you'll entertain his lordship till I return. (*Exit.*)

LORD T: 'Pon honour, I am not sorry for the coming in of these old tabbies, and
am much obliged to her ladyship for leaving us such an agreeable *tête-à-tête*.

HAR: Your lordship will find me extremely bad company.

LORD T: Not in the least, my dear! We'll entertain ourselves one way or other, I'll
warrant you. 'Egad! I think it a mighty good opportunity to establish a better
acquaintance with you.

HAR: I don't understand you.

LORD T: No? Why then I'll speak plainer. (*pausing and looking her full in the face*)
You're a damned fine piece, 'pon honour!

HAR: Sir! How!

LORD T: Oh, ma'am, I'll show you how.

HAR: If this be your lordship's polite conversation, I shall leave you to amuse yourself in soliloquy (*going*).

LORD T: No, no, no, madam, that must not be (*stopping her*). This place, that
chamber, the opportunity, all conspire to make me happy, and you shall not
deny me.

HAR: How, sir! You don't intend to do me any violence!

LORD T: 'Pon honour, ma'am, it will be doing great violence to myself, if I do not.
You must excuse me (*struggling with her*).

---

impertinence: irrelevant chatter.

HAR: Help! help! murder! help!

LORD T: Your helping will signify nothing; nobody will come (*struggling*).

HAR: For heaven's sake! Sir! My lord! (*noise within*)

LORD T: Pox on't, what noise? Then I must be quick (*still struggling*).

HAR: Murder! help! help!

        (*Enter* CHARLES, *hastily*.)

CHAR: What do I hear? My Harriot's voice calling for help? Ha! (*seeing them*) Is it possible? Turn, ruffian! (*drawing*) I'll find you employment.

LORD T: You are a most impertinent scoundrel, and I'll whip you through the lungs, 'pon honour.

        (*They fight.* HARRIOT *runs out screaming* 'Help' *etc. Then enter* LADY FREELOVE, SIR HARRY BEAGLE, *and* SERVANTS.)

LADY F: How's this? Swords drawn in my house! Part them! (*They are parted.*) This is the most impudent thing!

LORD T: Well, rascal, I shall find a time; I know you, sir!

CHAR: The sooner the better. I know your lordship too.

SIR H: (*to* LADY FREELOVE) I'faith, madam, we had like to have been in at the death.

LADY F: What is all this? (*to* CHARLES) Pray, sir, what is the meaning of your coming hither to raise this disturbance? Do you take my house for a brothel?

CHAR: Not I, indeed, madam! But I believe his lordship does.

LORD T: Impudent scoundrel!

LADY F: Your conversation, sir, is as insolent as your behaviour. Who are you? What brought you here?

CHAR: I am one, madam, always ready to draw my sword in defence of innocence in distress, and more especially in the cause of that lady I delivered from his lordship's fury; in search of whom I troubled your ladyship's house.

LADY F: Her lover, I suppose? or bully, or what?

CHAR: At your ladyship's service; though not quite so violent in my passion as his lordship there.

LORD T: Impertinent rascal!

LADY F: You shall be made to repent of this insolence.

LORD T: Your ladyship may leave that to me.

CHAR: Ha, ha!

SIR H: But pray what is become of the lady all this while? Why, Lady Freelove, you told me she was not here, and, i'faith, I was just drawing off another way, if I had not heard the view-hollow.

LADY F: You shall see her immediately, sir. Who's there? (*Enter* SERVANT.) Where is Miss Russet?

SERV: Gone out, madam.

LADY F: Gone out! Where?

SERV: I don't know, madam. But she ran down the back stairs crying for help, crossed the servants' hall in tears, and took a chair at the door.

LADY F: Blockheads! to let her go out in a chair alone! Go and enquire after her immediately.

        (*Exit* SERVANT.)

SIR H: Gone! What a pox had I just run her down, and is the little puss stole away at last?

LADY F: (*to* SIR HARRY) Sir, if you will walk in with his lordship and me, perhaps you may hear some tidings of her; though it is most probable she may be gone to her father. I don't know any other friend she has in town.

CHAR: I am heartily glad she is gone. She is safer anywhere than in this house.

LADY F: Mighty well, sir! My lord! Sir Harry! I attend you.

LORD T: (*to* CHARLES) You shall hear from me, sir!

CHAR: Very well, my lord!

SIR H: Stole away! pox on't! stole away.

> (*Exeunt* SIR HARRY *and* LORD TRINKET. *Manent* CHARLES *and* LADY FREELOVE.)

LADY F: Before I follow the company, give me leave to tell you, sir, that your behaviour here has been so extraordinary —

CHAR: My treatment here, madam, has indeed been very extraordinary.

LADY F: Indeed! Well; no matter. Permit me to acquaint you, sir, that there lies your way out, and that the greatest favour you can do me is to leave the house immediately.

CHAR: That your ladyship may depend on. Since you have put Miss Harriot to flight, you may be sure of not being troubled with my company. I'll after her immediately. I can't rest till I know what is become of her.

LADY F: If she has any regard for her reputation, she'll never put herself into such hands as yours.

CHAR: Oh, madam, there can be no doubt of her regard to that, by her leaving your ladyship.

LADY F: Insolent monster!

CHAR: Poor lady!

LADY F: Begone this moment.

CHAR: Immediately — My dear Harriot! Would I could have spoken with her! — But she was in danger, and I delivered her. — That's comfort still — and yet —

LADY F: Leave my house!

CHAR: Directly. A charming house! and a charming lady of the house too! ha! ha!

LADY F: Vulgar fellow!

CHAR: Fine lady!

> (*Exeunt severally.*)

ACT III

SCENE 1.   LADY FREELOVE'*s. Enter* LADY FREELOVE, *and* LORD TRINKET.

LORD T: *Doucement, doucement*, my dear Lady Freelove! excuse me! I meant no harm, 'pon honour.

LADY F: Indeed, indeed, my Lord Trinket, this is absolutely intolerable. What! to offer rudeness to a young lady in my house! What will the world say of it?

LORD T: Just what the world pleases. It does not signify a doit what they say. However, I ask pardon; but, 'egad, I thought it was the best way.

LADY F: For shame, for shame, my lord! I am quite hurt at your want of discretion.

LORD T: 'Pon honour, now, I am always for taking them by a *coup de main*. I never knew it fail before.

LADY F: Leave the whole conduct of this affair to me, or I'll have done with it at once. How strangely you have acted! There I went out of the way on purpose to serve you, by keeping off that looby Sir Harry Beagle, and preventing him or her father from seeing the girl, till we had some chance of managing her ourselves, and then you chose to make a disturbance, and spoilt all.

LORD T: Devil take Sir Harry, and t'other scoundrel too! That they should come driving hither just at so critical an instant! And that the wild little thing should take wing, and fly away the Lord knows whither!

LADY F: Ay! And there again you were indiscreet past redemption. To let her know that her father was in town, and where he was to be found too! For there I am confident she must be gone, as she is not acquainted with one creature in London.

LORD T: Why, a father is in these cases the *pis-aller*, I must confess. 'Pon honour, Lady Freelove, I can scarce believe this obstinate girl a relation of yours. Such narrow notions! I'll swear, there is less trouble in getting ten women of the *première volée*, than in conquering the scruples of a silly girl in that style of life.

LADY F: Come, come, my lord, a truce with your reflections on my niece! Let us consider what is best to be done.

LORD T: E'en just what your ladyship thinks proper. For my part, I am entirely *dérangé*.

LADY F: Will you submit to be governed by me then?

LORD T: I'll be all obedience: your ladyship's slave, 'pon honour.

LADY F: Why then, as this is rather an ugly affair in regard to me, as well as your lordship, and may make some noise, I think it absolutely necessary, merely to save appearances, that you should wait on her father, palliate matters as well as you can, and make a formal repetition of your proposal of marriage.

LORD T: Your ladyship is perfectly in the right. You are quite *au fait* of the affair. It shall be done immediately; and then your reputation will be safe, and my conduct justified to all the world. But should the old rustic continue as stubborn as his daughter, your ladyship, I hope, has no objections to my being a little *rusé*; for I must have her, 'pon honour.

LADY F: Not in the least.

LORD T: Or if a good opportunity should offer, and the girl should be still untractable —

LADY F: Do what you will; I wash my hands of it. She's out of my care now, you know. But you must beware of your rivals. One, you know, is in the house with her, and the other will lose no opportunities of getting to her.

LORD T: As to the fighting gentleman, I shall cut out work for him in his own way. I'll send him a *petit billet* tomorrow morning and then there can be no great difficulty in outwitting her bumpkin father, and the baronet.

(*Enter* SERVANT.)

SERV: Captain O'Cutter to wait on your ladyship.

LADY F: Oh the hideous fellow! The Irish sailorman, for whom I prevailed on your

lordship to get the post of a regulating captain. I suppose he is come to load
me with his odious thanks. I won't be troubled with him now.

LORD T: Let him in, by all means. He is the best creature to laugh at in nature. He
is a perfect sea-monster, and always looks and talks as if he was upon deck.
Besides, a thought strikes me, he may be of use.

LADY F: Well, send the creature up then. (*Exit* SERVANT.) But what fine thought
is this?

LORD T: A *coup de maître*, 'pon honour! I intend — but hush! here the porpoise
comes.

(*Enter* CAPTAIN O'CUTTER.)

LADY F: Captain, your humble servant! I am very glad to see you.

O'CUT: I am much oblaged to you, my lady! Upon my conscience, the wind
favours me at all points. I have no sooner got under way to tank your ladyship, but I have borne down upon my noble friend his lordship too. I hope
your lordship's well.

LORD T: Very well, I thank you, captain. But you seem to be hurt in the service.
What is the meaning of that patch over your right eye?

O'CUT: Some advanced wages from my new post, my lord! This pressing is hot
work, though it entitles us to no smart-money.

LADY F: And pray in what perilous adventure did you get that scar, captain?

O'CUT: Quite out of my ilement, indeed, my lady! I got it in an engagement by
land. A day or two ago I spied tree stout fellows, belonging to a marchant-
man. They made down Wapping. I immadiately gave my lads the signal to
chase, and we bore down right upon them. They tacked, and lay to. We gave
them a tundering broadside, which they resaved like men; and one of them
made use of small arms, which carried off the weadermost corner of Ned
Gage's hat; so I immadiately stood in with him, and raked him, but resaved
a wound on my starboord eye, from the stock of the pistol. However, we
took them all, and they now lie under the hatches, with fifty more, a-boord
a tinder off the Tower.

LORD T: Well done, noble captain! But, however, you will soon have better
employment; for I think the next step to your present post is commonly a
ship.

O'CUT: The sooner the better, my lord. Honest Terence O'Cutter shall never flinch,
I'll warrant you; and has had as much seen-sarvice as any man in the navy.

LORD T: You may depend on my good offices, captain. But in the meantime it is
in your power to do me a favour.

O'CUT: A favour, my lord! Your lordship does me honour. I would go round the
world, from one end to the other, by day or by night, to sarve your lordship,
or my good lady here.

LORD T: (*aside to* LADY FREELOVE) Dear madam, the luckiest thought in
nature. The favour I have to ask of you, captain, need not carry you so far
out of your way. The whole affair is, that there are a couple of impudent

---

regulating: supervising recruitment.
smart-money: compensation for injury.
seen-sarvice: experienced, skilled service.

fellows at an inn in Holborn, who have affronted me, and you would oblige me infinitely, by pressing them into his Majesty's service.

LADY F: (*aside to* LORD TRINKET) Now I understand you. Admirable!

O'CUT: With all my heart, my lord, and tank you too, fait. But, by the by, I hope they are not housekeepers, or freemen of the city. There's the devil to pay in meddling with them; they bodder one so about liberty and property and stuff. It was but t'other day that Jack Trowser was carried before my lord-mayor, and lost above a twelve-month's pay, for nothing at all — at all.

LORD T: I'll take care you shall be brought into no trouble. These fellows were formerly my grooms. If you'll call on me in the morning, I'll go with you to the place.

O'CUT: I'll be with your lordship, and bring with me four or five as pretty boys as you'd wish to clap your two lucking eyes upon of a summer's day.

LORD T: I am much obliged to you. But, captain, I have another little favour to beg of you.

O'CUT: Upon my shoul, and I'll do it.

LORD T: What, before you know it?

O'CUT: Fore and aft, my lord.

LORD T: A gentleman has offended me in a point of honour.

O'CUT: Cut his troat.

LORD T: Will you carry him a letter from me?

O'CUT: Indeed and I will; and I'll take you in tow too, and you shall engage him yard-arm and yard-arm.

LORD T: Why then, captain, you'll come a little earlier tomorrow morning than you proposed, that you may attend him with my *billet*, before you proceed on the other affair.

O'CUT: Never fear it, my lord! Your servant! My ladyship, your humble servant!

LADY F: Captain, yours! Pray give my service to my friend Mrs O'Cutter. How does she do?

O'CUT: I tank your ladyship's axing: the dear crature is purely tight and well.

LORD T: How many children have you, captain?

O'CUT: Four, and please your lordship, and another upon the stocks.

LORD T: When it is launched, I hope to be at the christening. I'll stand godfather, captain.

O'CUT: Your lordship's very good.

LORD T: Well, you'll come tomorrow.

O'CUT: Oh, I'll not fail, my lord! Little Terence O'Cutter never fails, fait, when a troat is to be cut. (*Exit.*)

LADY F: Ha, ha, ha! But sure you don't intend to ship off both her father and her country lover for the Indies?

LORD T: Oh no! Only let them contemplate the inside of a ship for a day or two.

LADY F: Well, but after all, my lord, this is a very bold undertaking. I don't think you'll be able to put it in practice.

LORD T: Nothing so easy, 'pon honour. To press a gentleman, a man of quality, one of us, would not be so easy, I grant you. But these fellows, you know, have not half so decent an appearance as one of my footmen; and from their behaviour, conversation, and dress, it is very possible to mistake them for grooms and ostlers.

LADY F: There may be something in that, indeed. But what use do you propose to make of this stratagem?

LORD T: Every use in nature. This artifice must at least take them out of the way for some time; and in the meanwhile measures may be concerted to carry off the girl.

(*Enter* SERVANT.)

SERV: Mrs Oakly, madam, is at the door, in her chariot, and desires to have the honour of speaking to your ladyship on particular business.

LORD T: Mrs Oakly! What can that jealous-pated woman want with you?

LADY F: No matter what. I hate her mortally. Let her in.

(*Exit* SERVANT.)

LORD T: What wind blows her hither?

LADY F: A wind that must blow us some good.

LORD T: How? I was amazed you chose to see her.

LADY F: How can you be so slow of apprehension? She comes, you may be sure, on some occasion relating to this girl; in order to assist young Oakly perhaps, to soothe me, and gain intelligence, and so forward the match; but I'll forbid the banns, I warrant you. Whatever she wants, I'll draw some sweet mischief out of it. But away, away! I think I hear her. Slip down the backstairs − or − stay − now I think on't, go out this way; meet her, and be sure to make her a very respectful bow, as you go out.

LORD T: Hush! Here she is.

(*Enter* MRS OAKLY. LORD TRINKET *bows and exit.*)

MRS OAK: I beg pardon for giving your ladyship this trouble.

LADY F: I am always glad of the honour of seeing Mrs Oakly.

MRS OAK: There is a letter, madam, just come from the country, which has occasioned some alarm in our family. It comes from Mr Russet.

LADY F: Mr Russet!

MRS OAK: Yes, from Mr Russet, madam; and is chiefly concerning his daughter. As she has the honour of being related to your ladyship, I took the liberty of waiting on you.

LADY F: She is indeed, as you say, madam, a relation of mine; but after what has happened, I scarce know how to acknowledge her.

MRS OAK: Has she been so much to blame, then?

LADY F: So much, madam! Only judge for yourself. Though she had been so indiscreet, not to say indecent in her conduct, as to elope from her father, I was in hopes to have hushed up that matter, for the honour of our family. But she has run away from me too, madam; went off in the most abrupt manner, not an hour ago.

MRS OAK: You surprise me. Indeed her father, by his letter, seems apprehensive of the worst consequences. But does your ladyship imagine any harm has happened?

LADY F: I can't tell; I hope not; but, indeed, she is a strange girl. You know, madam, young women can't be too cautious in their conduct. She is, I am sorry to declare it, a very dangerous person to take into a family.

MRS OAK: Indeed! (*alarmed*)

LADY F: If I was to say all I know!

MRS OAK: Why, sure, your ladyship knows of nothing that has been carried on clandestinely between her and Mr Oakly! (*in disorder*)

LADY F: Mr Oakly!

MRS OAK: Mr Oakly! no, not Mr Oakly — that is, not my husband: I don't mean him — not him — but his nephew, young Mr Oakly.

LADY F: (*aside*) Jealous of her husband! So, so! Now I know my game.

MRS OAK: But pray, madam, give me leave to ask, was there anything very particular in her conduct, while she was in your ladyship's house?

LADY F: Why, really, considering she was here scarce a week, her behaviour was rather mysterious. Letters and messages, to and fro, between her and I don't know who. I suppose you know that Mr Oakly's nephew has been here, madam.

MRS OAK: I was not sure of it. Has he been to wait on your ladyship already on this occasion?

LADY F: To wait on me! The expression is much too polite for the nature of his visit. My Lord Trinket, the nobleman whom you met as you came in, had, you must know, madam, some thoughts of my niece; and as it would have been an advantageous match, I was glad of it: but I believe after what he has been witness to this morning, he will drop all thoughts of it.

MRS OAK: I am sorry that any relation of mine should so far forget himself —

LADY F: It's no matter; his behaviour indeed, as well as the young lady's, was pretty extraordinary. And yet, after all, I don't believe *he* is the object of her affections.

MRS OAK: (*much alarmed*) Ha!

LADY F: She has certainly an attachment somewhere, a strong one; but his lordship, who was present all the time, was convinced, as well as myself, that Mrs Oakly's nephew was rather a convenient friend, a kind of go-between, than the lover. Bless me, madam, you change colour! You seem uneasy! What's the matter?

MRS OAK: Nothing — madam — nothing! A little shocked that my husband should behave so.

LADY F: Your husband, madam!

MRS OAK: His nephew, I mean. His unpardonable rudeness! But I am not well; I am sorry I have given your ladyship so much trouble; I'll take my leave.

LADY F: I declare, madam, you frighten me. Your being so visibly affected makes me quite uneasy: I hope I have not said anything — I really don't believe your husband is in fault. Men, to be sure, allow themselves strange liberties. But I think, nay I am sure, it cannot be so. It is impossible. Don't let what I have said, have any effect on you.

MRS OAK: No, it has not — I have no idea of such a thing. Your ladyship's most obedient. (*Going, returns.*) But, sure, madam, you have not heard, or don't know anything —

LADY F: Come, come, Mrs Oakly, I see how it is, and it would not be kind to say all I know. I dare not tell you what I have heard. Only be on your guard. There can be no harm in that. Do you be against giving the girl any countenance, and see what effect it has.

MRS OAK: I will. I am much obliged — But does it appear to your ladyship, then, that Mr Oakly —

LADY F: No, not at all. Nothing in't, I dare say. I would not create uneasiness in a family: but I am a woman myself, have been married, and can't help feeling for you. But don't be uneasy; there's nothing in't, I dare say.

MRS OAK: I think so. Your ladyship's humble servant.

LADY F: Your servant, madam. Pray don't be alarmed; I must insist on your not making yourself uneasy.

MRS OAK: Not at all alarmed; not in the least uneasy. Your most obedient. (*Exit.*)

LADY F: Ha, ha, ha! There she goes, brimful of anger and jealousy, to vent it all on her husband. Mercy on the poor man! (*Enter* LORD TRINKET.) Bless me, my lord! I thought you were gone.

LORD T: Only into the next room. My curiosity would not let me stir a step further. I heard it all, and was never more diverted in my life, 'pon honour. Ha, ha, ha!

LADY F: How the silly creature took it! Ha, ha, ha!

LORD T: Ha, ha, ha! My dear Lady Freelove, you have a deal of ingenuity, a deal of *esprit*, 'pon honour.

LADY F: A little shell thrown into the enemy's works, that's all.

BOTH: Ha, ha, ha, ha!

LADY F: But I must leave you. I have twenty visits to pay. You'll let me know how you succeed in your secret expedition.

LORD T: That you may depend on.

LADY F: Remember then that tomorrow morning I expect to see you. At present your lordship will excuse me. Who's there? (*calling to the servants*) Send Epingle into my dressing room. (*Exit.*)

LORD T: (*alone*) So! If O'Cutter and his myrmidons are alert, I think I can't fail of success; and then *prenez garde*, Mademoiselle Harriot! This is one of the drollest circumstances in nature. Here is my Lady Freelove, a woman of sense, a woman that knows the world too, assisting me in this design. I never knew her ladyship so much out. How, in the name of wonder, can she imagine that a man of quality, or any man else, 'egad, would marry a fine girl, after — Not I, 'pon honour. No, no! when I have had the *entamure*, let who will take the rest of the loaf. (*Exit.*)

SCENE 2.   *Scene changes to* MR OAKLY*'s. Enter* HARRIOT, *following a* SERVANT.

HAR: Not at home! Are you sure that Mrs Oakly is not at home, sir?

SERV: She is just gone out, madam.

HAR: I have something of consequence — If you will give me leave, sir, I will wait till she returns.

SERV: You would not see her, if you did, madam. She has given positive orders not to be interrupted with any company today.

HAR: Sure, sir, if you were to let her know that I had particular business —

---

entamure: first slice (e.g. of a loaf).

SERV: I should not dare to trouble her, indeed, madam.

HAR: How unfortunate this is! What can I do? Pray, sir, can I see *Mr* Oakly then?

SERV: Yes, madam: I'll acquaint my master, if you please.

HAR: Pray do, sir.

SERV: Will you favour me with your name, madam?

HAR: Be pleased, sir, to let him know that a lady desires to speak with him.

SERV: I shall, madam. (*Exit* SERVANT.)

HAR: (*alone*) I wish I could have seen Mrs Oakly! What an unhappy situation am I reduced to! What will the world say of me? And yet what could I do? Charles, I must own, has this very day revived much of my tenderness for him; and yet I dread the wildness of his disposition. I must now, however, solicit Mr Oakly's protection and beg leave to remain for some time in his house; a circumstance (all things considered) rather disagreeable to a delicate mind, and which nothing, but the absolute necessity of it, could excuse. Good heavens, what a multitude of difficulties and distresses am I thrown into by my father's obstinate perseverance to force me into a marriage which my soul abhors.
  (*Enter* OAKLY.)

OAK: (*at entering*) Where is this lady? (*seeing her*) Bless me, Miss Russet, is it you? — (*aside*) Was ever anything so unlucky? (*aloud*) Is it possible, madam, that I see you here?

HAR: It is too true, sir! And the occasion on which I am now to trouble you, is so much in need of an apology, that —

OAK: Pray make none, madam! — (*aside*) If my wife should return before I get her out of the house again!

HAR: I dare say, sir, you are not quite a stranger to the attachment your nephew has professed to me.

OAK: I am not, madam! I hope Charles has not been guilty of any baseness toward you. If he has, I'll never see his face again.

HAR: I have no cause to accuse him. But —

OAK: But what, madam? Pray be quick! — (*aside*) The very person in the world I would not have seen!

HAR: You seem uneasy, sir!

OAK: No, nothing at all. Pray go on, madam!

HAR: I am at present, sir, through a concurrence of strange accidents, in a very unfortunate situation; and do not know what will become of me, without your assistance.

OAK: I'll do everything in my power to serve you. I know of your leaving your father, by a letter we have had from him. Pray let me know the rest of your story.

HAR: My story, sir, is very short. When I left my father's, I came immediately to London, and took refuge with a relation, where, instead of meeting with the protection I expected, I was alarmed with the most infamous designs upon my honour. It is not an hour ago since your nephew rescued me from the attempts of a villain. I tremble to think that I left him actually engaged in a duel.

OAK: He is very safe. He has just sent home the chariot from the St Alban's tavern, where he dines today. But what are your commands for me, madam?

HAR: I am heartily glad to hear of his safety. The favour, sir, I would now request of you is, that you will suffer me to remain for a few days in your house.

OAK: Madam!

HAR: And that, in the meantime, you will use your utmost endeavours to reconcile me to my father, without his forcing me into a marriage with Sir Harry Beagle.

OAK: This is the most perplexing situation! Why did not Charles take care to bestow you properly?

HAR: It is most probable, sir, that I should not have consented to such a measure myself. The world is but too apt to censure, even without a cause: and if you are so kind as to admit me into your house, I must desire you not to consider Mr Oakly in any other light than as your nephew; as, in my present circumstances, I have particular objections to it.

OAK: What an unlucky circumstance! Upon my soul, madam, I would do anything to serve you; but being in my house creates a difficulty that —

HAR: I hope, sir, you do not doubt the truth of what I have told you.

OAK: I religiously believe every tittle of it, madam; but I have particular family considerations, that —

HAR: Sure, sir, you cannot suspect me to be base enough to form any connections in your family, contrary to your inclination, while I am living in your house.

OAK: Such connections, madam, would do me and all my family great honour. I never dreamed of any scruples on that account. What can I do? Let me see — let me see — suppose — (*pausing*)

(*Enter* MRS OAKLY *behind, in a capuchin tippet, etc.*)

MRS OAK: I am sure I heard the voice of a woman conversing with my husband. Ha! (*seeing* HARRIOT) It is so, indeed! Let me contain myself! I'll listen.

HAR: I see, sir, you are not inclined to serve me. Good heavens, what am I reserved to? Why, why did I leave my father's house, to expose myself to greater distresses? (*ready to weep*)

OAK: I would do anything for your sake; indeed I would. So, pray be comforted; and I'll think of some proper place to bestow you in.

MRS OAK: So, so!

HAR: What place can be so proper as your own house?

OAK: My dear madam, I — I —

MRS OAK: My *dear* madam! Mighty well!

OAK: Hush! hark! what noise? No, nothing. But I'll be plain with you, madam; we may be interrupted. The family consideration I hinted at, is nothing else than my wife. She is a little unhappy in her temper, madam; and if you were to be admitted into the house, I don't know what might be the consequence.

MRS OAK: Very fine!

HAR: My behaviour, sir —

OAK: My dear life, it would be impossible for you to behave in such a manner as not to give her suspicion.

HAR: But if your nephew, sir, took everything upon himself —

OAK: Still that would not do, madam. Why, this very morning, when the letter

---

capuchin: cloak with hood.

came from your father, though I positively denied any knowledge of it, and
Charles owned it, yet it was almost impossible to pacify her.

MRS OAK: The letter! How have I been bubbled!

HAR: What shall I do? What will become of me?

OAK: Why, look ye, my dear madam, since my wife is so strong an objection, it is
absolutely impossible for me to take you into the house. Nay, if I had not
known she was gone out, just before you came, I should be uneasy at your
being here even now. So we must manage as well as we can: I'll take a private
lodging for you a little way off, unknown to Charles or my wife, or anybody;
and if Mrs Oakly should discover it at last, why the whole matter will light
upon Charles, you know.

MRS OAK: Upon Charles!

HAR: How unhappy is my situation! (*weeping*) I am ruined forever.

OAK: Ruined! Not at all. Such a thing as this has happened to many a young lady
before you, and all has been well again. Keep up your spirits! I'll contrive, if
I possibly can, to visit you every day.

MRS OAK: (*advancing*) Will you so? Oh, Mr Oakly! have I discovered you at last?
I'll visit you, indeed. And you, my *dear* madam, I'll —

HAR: Madam, I don't understand —

MRS OAK: I understand the whole affair, and have understood it for some time
past. You shall have a private lodging, miss! It is the fittest place for you, I
believe. How dare you look me in the face?

OAK: For heaven's sake, my love, don't be so violent. You are quite wrong in this
affair; you don't know who you are talking to. That lady is a person of
fashion.

MRS OAK: Fine fashion, indeed! To seduce other women's husbands?

HAR: Dear madam, how can you imagine —

OAK: I tell you, my dear, this is the young lady that Charles —

MRS OAK: Mighty well! But that won't do, sir. Did not I hear you lay the whole
intrigue together? Did not I hear your fine plot of throwing all the blame
upon Charles?

OAK: Nay, be cool a moment. You must know, my dear, that the letter which
came this morning, related to this lady.

MRS OAK: I know it.

OAK: And since that, it seems, Charles has been so fortunate as to —

MRS OAK: Oh, you deceitful man! That trick is too stale to pass again with me. It is
plain now what you meant by your proposing to take her into the house this
morning. But the gentlewoman could introduce herself, I see.

OAK: Fie, fie, my dear! She came on purpose to enquire for you.

MRS OAK: For me! Better and better! Did not she watch her opportunity, and
come to you just as I went out? But I am obliged to you for your visit,
madam. It is sufficiently paid. Pray, don't let me detain you.

OAK: For shame, for shame, Mrs Oakly! How can you be so absurd? Is this proper
behaviour to a lady of her character!

---

bubbled: tricked (Italian *bubbola* — a fib).

MRS OAK: I have heard her character. Go, my fine runaway madam! Now you've eloped from your father, and run away from your aunt, go! You shan't stay here, I promise you.

OAK: Prithee, be quiet. You don't know what you are doing. She shall stay.

MRS OAK: She shan't stay a minute.

OAK: She shall stay a minute, an hour, a day, a week, a month, a year! 'Sdeath, madam, she shall stay forever, if I choose it.

MRS OAK: How!

HAR: For heaven's sake, sir, let me go. I am frighted to death.

OAK: Don't be afraid, madam! She shall stay, I insist upon it.

RUS: (*within*) I tell you, sir, I will go up. I am sure that the lady is here, and nothing shall hinder me.

HAR: Oh, my father, my father! (*Faints away.*)

OAK: See! She faints. (*catching her*) Ring the bell! Who's there?

MRS OAK: What, take her in your arms too! I have no patience.

(*Enter* RUSSET *and* SERVANTS.)

RUS: Where is this — Ha! Fainting! (*running to her*) Oh, my dear Harriot! my child! my child!

OAK: Your coming so abruptly shocked her spirits. But she revives. How do you, madam?

HAR: (*to* RUSSET) Oh, sir!

RUS: Oh, my dear girl! How could you run away from your father, that loves you with such fondness! But I was sure I should find you here.

MRS OAK: There, then! Sure he should find her here! Did not I tell you so? Are not you a wicked man to carry on such base underhand doings, with a gentleman's daughter?

RUS: Let me tell you, sir, whatever you may think of the matter, I shall not easily put up with this behaviour. How durst you encourage my daughter to an elopement, and receive her in your house?

MRS OAK: There, mind that! The thing is as plain as the light.

OAK: I tell you, you misunderstand —

RUS: Look you, Mr Oakly, I shall expect satisfaction from your family for so gross an affront. Zounds, sir, I am not to be used ill by any man in England!

HAR: My dear sir, I can assure you —

RUS: Hold your tongue, girl! You'll put me in a passion.

OAK: Sir, this is all a mistake.

RUS: A mistake! Did not I find her in your house?

OAK: Upon my soul, she has not been in the house above —

MRS OAK: Did not I hear you say you would take her a lodging? a private lodging?

OAK: Yes; but that —

RUS: Has not this affair been carried on a long time, in spite of my teeth?

OAK: Sir, I never troubled myself —

MRS OAK: Never troubled yourself! Did not you insist on her staying in the house, whether I would or not?

OAK: No.

RUS: Did not you send to meet her, when she came to town?

OAK: No.

MRS OAK: Did not you deceive me about the letter this morning?

OAK: No, no, no. I tell you, no.

MRS OAK: Yes, yes, yes. I tell you, yes.

RUS: Shan't I believe my own eyes?

MRS OAK: Shan't I believe my own ears?

OAK: I tell you, you are both deceived.

RUS: Zounds, sir, I'll have satisfaction.

MRS OAK: I'll stop these fine doings, I warrant you.

OAK: 'Sdeath, you will not let me speak! And you are both alike, I think. I wish you were married to one another, with all my heart.

MRS OAK: Mighty well! mighty well!

RUS: I shall soon find a time to talk with you.

OAK: Find a time to talk! You have talked enough now for all your lives.

MRS OAK: Very fine! Come along, sir! Leave that lady with her father. Now she is in the properest hands. (*Exit.*)

OAK: I wish I could leave you in his hands. (*Going, returns.*) I shall follow you, madam! One word with you, sir! The height of your passion, and Mrs Oakly's strange misapprehension of this whole affair, makes it impossible to explain matters to you at present. I will do it when you please, and how you please. (*Exit.*)

        (*Manent* RUSSET *and* HARRIOT.)

RUS: Yes, yes; I'll have satisfaction. – So, madam! I have found you at last. You have made a fine confusion here.

HAR: I have, indeed, been the innocent cause of a great deal of confusion.

RUS: Innocent! What business had you to be running hither after –

HAR: My dear sir, you misunderstand the whole affair. I have not been in this house half an hour.

RUS: Zounds, girl, don't put me in a passion! You know I love you; but a lie puts me in a passion! But come along; we'll leave this house directly. (CHARLES *singing without.*) Heyday! What now?

        (*After a noise without, enter* CHARLES, *drunk.*)

CHAR: 'But my wine neither nurses nor babies can bring,
    And a big-bellied bottle's a mighty good thing.' (*singing*)
What's here, a woman? Harriot! Impossible! My dearest, sweetest Harriot! I have been looking all over the town for you, and at last, when I was tired – and weary – and disappointed – why then the honest major and I sat down together, to drink your health in pint bumpers (*running up to her*).

RUS: Stand off! How dare you take any liberties with my daughter before me? Zounds, sir, I'll be the death of you!

CHAR: Ha, 'squire Russet too! You jolly old cock, how do you? But, Harriot! my dear girl! (*taking hold of her*) My life, my soul, my –

RUS: Let her go, sir! Come away, Harriot! Leave him this instant, or I'll tear you asunder (*pulling her*).

HAR: There needs no violence to tear me from a man who could disguise himself in such a gross manner, at a time when he knew I was in the utmost distress. (*Disengages herself, and exit with* RUSSET.)

CHAR: (*alone*) Only hear me, sir! madam! My dear Harriot! Mr Russet! Gone!

She's gone; and 'egad in very ill humour, and in very bad company! I'll go after her. But hold! I shall only make it worse, as I did, now I recollect, once before. How the devil came they here? Who would have thought of finding her in my own house? My head turns round with conjectures. I believe I am drunk, very drunk; so 'egad, I'll e'en go and sleep myself sober, and then enquire the meaning of all this. 'For, I love Sue, and Sue loves me, etc.' (*Exit singing.*)

ACT IV

SCENE 1.   OAKLY'*s. Enter* MRS OAKLY *and* MAJOR OAKLY.

MAJ: Well, well! but, sister!

MRS OAK: I will know the truth of this matter. Why can't you tell me the whole story?

MAJ: I'll tell you nothing. There's nothing to tell. You know the truth already. Besides, what have I to do with it? Suppose there was a disturbance yesterday, what's that to me? Was I here? It's no business of mine.

MRS OAK: Then why do you study to make it so? Am I not well assured that this mischief commenced at your house in the country? And now you are carrying it on in town.

MAJ: This is always the case in family squabbles. My brother has put you out of humour, and you choose to vent your spleen upon me.

MRS OAK: Because I know that you are the occasion of his ill usage. Mr Oakly never behaved in such a manner before.

MAJ: I! Am I the occasion of it?

MRS OAK: Yes, you. I am sure on't.

MAJ: I am glad on't with all my heart.

MRS OAK: Indeed!

MAJ: Ay, indeed; and you are the more obliged to me. Come, come, sister, it's time you should reflect a little. My brother is become a public jest; and by and by, if this foolish affair gets wind, the whole family will be the subject of town-talk.

MRS OAK: And well it may, when you take so much pains to expose us. The little disquiets and uneasinesses of other families are kept secret; but here quarrels are fomented, and afterwards industriously made public. And you, sir, you have done all this. You are my greatest enemy!

MAJ: Your truest friend, sister.

MRS OAK: But it's no wonder. You have no feelings of humanity, no sense of domestic happiness, no idea of tenderness or attachment to any woman.

MAJ: No idea of plague and disquiet! No, no! And yet I can love a woman, for all that, heartily; as you say, tenderly. But then I always choose a woman should show a little love for me too.

MRS OAK: Cruel insinuation! But I defy your malice. Mr Oakly can have no doubt of my affection for him.

MAJ: Nor I neither! And yet your affection, such as it is, has all the evil properties of aversion. You absolutely kill him with kindness. Why, what a life he leads! He serves for nothing but a mere whetstone of your ill humour.

MRS OAK: Pray now, sir —

MAJ: The violence of your temper makes his house uncomfortable to him, poisons his meals, and breaks his rest.

MRS OAK: I beg, Major Oakly, that —

MAJ: This it is to have a wife that dotes upon one! The least trifle kindles your suspicion; you take fire in an instant, and set the whole family in a blaze.

MRS OAK: This is beyond all patience. No, sir, 'tis you are the incendiary; you are the cause of — I can't bear such — (*ready to weep*) From this instant, sir, I forbid you my house. However Mr Oakly may treat me himself, I'll never be made the sport of all his insolent relations. (*Exit.*)

MAJ: (*alone*) Yes, yes, I knew I should be turned out of doors. There she goes; back again to my brother directly. Poor gentleman! 'Slife, if he was but half the man that I am, I'd engage to keep her going to and fro all day, like a shuttlecock. (*Enter* CHARLES.) What, Charles!

CHAR: Oh, major! Have you heard of what happened after I left you yesterday?

MAJ: Heard! Yes, yes; I have heard it plain enough. But, poor Charles! Ha, ha, ha, ha! What a scene of confusion! I would give the world to have been there.

CHAR: And I would give the world to have been anywhere else. Cursed fortune!

MAJ: To come in so opportunely at the tail of an adventure! Was not your mistress mighty glad to see you? You were very fond of her, I dare say.

CHAR: I am upon the rack. Who can tell what rudeness I might offer her? I can remember nothing! I deserve to lose her. To make myself a beast! and at such a time too! Oh, fool, fool, fool!

MAJ: Prithee, be quiet, Charles! Never vex yourself about nothing; this will all be made up the first time you see her.

CHAR: I should dread to see her! And yet the not knowing where she is, distracts me. Her father may force her to marry Sir Harry Beagle immediately.

MAJ: Not he, I promise you. She'd run plumb into your arms first, in spite of her father's teeth.

CHAR: But then her father's violence, and the mildness of her disposition —

MAJ: Mildness! ridiculous! Trust to the spirit of the sex in her. I warrant you, like all the rest, she'll have perverseness enough not to do as her father would have her.

CHAR: Well, well! But then my behaviour to her; to expose myself in such a condition to her again! the very occasion of our former quarrel!

MAJ: Quarrel! ha, ha, ha! What signifies a quarrel with a mistress? Why, the whole affair of making love, as they call it, is nothing but quarrelling and making it up again. They quarrel o' purpose to kiss and be friends.

CHAR: Then, indeed, things seemed to be taking a fortunate turn. To renew our difference at such a time! just when I had some reason to hope for a reconciliation. May wine be my poison, if ever I am drunk again!

MAJ: Ay, ay, so every man says the next morning.

CHAR: Where, where can she be? Her father would hardly have carried her back to Lady Freelove's, and he has no house in town himself, nor Sir Harry. I don't know what to think. I'll go in search of her, though I don't know where to direct myself.

(*Enter* SERVANT.)

SERV: A gentleman, sir, that calls himself Captain O'Cutter, desires to speak with you.

CHAR: Don't trouble me! I'll see nobody: I'm not at home!

SERV: The gentleman says he has very particular business, and he must see you.

CHAR: *What's* his name? *Who* did you say?

SERV: Captain O'Cutter, sir.

CHAR: Captain O'Cutter! I never heard of him before. Do you know anything of him, major?

MAJ: Not I. But you hear he has particular business. I'll leave the room.

CHAR: He can have no business that need be a secret to you. Desire the captain to walk up. (*Exit* SERVANT.) What would I give if this unknown captain were to prove a messenger from my Harriot!

(*Enter* CAPTAIN O'CUTTER.)

O'CUT: Jontlemen, your sarvant! Is either of your names Charles Oakly, Esq?

CHAR: Charles Oakly, sir, is my name, if you have any business with it.

O'CUT: Avast, avast, my dear! I have a little business with your name; but as I was to let nobody know it, I can't mention it, till you clear the decks, fait (*pointing to the* MAJOR).

CHAR: This gentleman, sir, is my most intimate friend, and anything that concerns me may be mentioned before him.

O'CUT: Oh, if he's your friend, my dear, we may do all above-board. It's only about your deciding a deferance with my Lord Trinket. He wants to show you a little warm work; and as I was steering this way, he desired me to bring you this letter (*giving a letter*).

MAJ: How, sir, a challenge?

O'CUT: Yes, fait, a challenge. I am to be his lordship's second; and if you are fond of a hot berth, and will come along with that jontleman, we'll all go to it together, and make a little line of battle ahead of our own, my dear!

CHAR: (*reading*) Ha! What's this? (*aside*) This may be useful.

MAJ: Sir, I am infinitely obliged to you! (*aside*) A rare fellow this! Yes, yes, I'll meet all the good company: I'll be there in my waistcoat and pumps, and take a morning's breathing with you. Are you very fond of fighting, sir?

O'CUT: Indeed and I am. I love it better than salt beef or biscuit. I love it better than grog.

MAJ: But pray, sir, how are you interested in this difference? Do you know what it is about?

O'CUT: Oh, the devil burn me, not I. What signifies what it's about, you know, so we do but tilt a little?

MAJ: What! Fight and not know for what?

O'CUT: When the signal's out for engaging, what signifies talking?

MAJ: I fancy, sir, a duel is a common breakfast with you. I'll warrant now, you have been engaged in many such affairs.

O'CUT: Upon my shoul, and I have; sea or land, it's all one to little Terence O'Cutter. When I was last in Dublin, I fought one jontleman for cheating me out of a tousand pounds; I fought two of the Mermaid's crew about Sally

Macguire, tree about politics; and one about the playhouse in Smock-Alley. But, upon my fait, since I am in England, I have done nothing at all, at all!

CHAR: (*aside*) This is lucky! But my transport will discover me. Will you be so kind, sir, (*to* O'CUTTER) as to make my compliments to his lordship, and assure him that I shall do myself the honour of waiting on him.

O'CUT: Indeed, and I will. (*to* MAJOR OAKLY) Arrah, my dear, won't you come too?

MAJ: Depend upon't. We'll go through the whole exercise; Carte, tierce, and segoon, captain!

CHAR: (*aside*) Now to get my intelligence. I think the time, sir, his lordship appoints, in his letter, is — a —

O'CUT: You say right — six o'clock.

CHAR: And the place — a — a — is — I think, behind Montague House?

O'CUT: No, my dear! avast! by the ring in Hyde Park, fait. I settled it there myself, for fare of interruption.

CHAR: True, as you say, the ring in Hyde Park: I had forgot. Very well, I'll not fail you, sir.

O'CUT: Devil burn me, nor I. Upon my shoul, little Terence O'Cutter will see fair play, or he'll know the rason. And so, my dear, your sarvant. (*Exit.*)

MAJ: Ha, ha, ha! What a fellow! He loves fighting, like a game-cock.

CHAR: Oh, uncle! The luckiest thing in the world!

MAJ: What, to have the chance of being run through the body! I desire no such good fortune.

CHAR: Wish me joy, wish me joy! I have found her; my dear girl, my Harriot! She is at an inn in Holborn, major!

MAJ: The devil she is! How do you know?

CHAR: Why, this dear, delightful, charming, blundering captain has delivered me a wrong letter.

MAJ: A wrong letter!

CHAR: Yes, a letter from Lord Trinket to Lady Freelove.

MAJ: The devil! What are the contents?

CHAR: The news I told you just now, that she's at an inn in Holborn: and, besides, an excuse from my lord, for not waiting on her ladyship this morning, according to his promise, as he shall be entirely taken up with his design upon Harriot.

MAJ: So, so! a plot between the lord and the lady!

CHAR: What his plot is I don't know, but I shall beg leave to be made a party in it. So perhaps his lordship and I may meet, and *decide* our *deferance*, as the captain calls it, before tomorrow morning. There! read, read, man! (*giving the letter*)

MAJ: (*reading*) Um — um — um — very fine! And what do you propose doing?

CHAR: To go thither immediately.

Smock-Alley: one of the two Dublin theatres.
my transport will discover me: my joy will give me away.

MAJ: Then you shall take me with you. Who knows what his lordship's designs may be? I begin to suspect foul play.

CHAR: No, no; pray mind your own business. If I find there is any need of your assistance, I'll send for you.

MAJ: You'll manage this affair like a boy now — go on rashly, with noise and bustle, and fury, and get yourself into another scrape.

CHAR: No, no; let me alone; I'll go *incog.*; leave my chariot at some distance; proceed prudently, and take care of myself, I warrant you. I did not imagine that I should ever rejoice at receiving a challenge; but this is the most fortunate accident that could possibly have happened. B'ye, b'ye, uncle! (*Exit hastily.*)

MAJ: (*alone*) I don't half approve this; and yet I can hardly suspect his lordship of any very deep designs neither. Charles may easily outwit him. Hark ye, William! (*seeing a servant at some distance*)
                    (*Enter* SERVANT.)

SERV: Sir!

MAJ: Where's my brother?

SERV: In his study, alone, sir!

MAJ: And how is he, William?

SERV: Pretty well, I believe, sir.

MAJ: Ay, ay, but is he in good humour, or —

SERV: I never meddle in family affairs, not I, sir. (*Exit.*)

MAJ: (*alone*) Well said, William! No bad hint for me, perhaps! What a strange world we live in! No two people in it love one another better than my brother and sister, and yet the bitterest enemies could not torment each other more heartily. Ah, if he had but half my spirit! And yet he don't want it neither. But I know his temper: he pieces out the matter with maxims, and scraps of philosophy, and odds and ends of sentences: 'I must live in peace' — 'Patience is the best remedy' — 'anything for a quiet life' — and so on! However, yesterday, to give him his due, he behaved like a man. Keep it up, brother! keep it up! or it's all over with you. Since mischief is on foot, I'll e'en set it forwards on all sides. I'll in to him directly, read him one of my morning lectures, and persuade him, if I possibly can, to go out with me immediately; or work him up to some open act of rebellion against the sovereign authority of his lady-wife. Zounds, brother, rant, and roar, and rave, and turn the house out of the window. If I was a husband! 'Sdeath, what a pity it is that nobody knows how to manage a wife, but a bachelor. (*Exit.*)

SCENE 2.   *Scene changes to the Bull and Gate Inn.*

HAR: (*alone*) What will become of me? My father is enraged, and deaf to all remonstrances; and here I am to remain, by his positive orders, to receive this booby baronet's odious addresses. Among all my distresses, I must confess that Charles's behaviour yesterday is not the least. So wild! So given up to excesses! And yet, I am ashamed to own it even to myself, I love him; and

---

don't want it: isn't without it.

death itself shall not prevail on me to give my hand to Sir Harry. But here he comes! What shall I do with him?

(*Enter* SIR HARRY BEAGLE.)

SIR H: Your servant, miss! What, not speak? Bashful mayhap. Why then I will. Look'e, miss, I am a man of few words. What signifies haggling? It looks just like a dealer. What d'ye think of me for a husband? I am a tight young fellow − sound wind and limb − free from all natural blemishes, rum all over, damme.

HAR: Sir, I don't understand you. Speak English, and I'll give you an answer.

SIR H: English! Why so I do, and good plain English too. What d'ye think of me for a husband? That's English, e'nt it? I know none of your French lingo, none of your *parlyvoos*, not I. What d'ye think of me for a husband? The 'squire says you shall marry me.

HAR: (*aside*) What shall I say to him? I had best be civil. − I think, sir, you deserve a much better wife, and beg −

SIR H: Better! No, no, though you're so knowing, I'm not to be taken in so. You're a fine thing: your points are all good.

HAR: Sir Harry! Sincerity is above all ceremony. Excuse me if I declare, I never will be your wife. And if you have a real regard for me, and my happiness, you will give up all pretension to me. Shall I beseech you, sir, to persuade my father not to urge a marriage, to which I am determined never to consent?

SIR H: Hey! how! what! be off! Why, it's a match, miss! It's done and done on both sides.

HAR: For heaven's sake, sir, withdraw your claim to me. I never can be prevailed on − indeed I can't.

SIR H: What, make a match and then draw stakes! That's doing of nothing − Play or pay, all the world over.

HAR: Let me prevail on you, sir! I am determined not to marry you, at all events.

SIR H: But your father's determined you shall, miss! So the odds are on my side. I am not quite sure of my horse, but I have the rider hollow.

HAR: Your horse, sir! − d'ye take me for − but I forgive you. I beseech you come into my proposal. It will be better for us both in the end.

SIR H: I can't be off.

HAR: Let me entreat you.

SIR H: I tell you, it's unpossible.

HAR: Pray, pray do, sir.

SIR H: I can't, damme.

HAR: I beseech you.

SIR H: (*Whistles.*)

HAR: How! Laughed at?

SIR H: (*singing*) 'Will you marry me, dear Ally, Ally Croker?'

HAR: Marry you? I had rather be married to a slave, a wretch − You! (*Walks about.*)

SIR H: A fine going thing. She has a deal of foot, treads well upon her pasterns, goes above her ground −

---

rum: manly (perhaps a gipsy word).

HAR: Peace, wretch! Do you talk to me as if I were your horse.

SIR H: Horse! Why not speak of my horse! If your fine ladies had half as many good qualities, they would be much better bargains.

HAR: And if their wretches of husbands liked them half so well as they do their horses, they would lead better lives.

SIR H: Mayhap so: but what signifies talking to you? The 'squire shall know your tricks! He'll doctor you! I'll go and talk to him.

HAR: Go anywhere, so that you go from me.

SIR H: He'll break you in! If you won't go in a snaffle, you must be put in a curb. He'll break you, damme! (*Exit.*)

HAR: (*alone*) A wretch! But I was to blame to suffer his brutal behaviour to ruffle my temper. I could expect nothing else from him, and he is below my anger. How much trouble has this odious fellow caused both to me and my poor father! I never disobeyed him before, and my denial now makes him quite unhappy. In anything else I would be all submission; and even now, while I dread his rage, my heart bleeds for his uneasiness. I wish I could resolve to obey him!

> (*Enter* RUSSET.)

RUS: Are not you a sad girl! a perverse, stubborn, obstinate —

HAR: My dear sir —

RUS: Look ye, Harriot, don't speak. You'll put me in a passion. Will you have him? Answer me that. Why don't the girl speak? Will you have him?

HAR: Dearest sir, there is nothing in the world else —

RUS: Why there! there! look ye there! Zounds, you shall have him! Hussy, you shall have him! You shall marry him tonight! Did not you promise to receive him civilly? How came you to affront him?

HAR: Sir, I did receive him very civilly; but his behaviour was so insolent and insupportable —

RUS: Insolent! Zounds, I'll blow his brains out. Insolent to my dear Harriot! A rogue! a villain! a scoundrel! I'll — but it's a lie! I know it's a lie! He durst not behave insolent. Will you have him? Answer me that. Will you have him? Zounds, you shall have him!

HAR: If you have any love for me, sir —

RUS: Love for you! You know I love you; you know your poor fond father dotes on you to madness: I would not force you, if I did not love you. Don't I want you to be happy? But I know what you would have: you want young Oakly, a rake-helly, drunken —

HAR: Release me from Sir Harry, and if I ever marry against your consent, renounce me forever.

RUS: I *will* renounce you, unless you'll have Sir Harry.

HAR: Consider, my dear sir, you'll make me miserable. I would die to please you, but cannot prostitute my hand to a man my heart abhors. Absolve me from this hard command, and in everything else it will be happiness to obey you.

RUS: You'll break my heart, Harriot, you'll break my heart. Make you miserable! Don't I want to make you happy? Is not he the richest man in the county? That will make you happy. Don't all the pale-faced girls in the country long to get him? And yet you are so perverse, and wayward, and stubborn. Zounds, you shall have him!

HAR: For heaven's sake, sir —

RUS: Hold your tongue, Harriot! I'll hear none of your nonsense. You shall have him, I tell you, you shall have him! He shall marry you this very night. I'll go for a licence and a parson immediately. Zounds, why do I stand arguing with you? An't I your father? Have not I a right to dispose of you? You shall have him!

HAR: Sir!

RUS: I won't hear a word. You shall have him! (*Exit.*)

HAR: (*alone*) Sir! Hear me! But one word! He will not hear me, and is gone to prepare for this odious marriage. I will die before I consent to it. 'You *shall* have him!' Oh, that fathers would enforce their commands by better arguments! And yet I pity him, while he afflicts me. He upbraided me with Charles's wildness and intemperance; alas! but too justly! I see that he is wedded to his excesses; and I ought to conquer an affection for him which will only serve to make me unhappy. (*Enter* CHARLES *in a frock-coat etc.*) Ha! What do I see? (*screaming*)

CHAR: Peace, my love! My dear life, make no noise! I have been hovering about the house this hour. I just now saw your father and Sir Harry go out, and have seized this precious opportunity to throw myself at your feet.

HAR: You have given yourself, sir, a great deal of needless trouble. I did not expect or hope for the favour of such a visit.

CHAR: Oh, my dear Harriot, your words and looks cut me to the soul! You can't imagine what I suffer, and have suffered, since last night. And yet I have in some fond moments flattered myself that the service I was so fortunate as to do you at Lady Freelove's would plead a little in my favour.

HAR: You may remember, sir, that you took a very early opportunity of cancelling that obligation.

CHAR: I do remember it with shame and despair. But may I perish, if my joy at having delivered you from a villain, was not the cause! My transport more than half intoxicated me, and wine made an easy conquest over me. I tremble to think lest I should have behaved in such a manner as you cannot pardon.

HAR: Whether I pardon you or no, sir, is a matter of mighty little consequence.

CHAR: Oh, my Harriot! Upbraid me, reproach me, do anything but look and talk with that air of coldness and indifference. Must I lose you for one offence, when my soul dotes on you, when I love you to distraction!

HAR: Did it appear like love, your conduct yesterday? To lose yourself in riot, when I was exposed to the greatest distresses!

CHAR: I feel, I feel my shame, and own it.

HAR: You confess that you don't know in what manner you behaved. Ought not I to tremble at the very thoughts of a man devoted to a vice which renders him no longer a judge or master of his own conduct?

CHAR: Abandon me, if ever I am guilty of it again. Oh, Harriot! I am distracted with ten thousand fears and apprehensions of losing you forever. The chambermaid, whom I bribed to admit me to you, told me that when the two gentlemen went out they talked of a licence. What am I to think? Is it possible that

you can resign yourself to Sir Harry Beagle? (HARRIOT *pauses.*) Can you
then consent to give your hand to another? No; let me once more deliver you.
Let us seize this lucky moment! My chariot stands at the corner of the next
street. Let me gently force you, while their absence allows it, and convey you
from the brutal violence of a constrained marriage.

HAR: I will wait the event, be it what it may. Oh, Charles, I am too much inclined –
They shan't force me to marry Sir Harry. But your behaviour! Not half an
hour ago, my father reproached me with the looseness of your character
(*weeping*).

CHAR: I see my folly, and am ashamed of it. You have reclaimed me, Harriot! On
my soul, you have. If all women were as attentive as yourself to the morals of
their lovers, a libertine would be an uncommon character. But let me persuade
you to leave this place, while you may. Major Oakly will receive us at his
house with pleasure. I am shocked at the thoughts of what your stay here
may reserve you to.

HAR: No; I am determined to remain. To leave my father again, to go off openly
with a man, of whose libertine character he has himself so lately been a witness, would justify his anger, and impeach my reputation.

CHAR: Fool! fool! How unhappy have I made myself! Consider, my Harriot, the
peculiarity of your situation; besides, I have reason to fear other designs
against you.

HAR: From other designs I can be nowhere so secure as with my father.

CHAR: Time flies. Let me persuade you!

HAR: I am resolved to stay here.

CHAR: You distract me. For heaven's sake –

HAR: I will not think of it.

CHAR: Consider, my angel! –

HAR: I do consider, that your conduct has made it absolutely improper for me to
trust myself to your care.

CHAR: My conduct! Vexation! 'Sdeath! But then, my dear Harriot, the danger you
are in, the necessity –

(*Enter* CHAMBERMAID.)

CHAMB: Oh law, ma'am! such a terrible accident! As sure as I am here, there's a
press-gang has seized the two gemmin, and is carrying them away, thof so be
one an'em says as how he's a knight and baronight, and that t'other's a 'squire
and a housekeeper.

HAR: Seized by a press-gang! Impossible.

CHAR: Oh, now the design comes out. But I'll balk his lordship.

CHAMB: Lack-a-dasy, ma'am, what can we do? There is master, and John Ostler,
and Bootcatcher, all gone a'ter 'em. There is such an uproar as never was!
(*Exit.*)

HAR: If I thought this was your contrivance, sir, I would never speak to you again.

CHAR: I would sooner die than be guilty of it. This is Lord Trinket's doing, I am
sure. I knew he had some scheme in agitation, by a letter I intercepted this
morning. (HARRIOT *screams.*) Ha! Here he comes! Nay, then, it's plain
enough. Don't be frightened, my love! I'll protect you. But now I must desire
you to follow my directions.

(*Enter* LORD TRINKET.)

LORD T: Now, madam! Pox on't, he here again! Nay, then! (*drawing*) Come, sir! You're unarmed, I see. Give up the lady: give her up, I say; or I am through you in a twinkling (*going to make a pass at* CHARLES).

CHAR: Keep your distance, my lord! I have arms (*producing a pistol*). If you come a foot nearer, you have a brace of balls through your lordship's head.

LORD T: How? what's this? pistols!

CHAR: At your lordship's service. Sword and pistol, my lord! Those, you know, are our weapons. If this misses, I have the fellow to't in my pocket. Don't be frighted, madam! His lordship has removed your friends and relations, but he will take great care of you. Shall I leave you with him?

HAR: Cruel Charles! You know I *must* go with you now.

CHAR: A little away from the door, if your lordship pleases (*waving his hand*).

LORD T: Sir! 'Sdeath! Madam!

CHAR: A little more round, my lord! (*waving*)

LORD T: But, sir! Mr Oakly!

CHAR: I have no leisure to talk with your lordship now. A little more that way, if you please (*waving*). You know where I live. If you have any commands for Miss Russet, you will hear of her too at my house. Nay, keep back, my lord! (*presenting*) Your lordship's most obedient humble servant! (*Exit with* HARRIOT.)

LORD T: (*looking after him, and pausing for a short time*) I cut a mighty ridiculous figure here, 'pon honour. So, I have been concerting this deep scheme merely to serve him. Oh, the devil take such intrigues, and all silly country girls, that can give up a man of quality and figure, for a fellow that nobody knows! (*Exit.*)

ACT V

SCENE 1.   LADY FREELOVE'*s. Enter* LORD TRINKET, LADY FREE-LOVE *with a letter, and* CAPTAIN O'CUTTER.

LORD T: Was ever anything so unfortunate? Pox on't, captain, how could you make such a strange blunder?

O'CUT: I never tought of a blunder. I was to daliver two letters, and if I gave them one a-piece I tought it was all one, fait.

LADY F: And so, my lord, the ingenious captain gave the letter intended for me to young Oakly, and here he has brought me a challenge.

LORD T: Ridiculous! Never was anything so *mal-à-propos*. Did not you read the direction, captain?

O'CUT: Who, me! Devil burn me, not I. I never rade at all.

LORD T: 'Sdeath, how provoking! When I had secured the servants, and got all the people out of the way; when everything was *en train*!

LADY F: Nay, never despair, my lord! Things have happened unluckily, to be sure; and yet, I think I could hit upon a method to set everything to right again.

LORD T: How, how, my dear Lady Freelove, how?

LADY F: Suppose, then, your lordship was to go and deliver these country gentlemen from their confinement; make them believe it was a plot of young

Oakly's to carry off my niece; and so make a merit of your own services with the father.

LORD T: Admirable! I'll about it immediately.

O'CUT: Has your lordship any occasion for my sarvice, in this expedition?

LORD T: Oh, no. Only release me these people, and then keep out of the way, dear captain!

O'CUT: With all my heart, fait! But you are all wrong. This will not signify a brass farding. If you would let me alone, I would give him a salt eel, I warrant you. But, upon my credit, there's nothing to be done without a little tilting. (*Exit.*)

LADY F: Ha, ha! poor captain!

LORD T: But where shall I carry them, when I have delivered them?

LADY F: To Mr Oakly's, by all means. You may be sure my niece is there.

LORD T: To Mr Oakly's! Why, does your ladyship consider, 'tis going directly into the fire of the enemy? Throwing the *démenti* full in their teeth?

LADY F: So much the better. Face your enemies: nay, you shall outface them too. Why, where's the difference between truths and untruths, if you do but stick close to the point? Falsehood would scarce ever be detected, if we had confidence enough to support it.

LORD T: Nay, I don't want *bronze* upon occasion: but, to go amongst a whole troop of people, sure to contradict every word I say, is so dangerous —

LADY F: To leave Russet alone amongst them would be ten times more dangerous. You may be sure that Oakly's will be the first place he will go to after his daughter; where, if you don't accompany him, he will be open to all their suggestions. They'll be all in one story, and nobody there to contradict them: and then their dull truth would triumph; which must not be. No, no; positively, my lord, you must battle it out.

LORD T: Well! I'll go, 'pon honour; and, if I could depend on your ladyship, as a *corps de reserve* —

LADY F: I'll certainly meet you there. Tush! My lord, there's nothing in it. It's hard, indeed, if two persons of condition can't bear themselves out against such trumpery folks as the family of the Oaklys.

LORD T: Odious low people! But I lose time. I must after the captain. And so, till we meet at Mr Oakly's, I kiss your ladyship's hands. You won't fail me?

LADY F: You may depend on me.

        (*Exit* LORD TRINKET.)

LADY F: (*alone*) So, here is fine work! This artful little hussy has been too much for us all. Well! what's to be done? Why, when a woman of fashion gets into a scrape, nothing but a fashionable assurance can get her out of it again. I'll e'en go boldly to Mr Oakly's, as I have promised; and, if it appears practicable, I will forward Lord Trinket's match; but if I find that matters have taken another turn, his lordship must excuse me. In that case, I'll fairly drop him, seem a perfect stranger to all his intentions, and give my visit an air of congratulation to my niece and any other husband which fortune, her wise father, or her ridiculous self, has provided for her. (*Exit.*)

---

want bronze: lack impudence.

SCENE 2.   *Scene changes to* MRS OAKLY*'s dressing room.*

MRS OAK: (*alone*) This is worse and worse! He never held me so much in contempt before. To go out without so much as speaking to me, or taking the
least notice! I am obliged to the major for this. How could he take him out?
And how could Mr Oakly go with him?
               (*Enter* TOILET.)

MRS OAK: Well, Toilet!

TOIL: My master is not come back yet, ma'am.

MRS OAK: Where is he gone?

TOIL: I don't know, I can assure your ladyship.

MRS OAK: Why don't you know? You know nothing! But I warrant, you know
well enough, if you would tell. You shall never persuade me but you knew of
Mr Oakly's going out today.

TOIL: I wish I may die, ma'am, upon my honour, and I protest to your ladyship, I
knew nothing in the world of the matter, no more than the child unborn.
There is Mr Paris, my master's gentleman, knows —

MRS OAK: What does he know?

TOIL: That I knew nothing about it, till after my master was gone.

MRS OAK: Where is Paris? What is he doing?

TOIL: He is in my master's room, ma'am.

MRS OAK: Bid him come here.

TOIL: Yes, ma'am. (*Exit.*)

MRS OAK: He is certainly gone after this young flirt. His confidence, and the
major's insolence, provoke me beyond expression. (*Re-enter* TOILET *with*
PARIS.) Where's your master?

PAR: *Il est sorti.*

MRS OAK: Where is he gone?

PAR: Ah, madame! *Je n'en sais rien.* I know noting of it.

MRS OAK: Nobody knows anything. Why did not you tell me he was going out?

PAR: I dress him; *Je ne m'en soucis plus.* He go where he will; I have no bisness wis
it.

MRS OAK: Yes, you should have told me; that was your business; and if you don't
mind your business better, you shan't stay here, I can tell you, sir.

PAR: *Voilà! quelque chose d'extraordinaire!*

MRS OAK: Don't stand jabbering and shrugging your shoulders; but go, and
enquire — go — and bring me word where he is gone.

PAR: I don't know vat I am do: I'll ask-a Jean.

MRS OAK: Bid John come here.

PAR: *De tout mon coeur. Jean! ici! Jean!* Speak mi ladi! (*Exit.*)

MRS OAK: Impudent fellow! His insolent gravity and indifference are insupportable. Toilet!

TOIL: Ma'am.

MRS OAK: Where's John? Why don't he come? Why do you stand with your hands
before you? Why don't you fetch him?

TOIL: Yes, ma'am: I'll go this minute. Oh! here! John! my lady wants you.
               (*Enter* JOHN.)

MRS OAK: Where's your master?

JOHN: Gone out, madam.

MRS OAK: Why did not you go with him?

JOHN: Because he went out in the major's chariot, madam.

MRS OAK: Where did they go to?

JOHN: To the major's, I suppose, madam.

MRS OAK: Suppose! Don't you know?

JOHN: I believe so; but can't tell for certain, indeed, madam.

MRS OAK: Believe! and suppose! and don't know! and can't tell! You are all fools!
    Go about your business! (JOHN *going*) Come here! (*Returns.*) Go to the
    major's. — No; it does not signify. Go along! (JOHN *going*) Yes, hark ye!
    (*Returns.*) Go to the major's, and see if your master is there.

JOHN: Give your compliments, madam?

MRS OAK: My compliments, blockhead! Get along! (JOHN *going*) Come hither!
    (*Returns.*) Can't you go to the major's, and bring me word if Mr Oakly is
    there, without taking any further notice?

JOHN: Yes, ma'am!

MRS OAK: Well! why don't you go, then? And make haste back. And, d'ye hear?
    John!
                (JOHN, *going, returns.*)

JOHN: Madam.

MRS OAK: Nothing at all — go along! (JOHN *goes.*) How uneasy Mr Oakly makes
    me! — Hark ye! John!
                (JOHN *returns.*)

JOHN: Madam.

MRS OAK: Send the porter here.

JOHN: Yes, madam.
                (*Exit* JOHN.)

TOIL: (*aside*) So! She's in a rare humour! I shall have a fine time on't. — Will your
    ladyship choose to dress?

MRS OAK: Prithee, creature, don't tease me with your fiddle-faddle stuff — I have
    a thousand things to think of. Where is the porter? Why has not that booby
    sent him? What is the meaning —
                (*Re-enter* JOHN.)

JOHN: Madam, my master is this moment returned with Major Oakly, and my
    young master, and the lady that was here yesterday.

MRS OAK: Very well. (*Exit* JOHN.) Returned! Yes, truly, he is returned; and in a
    very extraordinary manner. This is setting me at open defiance. But I'll go
    down, and show them I have too much spirit to endure such usage (*going*).
    Or, stay — I'll not go amongst his company — I'll go out. Toilet!

TOIL: Ma'am.

MRS OAK: Order the coach; I'll go out. (TOILET *going*) Toilet! stay! I'll e'en go
    down to them. — No. — Toilet!

TOIL: Ma'am.

MRS OAK: Order me a boiled chicken. — I'll not go down to dinner. — I'll dine in
    my own room; and sup there. — I'll not see his face these three days.
                (*Exeunt.*)

SCENE 3.   *Scene changes to another room. Enter* OAKLY, MAJOR OAKLY, CHARLES, *and* HARRIOT.

CHAR: My dear Harriot, do not make yourself so uneasy.

HAR: Alas! I have too much cause for my uneasiness. Who knows what that vile lord has done with my father?

OAK: Be comforted, madam. We shall soon hear of Mr Russet; and all will be well, I dare say.

HAR: You are too good to me, sir! But, I can assure you, I am not a little concerned on your account, as well as my own; and, if I did not flatter myself with the hopes of explaining everything to Mrs Oakly's satisfaction, I should never forgive myself for having disturbed the peace of such a worthy family.

MAJ: Don't mind that, madam! They'll be very good friends again. This is nothing among married people. — 'Sdeath, here she is! — No; it's only Mrs Toilet.
          (*Enter* TOILET.)

OAK: Well, Toilet, what now? (TOILET *whispers.*) Not well? Can't come down to dinner? Wants to see me above? — Hark ye, brother; what shall I do?

MAJ: If you go, you're undone.

HAR: Go, sir! Go to Mrs Oakly. Indeed you had better.

MAJ: 'Sdeath, brother, don't budge a foot! This is all fractiousness and ill humour.

OAK: No; I'll not go. — Tell her I have company, and we shall be glad to see her here. (*Exit* TOILET.)

MAJ: That's right.

OAK: Suppose I go, and watch how she proceeds.

MAJ: What d'ye mean? You would not go to her! Are you mad?

OAK: By no means go to her. — I only want to know how she takes it. I'll lie *perdu* in my study, and observe her motions.

MAJ: I don't like this pitiful ambuscade-work; this bush-fighting. Why can't you stay here? Ay, ay! I know how it will be. She'll come bounce in upon you, with a torrent of anger and passion, or, if necessary, a whole flood of tears, and carry all before her at once.

OAK: You shall find that you're mistaken, major. Don't imagine, because I wish not to be void of humanity, that I am destitute of resolution. Now I am convinced I'm in the right, I'll support that right with ten times your steadiness.

MAJ: You talk this well, brother!

OAK: I'll *do* it well, brother!

MAJ: If you don't, you're undone.

OAK: Never fear, never fear! (*Exit.*)

MAJ: Well, Charles!

CHAR: I can't bear to see my Harriot so uneasy. I'll go immediately in quest of Mr Russet. Perhaps I may learn at the inn, where his lordship's ruffians have carried him.

RUS: (*without*) Here? Yes, yes; I know she's here, well enough. Come along, Sir Harry, come along.

HAR: He's here! my father! I know his voice. Where is Mr Oakly? Oh, now, good sir, (*to the* MAJOR) do but pacify him, and you'll be a friend indeed.
          (*Enter* RUSSET, LORD TRINKET, *and* SIR HARRY BEAGLE.)

LORD T: There, sir! I told you it was so.

RUS: Ay, ay, it is too plain. Oh, you provoking slut! Elopement after elopement! And, at last, to have your father carried off by violence! To endanger my life! Zounds, I am so angry, I dare not trust myself within reach of you!

CHAR: I can assure you, sir, that your daughter is entirely —

RUS: You assure me? You are the fellow that has perverted her mind — that has set my own child against me!

CHAR: If you will but hear me, sir —

RUS: I won't hear a word you say! — I'll have my daughter. — I won't hear a word!

MAJ: Nay, Mr Russet, hear reason. If you will but have patience —

RUS: I'll have no patience. — I'll have my daughter; and she shall marry Sir Harry tonight.

LORD T: That is dealing rather too much *en cavalier* with me, Mr Russet, 'pon honour. You take no notice of my pretensions, though my rank and family —

RUS: What care I for rank and family! I don't want to make my daughter a ranti-pole woman of quality. I'll give her to whom I please. Take her away, Sir Harry! She shall marry you tonight.

HAR: For heaven's sake, sir, hear me but a moment.

RUS: Hold your tongue, girl! Take her away, Sir Harry, take her away.

CHAR: It must not be.

MAJ: Only three words, Mr Russet —

RUS: Why don't the booby take her!

SIR H: Hold hard! hold hard! You are all on a wrong scent. Hold hard! I say, hold hard! Hark ye, squire Russet.

RUS: Well! What now?

SIR H: It was proposed, you know, to match me with Miss Harriot, but she can't take kindly to me. When one has made a bad bet, it is best to hedge off, you know; and so I have e'en swopped her with Lord Trinket here for his brown horse Nabob, that he bought of Lord Whistle-Jacket, for fifteen hundred guineas.

RUS: Swopped her? Swopped my daughter for a horse? Zounds, sir, what d'ye mean?

SIR H: Mean? Why I mean to be off, to be sure! It won't do; I tell you, it won't do. First of all, I knocked up myself and my horses, when they took for London; and now I have been stewed aboard a tender: I have wasted three stone at least. If I could have rid my match, it would not have grieved me. And so, as I said before, I have swopped her for Nabob.

RUS: The devil take Nabob, and yourself, and Lord Trinket, and —

LORD T: *Pardon! je vous demande pardon, monsieur* Russet, 'pon honour.

RUS: Death and the devil! I shall go distracted. My daughter plotting against me! The —

MAJ: Come, Mr Russet, I am your man, after all. Give me but a moment's hearing, and I'll engage to make peace between you and your daughter, and throw the blame where it ought to fall most deservedly.

---

rantipole: wild, rakish.
stewed: *stew* is a Middle English variant of *stow*; but he may mean *left to stew* or *sweat*.

SIR H: Ay, ay, that's right. Put the saddle on the right horse, my buck!

RUS: Well, sir! What d'ye say? Speak! I don't know what to do!

MAJ: I'll speak the truth, let who will be offended by it: I have proof presumptive and positive for you, Mr Russet. From his lordship's behaviour at Lady Free-love's, when my nephew rescued her, we may fairly conclude that he would stick at no measures to carry his point. There's proof presumptive. But, sir, we can give you proof positive too — proof under his lordship's own hand, that he, likewise, was the contriver of the gross affront that has just been offered you.

RUS: Hey! how!

LORD T: Every syllable romance, 'pon honour.

MAJ: Gospel, every word on't.

CHAR: This letter will convince you, sir. In consequence of what happened at Lady Freelove's, his lordship thought fit to send me a challenge; but the messenger blundered, and gave me this letter instead of it (*giving the letter*). I have the case which enclosed it in my pocket.

LORD T: Forgery, from beginning to end, 'pon honour.

MAJ: Truth, upon *my* honour. But read, Mr Russet; read and be convinced.

RUS: Let me see — let me see — (*reading*) — Um um — um — um — so! so! — um — um — um — Damnation! — 'Wish me success — obedient slave — Trinket.' — Fire and fury! How dare you do this?

LORD T: When you are cool, Mr Russet, I will explain this matter to you.

RUS: Cool? 'Sdeath and hell! I'll never be cool again! I'll be revenged! So my Harriot, my dear girl, is innocent at last! Say so, Harriot; tell me you are innocent (*embracing her*).

HAR: I am, indeed, sir! And happy beyond expression at your being convinced of it.

RUS: I am glad on't — I am glad on't — I believe you, Harriot! You were always a good girl.

MAJ: So she is, an excellent girl! Worth a regiment of such lords and baronets! Come, sir, finish everything handsomely at once. Come, Charles will have a handsome fortune.

RUS: Marry! She durst not do it.

MAJ: Consider, sir, they have long been fond of each other; old acquaintance — faithful lovers — turtles — and may be very happy.

RUS: Well, well; since things are so — I love my girl. Hark ye, young Oakly, if you don't make her a good husband, you'll break my heart, you rogue.

MAJ: I'll cut his throat, if he don't.

CHAR: Do not doubt it, sir! my Harriot has reformed me altogether.

RUS: Has she? Why then — there — heaven bless you both — there — now there's an end on't.

SIR H: So, my lord, you and I are both distanced — a hollow thing, damme.

LORD T: *N'importe.*

SIR H: (*aside*) Now this stake is drawn, my lord may be for hedging off, mayhap. Ecod! I'll go to Jack Speed's, and secure Nabob, and be out of town in an hour. Soho! Lady Freelove! yoicks! (*Exit.*)

(*Enter* LADY FREELOVE.)

LADY F: My dear Miss Russet, you'll excuse —

CHAR: Mrs Oakly, at your ladyship's service.

LADY F: Married?

HAR: Not yet, madam; but my father has been so good as to give his consent.

LADY F: I protest, I am prodigiously glad of it. My dear, I give you joy! and you,
    Mr Oakly! I wish you joy, Mr Russet, and all the good company! for I think
    they are most of them parties concerned.

MAJ: (aside) How easy, impudent, and familiar!

LADY F: Lord Trinket here too! I vow I did not see your lordship before.

LORD T: Your ladyship's most obedient slave (bowing).

LADY F: You seem grave, my lord! Come, come, I know there has been some
    difference between you and Mr Oakly. You must give me leave to be a
    mediator in this affair.

LORD T: Here has been a small fracas to be sure, madam! We are all blown, 'pon
    honour.

LADY F: Blown! What do you mean, my lord?

LORD T: Nay, your ladyship knows that I never mind these things, and I know
    that they never discompose your ladyship. But things have happened a little
    en travers: the little billet that I sent your ladyship has fallen into the hands
    of that gentleman (pointing to CHARLES); and so, there has been a little
    brouillerie about it; that's all.

LADY F: You talk to me, my lord, in a very extraordinary style. If you have been
    guilty of any misbehaviour, I am sorry for it; but your ill conduct can fasten
    no imputation on me. Miss Russet will justify me sufficiently.

MAJ: Had not your ladyship better appeal to my friend Charles here? The letter,
    Charles! out with it this instant!

CHAR: Yes, I have the credentials of her ladyship's integrity in my pocket. Mr
    Russet, the letter you read a little while ago was inclosed in this cover; which
    also I now think it my duty to put into your hands.

RUS: (reading) 'To the Right Honourable Lady Freelove.' 'Sdeath and hell! and
    now I recollect, the letter itself was pieced with scraps of French, and
    'madam', and 'your ladyship'. Fire and fury! Madam, how came you to use
    me so? I am obliged to you then, for the insult that has been offered me.

LADY F: What is all this? Your obligations to me, Mr Russet, are of a nature
    that —

RUS: Fine obligations! I dare say I am partly obliged to you too for the attempt on
    my daughter by that thing of a lord yonder, at your house. Zounds, madam,
    these are injuries never to be forgiven! They are the grossest affronts to me
    and my family. All the world shall know them! Zounds! I'll —

LADY F: Mercy on me! How boisterous are these country gentlemen! Why really,
    Mr Russet, you rave like a man in Bedlam; I'm afraid you'll beat me: and then
    you swear most abominably! How can you be so vulgar? I see the meaning of
    this low malice. But the reputations of women of quality are not so easily
    impeached. My rank places me above the scandal of little people, and I shall
    meet such petty insolence with the greatest ease and tranquillity. But you and
    your simple girl will be the sufferers. I had some thoughts of introducing her
    into the first company; but now, madam, I shall neither receive nor return

your visits, and will entirely withdraw my protection from the ordinary part of the family. (*Exit.*)

RUS: Zounds! what impudence! That's worse than all the rest.

LORD T: Fine presence of mind, faith! the true French *nonchalance*. But, good folks, why such a deal of rout and *tapage* about nothing at all? If mademoiselle Harriot had rather be Mrs Oakly than Lady Trinket — why — I wish her joy, that's all. Mr Russet, I wish you joy of your son-in-law — Mr Oakly, I wish you joy of the lady — and you, madam (*to* HARRIOT), of the gentleman. And, in short, I wish you all joy of one another, 'pon honour. (*Exit.*)

RUS: There's a fine fellow of a lord now! The devil's in your London folks of the first fashion, as you call them. They will rob you of your estate, debauch your daughter, or lie with your wife; and all, as if they were doing you a favour — 'pon honour! (*Bell rings violently.*)

MAJ: Hey! what now?

> (*Enter* OAKLY.)

OAK: D'ye hear, major, d'ye hear?

MAJ: Zounds! what a clatter! She'll pull down all the bells in the house.

OAK: My observations since I left you have confirmed my resolution. I see plainly that her good humour, and her ill humour, her smiles, her tears, and her fits, are all calculated to play upon me.

MAJ: Did not I always tell you so? It's the way with them all: they will be rough, and smooth, and hot, and cold, and all in a breath: anything to get the better of us.

OAK: She is in all moods at present, I promise you. I am at once angry and ashamed of her; and yet she is so ridiculous I can't help laughing at her. There has she been in her chamber, fuming and fretting, and dispatching a messenger to me every two minutes, servant after servant. Now she insists on my coming to her — now again she writes a note to entreat — then Toilet is sent to let me know that she is ill — absolutely dying — then, the very next minute, she'll never see my face again — she'll go out of the house directly. (*Bell rings.*) Again! Now the storm rises.

MAJ: It will soon drive this way then. Now, brother, prove yourself a man. You have gone too far to retreat.

OAK: Retreat! retreat! No, no! I'll preserve the advantage I have gained, I am determined.

MAJ: Ay, ay! keep your ground! fear nothing! Up with your noble heart! Good discipline makes good soldiers. Stick close to my advice, and you may stand buff to a tigress.

OAK: Here she is, by heavens. Now, brother!

MAJ: And now, brother! Now, or never!

> (*Enter* MRS OAKLY.)

MRS OAK: I think, Mr Oakly, you might have had humanity enough to have come to see how I did. You have taken your leave, I suppose, of all tenderness and

---

stand buff: confront without flinching.

affection! — But I'll be calm. — I'll not throw myself into a passion. — You want to drive me out of your house. — I see what you aim at, and will be aforehand with you. — Let me keep my temper! — I'll send for a chair, and leave the house this instant.

OAK: True, my love! I knew you would not think of dining in your own chamber alone, when I had company below. You shall sit at the head of the table, as you ought, to be sure, as you say, and make my friends welcome.

MRS OAK: Excellent raillery! Look ye, Mr Oakly, I see the meaning of all this affected coolness and indifference!

OAK: My dear, consider where you are!

MRS OAK: You would be glad, I find, to get me out of your house, and have all your flirts about you.

OAK: Before all this company! Fie!

MRS OAK: But I'll disappoint you; for I shall remain in it to support my due authority. As for you, Major Oakly —

MAJ: Heyday! what have I done?

MRS OAK: I think you might find better employment than to create divisions between married people! And you, sir —

OAK: Nay, but, my dear!

MRS OAK: Might have more sense, as well as tenderness, than to give ear to such idle stuff.

OAK: Lord! Lord!

MRS OAK: You and your wise counsellor there, I suppose, think to carry all your points with me.

OAK: Was ever anything —

MRS OAK: But it won't do, sir! You shall find that I will have my own way, and that I will govern my own family.

OAK: You had better learn to govern yourself, by half. Your passion makes you ridiculous. Did ever anybody see so much fury and violence? Affronting your best friends, breaking my peace, and disconcerting your own temper! And all for what? For nothing. 'Sdeath, madam, at these years you ought to know better!

MRS OAK: At these years! Very fine! Am I to be talked to in this manner?

OAK: Talked to! Why not? You have talked to me long enough, almost talked me to death, and I have taken it all, in hopes of making you quiet: but all in vain; for the more one bears, the worse you are. Patience, I find, is all thrown away upon you; and henceforward, come what may, I am resolved to be master of my own house.

MRS OAK: So, so! Master indeed! Yes, sir, and you'll take care to have mistresses enough too, I warrant you.

OAK: Perhaps I may; but they shall be quiet ones, I assure you.

MRS OAK: Indeed! And do you think I am such a tame fool as to sit quietly and bear all this? You shall know, sir, that I will resent this behaviour! You shall find that I have a spirit —

OAK: Of the devil.

MRS OAK: Intolerable! You shall find then that I will exert that spirit. I am sure I have need of it. As soon as the house is once cleared again, I'll shut my doors against all company. You shan't see a single soul for this month.

OAK: 'Sdeath! Madam, but I will. I'll keep open house for a year — I'll send cards to the whole town — *Mr* Oakly's rout! All the world will come. And I'll go among the world too. I'll be mewed up no longer.

MRS OAK: Provoking insolence! This is not to be endured. Look ye, Mr Oakly —

OAK: And look ye, Mrs Oakly, I will have my own way.

MRS OAK: Nay, then, let me tell you, sir —

OAK: And let me tell you, madam, I will not be crossed, I won't be made a fool!

MRS OAK: Why, you won't let me speak!

OAK: Because you don't speak as you ought. Madam, madam, you shan't look, nor walk, nor talk, nor think, but as I please!

MRS OAK: Was there ever such a monster? I can bear this no longer. (*Bursts into tears.*) Oh, you vile man! — I see through your design. — You cruel, barbarous, unhuman — Such usage to your poor wife! You'll be the death of her.

OAK: She shan't be the death of me, I am determined.

MRS OAK: That it should ever come to this! To be contradicted — (*sobbing*) — insulted — abused — hated — 'tis too much — my heart will burst with — oh — oh — (*Falls into a fit.* HARRIOT, CHARLES, *etc. run to her assistance.*)

OAK: (*interposing*) Let her alone.

HAR: Sir, Mrs Oakly —

CHAR: For heaven's sake, sir! She will be —

OAK: Let her alone, I say; I won't have her touched. Let her alone! If her passions throw her into fits, let the strength of them carry her through them.

HAR: Pray, my dear sir, let us assist her! She may —

OAK: I don't care. You shan't touch her. — Let her bear them patiently. She'll learn to behave better another time. — Let her alone, I say.

MRS OAK: (*rising*) Oh, you monster! — You villain! — You base man! Would you let me die for want of help? — Would you?

OAK: Bless me, madam, your fit is very violent! Take care of yourself.

MRS OAK: Despised! — ridiculed! — But I'll be revenged! — You shall see, sir —

OAK: (*singing*) *Tol-de-rol lol-de-rol lol-de-rol lol.*

MRS OAK: What, am I made a jest of? Exposed to all the world? If there's law or justice —

OAK: (*singing*) *tol-de-rol lol-de-rol lol-de-rol lol.*

MRS OAK: I shall burst with anger! Have a care, sir! You may regret this. — Scorned and made ridiculous! — No power on earth shall hinder my revenge (*going*).

HAR: (*interposing*) Stay, madam!

MRS OAK: Let me go. I cannot bear this place.

HAR: Let me beseech you, madam.

OAK: What does the girl mean?

MAJ: Courage, brother! You have done wonders. ⎫ (*aside*)

OAK: I think she'll have no more fits. ⎭

HAR: Stay, madam! pray stay! but one moment. I have been a painful witness of your uneasiness, and in great part the innocent occasion of it. Give me leave then —

MRS OAK: I did not expect, indeed, to have found you here again. But, however —

HAR: I see the agitation of your mind, and it makes me miserable. Suffer me to tell
you the real truth. I can explain everything to your satisfaction.

MRS OAK: May be so — I cannot argue with you.

CHAR: Pray, madam, hear her — for my sake — for your own — dear madam!

MRS OAK: Well, well; proceed.

OAK: I shall relapse; I cannot bear to see her so uneasy. } (aside)
MAJ: Hush, hush!

HAR: I understand, madam, that your first alarm was occasioned by a letter from
my father to your nephew.

RUS: I was in a bloody passion to be sure, madam! The letter was not over civil, I
believe, — I did not know but the young rogue had ruined my girl. — But
it's all over now, and so —

MRS OAK: You were here yesterday, sir?

RUS: Yes, I came after Harriot. I thought I should find my young madam with my
young sir, here.

MRS OAK: With Charles, did you say, sir?

RUS: Ay, with Charles, madam. The young rogue has been fond of her a long time,
and she of him, it seems.

MRS OAK: (aside) I fear I have been to blame.

RUS: I ask pardon, madam, for the disturbance I made in your house.

HAR: And the abrupt manner in which I came into it demands a thousand
apologies: but the occasion must be my excuse.

MRS OAK: (aside) How have I been mistaken! (to HARRIOT) But did not I over-
hear you and Mr Oakly —

HAR: Dear madam, you had but a partial hearing of our conversation. It related
entirely to this gentleman.

CHAR: To put it beyond doubt, madam, Mr Russet and my guardian have consented to our marriage; and we are in hopes that you will not withhold your
approbation.

MRS OAK: I have no further doubt; I see you are innocent, and it was cruel to
suspect you. You have taken a load of anguish off my mind; and yet your
kind interposition comes too late. Mr Oakly's love for me is entirely
destroyed (weeping).

OAK: I must go to her! } (aside)
MAJ: Not yet, not yet!

HAR: Do not disturb yourself with such apprehensions. I am sure Mr Oakly loves
you most affectionately.

OAK: I can hold no longer (going to her). My affection for you, madam, is as warm
as ever. Nothing can ever extinguish it. My constrained behaviour cut me to
the soul; for, within these few hours, it has been all constrained; and it was
with the utmost difficulty that I was able to support it.

MRS OAK: Oh, Mr Oakly, how have I exposed myself! What low arts has my
jealousy induced me to practise! I see my folly, and fear that you can never
forgive me.

OAK: Forgive you! — You are too good, my love! — Forgive you! — Can you forgive me? This change transports me. Brother! Mr Russet! Charles! Harriot! give me joy! I am the happiest man in the world.

MAJ: Joy, much joy to you both! though, by the by, you are not a little obliged to me for it. Did not I tell you I would cure all the disorders in your family? I beg pardon, sister, for taking the liberty to prescribe for you. My medicines have been somewhat rough, I believe, but they have had an admirable effect, and so don't be angry with your physician.

MRS OAK: I am indeed obliged to you, and I feel —

OAK: Nay, my dear, no more of this. All that's past must be utterly forgotten.

MRS OAK: I have not merited this kindness; but it shall hereafter be my study to deserve it. Away with all idle jealousies! and, since my suspicions have hitherto been groundless, I am resolved for the future never to suspect at all.

4. *The Marriage Contract*, No. 1 in a series of six paintings by William Hogarth of *Marriage à la Mode* (National Gallery). A satirical picture of negotiations between a grim, gouty nobleman and a rich merchant, while the young couple to be married appear indifferent to each other. The picture and the others are [...]

THE CLANDESTINE MARRIAGE

by David Garrick and George Colman the Elder

First performed at the Theatre Royal, Drury Lane,
20 February 1766, with the following cast:

LORD OGLEBY	Mr King
SIR JOHN MELVIL	Mr Holland
STERLING	Mr Yates
LOVEWELL	Mr Powell
CANTON	Mr Baddeley
BRUSH	Mr Palmer
SERJEANT FLOWER	Mr Love
TRAVERSE	Mr Lee
TRUEMAN	Mr Aickin
MRS HEIDELBERG	Mrs Clive
MISS STERLING	Miss Pope
FANNY	Mrs Palmer
BETTY	Mrs —
CHAMBERMAID	Miss Plym
TRUSTY	Miss Mills

Mrs — : so shown in first edition. In fact, Mrs Abington played the part.

PROLOGUE

WRITTEN BY MR GARRICK
SPOKEN BY MR HOLLAND

Poets and painters, who from Nature draw
Their best and richest stores, have made this law:
That each should neighbourly assist his brother,
And steal with decency from one another.
Tonight, your matchless Hogarth gives the thought,
Which from his canvas to the stage is brought.
And who so fit to warm the poet's kind,
As he who pictured morals and mankind?
But not the same their characters and scenes;
Both labour for one end, by different means:
Each, as it suits him, takes a separate road,
Their one great object, Marriage-à-la-mode!
Where titles deign with cits to have and hold,
And change rich blood for more substantial gold!
And honoured trade from interest turns aside,
To hazard happiness for titled pride.
The painter dead, yet still he charms the eye;
While England lives, his fame can never die:
But he who struts his hour upon the stage,
Can scarce extend his fame for half an age;
Nor pen nor pencil can the actor save,
The art, and artist, share one common grave.
    O let me drop one tributary tear
On poor Jack Falstaff's grave, and Juliet's bier!
You to their worth must testimony give;
'Tis in your hearts alone their fame can live.
Still as the scenes of life will shift away,
The strong impressions of their art decay.
Your children cannot feel what you have known;
They'll boast of Quins and Cibbers of their own:
The greatest glory of our happy few,
Is to be felt, and be approved by you.

ACT I

SCENE 1.   *A room in* STERLING's *house.* MISS FANNY *and* BETTY *meeting.*

BETTY: (*running in*) Ma'am! Miss Fanny! Ma'am!

FANNY: What's the matter! Betty!

HETTY: Oh la! ma'am! As sure as I'm alive, here is your husband —

FANNY: Hush! My dear Betty! If anybody in the house should hear you, I am ruined.

BETTY: Mercy on me! It has frighted me to such a degree, that my heart is come
          up to my mouth. But as I was a-saying, ma'am, here's that dear, sweet —

FANNY: Have a care, Betty.

BETTY: Lord! I'm bewitched, I think. But as I was a-saying, ma'am, here's Mr
          Lovewell just come from London.

FANNY: Indeed!

BETTY: Yes, indeed, and indeed, ma'am, he is. I saw him crossing the courtyard in
          his boots.

FANNY: I am glad to hear it. But pray now, my dear Betty, be cautious. Don't
          mention that word again, on any account. You know we have agreed never to
          drop any expressions of that sort for fear of an accident.

BETTY: Dear ma'am, you may depend upon me. There is not a more trustier
          creature on the face of the earth than I am. Though I say it, I am as secret as
          the grave — and if it's never told till I tell it, it may remain untold till Dooms-
          day for Betty.

FANNY: I know you are faithful — but in our circumstances we cannot be too
          careful.

BETTY: Very true, ma'am! — and yet I vow and protest there's more plague than
          pleasure with a secret; especially if a body mayn't mention it to four or five
          of one's particular acquaintance.

FANNY: Do but keep this secret a little while longer, and then I hope you may
          mention it to anybody. Mr Lovewell will acquaint the family with the nature
          of our situation as soon as possible.

BETTY: The sooner the better, I believe: for if he does not tell it, there's a little
          tell-tale, I know of, will come and tell it for him.

FANNY: Fie, Betty! (*blushing*)

BETTY: Ah! You may well blush. But you're not so sick, and so pale, and so wan,
          and so many qualms —

FANNY: Have done! I shall be quite angry with you.

BETTY: Angry! Bless the dear puppet! I am sure I shall love it as much as if it was
          my own. I meant no harm, Heaven knows.

FANNY: Well — say no more of this — it makes me uneasy. All I have to ask of
          you is to be faithful and secret, and not to reveal this matter till we disclose
          it to the family ourselves.

BETTY: Me reveal it! If I say a word, I wish I may be burned. I would not do you
          any harm for the world. And as for Mr Lovewell, I am sure I have loved the
          dear gentleman ever since he got a tide-waiter's place for my brother. But

---

tide-waiter: customs officer.

let me tell you both, you must leave off your soft looks to each other, and your whispers, and your glances, and your always sitting next to one another at dinner, and your long walks together in the evening. For my part, if I had not been in the secret, I should have known you were a pair of loviers at least, if not man and wife, as –

FANNY: See there now again. Pray be careful.

BETTY: Well – well – nobody hears me. Man and wife – I'll say so no more. What I tell you is very true for all that –

LOVE: (*calling within*) William!

BETTY: Hark! I hear your husband –

FANNY: What!

BETTY: I say, here comes Mr Lovewell. Mind the caution I give you – I'll be whipped now, if you are not the first person he sees or speaks to in the family. However, if you choose it, it's nothing at all to me – as you sow, you must reap – as you brew, so you must bake. I'll e'en slip down the back-stairs, and leave you together. (*Exit.*)

FANNY: (*alone*) I see, I see I shall never have a moment's ease till our marriage is made public. New distresses crowd in upon me every day. The solicitude of my mind sinks my spirits, preys upon my health, and destroys every comfort of my life. It shall be revealed, let what will be the consequence.

(*Enter* LOVEWELL.)

LOVE: My love! How's this? In tears? Indeed this is too much. You promised me to support your spirits, and to wait the determination of our fortune with patience. For my sake, for your own, be comforted! Why will you study to add to our uneasiness and perplexity?

FANNY: Oh, Mr Lovewell! The indelicacy of a secret marriage grows every day more and more shocking to me. I walk about the house like a guilty wretch: I imagine myself the object of the suspicion of the whole family; and am under the perpetual terrors of a shameful detection.

LOVE: Indeed, indeed, you are to blame. The amiable delicacy of your temper, and your quick sensibility, only serve to make you unhappy. To clear up this affair properly to Mr Sterling is the continual employment of my thoughts. Everything now is in a fair train. It begins to grow ripe for a discovery; and I have no doubt of its concluding to the satisfaction of ourselves, of your father, and the whole family.

FANNY: End how it will, I am resolved it shall end soon – very soon – I would not live another week in this agony of mind to be mistress of the universe.

LOVE: Do not be too violent neither. Do not let us disturb the joy of your sister's marriage with the tumult this matter may occasion! I have brought letters from Lord Ogleby and Sir John Melvil to Mr Sterling. They will be here this evening – and, I dare say, within this hour.

FANNY: I am sorry for it.

LOVE: Why so?

FANNY: No matter. Only let us disclose our marriage immediately!

LOVE: As soon as possible.

FANNY: But directly.

LOVE: In a few days, you may depend on it.

FANNY: Tonight — or tomorrow morning.

LOVE: That, I fear, will be impracticable.

FANNY: Nay, but you must.

LOVE: Must! Why?

FANNY: Indeed, you must. I have the most alarming reasons for it.

LOVE: Alarming indeed! For they alarm me, even before I am acquainted with
    them. What are they?

FANNY: I cannot tell you.

LOVE: Not tell me?

FANNY: Not at present. When all is settled, you shall be acquainted with every-
    thing.

LOVE: Sorry they are coming! Must be discovered! What can this mean! Is it
    possible you can have any reasons that need be concealed from me?

FANNY: Do not disturb yourself with conjectures — but rest assured, that though
    you are unable to divine the cause, the consequence of a discovery, be it what
    it will, cannot be attended with half the miseries of the present interval.

LOVE: You put me upon the rack. I would do anything to make you easy. But you
    know your father's temper. Money (you will excuse my frankness) is the
    spring of all his actions, which nothing but the idea of acquiring nobility or
    magnificence can ever make him forgo — and these he thinks his money will
    purchase. You know too your aunt's, Mrs Heidelberg's, notions of the splen-
    dour of high life, her contempt for everything that does not relish of what
    she calls Quality, and that from the vast fortune in her hands, by her late
    husband, she absolutely governs Mr Sterling and the whole family. Now, if
    they should come to the knowledge of this affair too abruptly, they might,
    perhaps, be incensed beyond all hopes of reconciliation.

FANNY: But if they are made acquainted with it otherwise than by ourselves, it
    will be ten times worse: and a discovery grows every day more probable. The
    whole family have long suspected our affection. We are also in the power of a
    foolish maidservant; and if we may even depend on her fidelity, we cannot
    answer for her discretion. Discover it therefore immediately, lest some acci-
    dent should bring it to light, and involve us in additional disgrace.

LOVE: Well — well — I meant to discover it soon, but would not do it too precipi-
    tately. I have more than once sounded Mr Sterling about it, and will attempt
    him more seriously the next opportunity. But my principal hopes are these.
    My relationship to Lord Ogleby, and his having placed me with your father,
    have been, you know, the first links in the chain of this connection between
    the two families; in consequence of which, I am at present in high favour with
    all parties: while they all remain thus well-affected to me, I propose to lay
    our case before the old lord; and if I can prevail on him to mediate in this
    affair, I make no doubt but he will be able to appease your father; and, being
    a lord and a man of quality, I am sure he may bring Mrs Heidelberg into good
    humour at any time. Let me beg you, therefore, to have but a little patience,
    as, you see, we are upon the very eve of a discovery that must probably be to
    our advantage.

FANNY: Manage it your own way. I am persuaded.

LOVE: But in the meantime make yourself easy.

FANNY: As easy as I can, I will. We had better not remain together any longer at present. Think of this business, and let me know how you proceed.

LOVE: Depend on my care! But, pray, be cheerful.

FANNY: I will.

> (*As she is going out, enter* STERLING.)

STERL: Heyday! Who have we got here!

FANNY: (*confused*) Mr Lovewell, sir!

STERL: And where are you going, hussy!

FANNY: To my sister's chamber, sir! (*Exit.*)

STERL: Ah, Lovewell! What! Always getting my foolish girl yonder into a corner! Well − well − let us but once see her elder sister fast-married to Sir John Melvil, we'll soon provide a good husband for Fanny, I warrant you.

LOVE: Would to heaven, sir, you would provide her one of my recommendation!

STERL: Yourself? Eh, Lovewell!

LOVE: With your pleasure, sir!

STERL: Mighty well!

LOVE: And I flatter myself that such a proposal would not be very disagreeable to Miss Fanny.

STERL: Better and better!

LOVE: And if I could but obtain your consent, sir −

STERL: What! You marry Fanny! No, no − that will never do, Lovewell! You're a good boy, to be sure − I have a great value for you − but can't think of you for a son-in-law. There's no *stuff* in the case, no money, Lovewell!

LOVE: My pretensions to fortune, indeed, are but moderate: but though not equal to splendour, sufficient to keep us above distress − add to which, that I hope by diligence to increase it − and have love, honour −

STERL: But not the *stuff*, Lovewell! Add one little round 0 to the sum total of your fortunes, and that will be the finest thing you can say to me. You know I've a regard for you − would do anything to serve you − anything on the footing of friendship − but −

LOVE: If you think me worthy of your friendship, sir, be assured that there is no instance in which I should rate your friendship so highly.

STERL: Psha! psha! That's another thing, you know. Where money or interest is concerned, friendship is quite out of the question.

LOVE: But where the happiness of a daughter is at stake, you would not scruple, sure, to sacrifice a little to her inclinations.

STERL: Inclinations! Why, you would not persuade me that the girl is in love with you − eh, Lovewell!

LOVE: I cannot absolutely answer for Miss Fanny, sir; but am sure that the chief happiness or misery of my life depends entirely upon her.

STERL: Why, indeed now, if your kinsman, Lord Ogleby, would come down handsomely for you − but that's impossible. No, no − 'twill never do − I must hear no more of this. Come, Lovewell, promise me that I shall hear no more of this.

LOVE: (*hesitating*) I am afraid, sir, I should not be able to keep my word with you, if I did promise you.

STERL: Why, you would not offer to marry her without my consent? Would you, Lovewell!

LOVE: (*confused*) Marry her, sir!

STERL: Ay, marry her, sir! — I know very well that a warm speech or two from such a dangerous young spark, as you are, will go much farther towards persuading a silly girl to do what she has more than a month's mind to do, than twenty grave lectures from fathers or mothers, or uncles or aunts, to prevent her. But you would not, sure, be such a base fellow, such a treacherous young rogue, as to seduce my daughter's affections, and destroy the peace of my family in that manner. I must insist on it that you give me your word not to marry her without my consent.

LOVE: Sir — I — I — as to that — I — I — I beg, sir — Pray, sir, excuse me on this subject at present.

STERL: Promise then, that you will carry this matter no further without my approbation.

LOVE: You may depend on it, sir, that it shall go no further.

STERL: Well — well — that's enough — I'll take care of the rest, I warrant you. Come, come, let's have done with this nonsense! What's doing in town? Any news upon 'Change?

LOVE: Nothing material.

STERL: Have you seen the currants, the soap, and Madeira, safe in the warehouses? Have you compared the goods with the invoice and bills of lading, and are they all right?

LOVE: They are, sir!

STERL: And how are stocks?

LOVE: Fell one and a half this morning.

STERL: Well — well — some good news from America, and they'll be up again. But how are Lord Ogleby and Sir John Melvil? When are we to expect them?

LOVE: Very soon, sir! I came on purpose to bring you their commands. Here are letters from both of them (*giving letters*).

STERL: Let me see — let me see — 'Slife, how his lordship's letter is perfumed! It takes my breath away (*opening it*). And French paper too! With a fine border of flowers and flourishes — and a slippery gloss on it that dazzles one's eyes. 'My dear Mr Sterling' (*reading*). Mercy on me! His lordship writes a worse hand than a boy at his exercise. But how's this? Eh! — 'with you tonight' — (*reading*) — 'Lawyers tomorrow morning.' — Tonight! — That's sudden indeed. — Where's my sister Heidelberg? She should know of this immediately. — Here, John! Harry! Thomas! (*calling the servants*) Hark ye, Lovewell!

LOVE: Sir!

STERL: Mind, now, how I'll entertain his lordship and Sir John. — We'll show your fellows at the other end of the town how we live in the city. — They shall eat gold — and drink gold — and lie in gold. — Here cook! butler! (*calling*). What signifies your birth and education, and titles? Money, money, that's the stuff that makes the great man in this country.

LOVE: Very true, sir!

STER: True, sir? — Why then have done with your nonsense of love and matrimony. You're not rich enough to think of a wife yet. A man of business should mind nothing but his business. — Where are these fellows? John! Thomas! (*calling*) — Get an estate, and a wife will follow of course. — Ah!

Lovewell! An English merchant is the most respectable character in the universe. 'Slife, man, a rich English merchant may make himself a match for the daughter of a Nabob. – Where are all my rascals? Here, William! (*Exit, calling.*)

LOVE: (*alone*) So! – As I suspected. – Quite averse to the match, and likely to receive the news of it with great displeasure. – What's best to be done? – Let me see! – Suppose I get Sir John Melvil to interest himself in this affair. He may mention it to Lord Ogleby with a better grace than I can, and more probably prevail on him to interfere in it. I can open my mind also more freely to Sir John. He told me, when I left him in town, that he had something of consequence to communicate, and that I could be of use to him. I am glad of it: for the confidence he reposes in me, and the service I may do him, will ensure me his good offices. – Poor Fanny! It hurts me to see her so uneasy, and her making a mystery of the cause adds to my anxiety. – Something must be done upon her account; for at all events, her solicitude shall be removed. (*Exit.*)

SCENE 2.   *Another chamber. Enter* MISS STERLING *and* MISS FANNY.

MISS STERL: Oh, my dear sister, say no more! This is downright hypocrisy. You shall never convince me that you don't envy me beyond measure. Well, after all it is extremely natural. It is impossible to be angry with you.

FANNY: Indeed, sister, you have no cause.

MISS STERL: And you really pretend not to envy me!

FANNY: Not in the least.

MISS STERL: And you don't in the least wish that you was just in my situation?

FANNY: No, indeed, I don't. Why should I?

MISS STERL: Why should you? What! On the brink of marriage, fortune, title? But I had forgot. There's that dear sweet creature Mr Lovewell in the case. You would not break your faith with your true love now for the world, I warrant you.

FANNY: Mr Lovewell! Always Mr Lovewell! Lord, what signifies Mr Lovewell, sister?

MISS STERL: Pretty peevish soul! Oh, my dear, grave, romantic sister! – A perfect philosopher in petticoats! Love and a cottage! Eh, Fanny! Ah, give me indifference and a coach and six!

FANNY: And why not the coach and six without the indifference? But, pray, when is this happy marriage of yours to be celebrated? I long to give you joy.

MISS STERL: In a day or two – I can't tell exactly. – Oh, my dear sister! – (*aside*) I must mortify her a little. – I know you have a pretty taste. Pray, give me your opinion of my jewels. How d'ye like the style of this esclavage? (*showing jewels*)

FANNY: Extremely handsome indeed, and well fancied.

MISS STERL: What d'ye think of these bracelets? I shall have a miniature of my father, set round with diamonds, to one, and Sir John's to the other. And this pair of ear-rings! Set transparent! Here, the tops, you see, will take off to wear in a morning, or in an undress. How d'ye like them? (*shows jewels*)

FANNY: Very much, I assure you. – Bless me; sister, you have a prodigious quantity of jewels – you'll be the very Queen of Diamonds.

MISS STERL: Ha! ha! ha! very well, my dear! I shall be as fine as a little queen
　　indeed. I have a bouquet to come home tomorrow — made up of diamonds,
　　and rubies, and emeralds, and topazes, and amethysts — jewels of all colours,
　　green, red, blue, yellow, intermixed — the prettiest thing you ever saw in your
　　life! The jeweller says I shall set out with as many diamonds as anybody in
　　town, except Lady Brilliant, and Polly What-d'ye-call-it, Lord Squander's
　　kept mistress.
FANNY: But what are your wedding-clothes, sister?
MISS STERL: Oh, white and silver to be sure, you know. I bought them at Sir
　　Joseph Lutestring's, and sat above an hour in the parlour behind the shop,
　　consulting Lady Lutestring about gold and silver stuffs, on purpose to
　　mortify her.
FANNY: Fie, sister! How could you be so abominably provoking?
MISS STERL: Oh, I have no patience with the pride of your city-knights' ladies.
　　Did you never observe the airs of Lady Lutestring dressed in the richest bro-
　　cade out of her husband's shop, playing crown-whist at Haberdasher's Hall?
　　While the civil smirking Sir Joseph, with a smug wig trimmed round his broad
　　face as close as a new-cut yew-hedge, and his shoes so black that they shine
　　again, stands all day in his shop, fastened to his counter like a bad shilling?
FANNY: Indeed, indeed, sister, this is too much. If you talk at this rate, you will
　　be absolutely a by-word in the city. You must never venture on the inside of
　　Temple Bar again.
MISS STERL: Never do I desire it — never, my dear Fanny, I promise you. Oh, how
　　I long to be transported to the dear regions of Grosvenor Square — far — far
　　from the dull districts of Aldersgate, Cheap, Candlewick, and Farringdon
　　Without and Within! My heart goes pit-a-pat at the very idea of being intro-
　　duced at Court! — gilt chariot! — piebald horses! — laced liveries! — and then
　　the whispers buzzing round the circle: 'Who is that young lady? Who is she?'
　　'Lady Melvil, ma'am!' Lady Melvil! My ears tingle at the sound. And then at
　　dinner, instead of my father perpetually asking: 'Any news upon 'Change?'
　　to cry: 'Well, Sir John! Anything new from Arthur's?' — or to say to some
　　other woman of quality: 'Was your ladyship at the Duchess of Rubber's last
　　night? — Did you call in at Lady Thunder's? In the immensity of crowd I
　　swear I did not see you — Scarce a soul at the opera last Saturday. — Shall I
　　see you at Carlisle House next Thursday?' — Oh, the dear beau-monde! I was
　　born to move in the sphere of the great world.
FANNY: And so, in the midst of all this happiness, you have no compassion for me
　　— no pity for us poor mortals in common life.
MISS STERL: (affectedly) You? You're above pity. You would not change con-
　　ditions with me — you're over head and ears in love, you know. Nay, for that
　　matter, if Mr Lovewell and you come together, as I doubt not you will, you
　　will live very comfortably, I dare say. He will mind his business — you'll
　　employ yourself in the delightful care of your family — and once in a season

---

Arthur's: upper-class club.
Carlisle House: London mansion of Earl of Carlisle, later used for society gatherings.

perhaps you'll sit together in a front box at a benefit-play, as we used to do at our dancing-master's, you know — and perhaps I may meet you in the summer with some other citizens at Tunbridge. For my part, I shall always entertain a proper regard for my relations. You shan't want my countenance, I assure you.

FANNY: Oh, you're too kind, sister!

        (*Enter* MRS HEIDELBERG.)

MRS HEIDEL: (*at entering*) Here this evening! I vow and pertest we shall scarce have time to provide for them. Oh, my dear! (*to* MISS STERLING) I am glad to see you're not quite in dishabille. Lord Ogleby and Sir John Melvil will be here tonight.

MISS STERL: Tonight, ma'am?

MRS HEIDEL: Yes, my dear, tonight. Do put on a smarter cap, and change those ordinary ruffles! Lord, I have such a deal to do, I shall scarce have time to slip on my Italian lutestring. Where is this dawdle of a housekeeper? (*Enter* MRS TRUSTY.) Oh, here, Trusty! Do you know that people of quality are expected here this evening?

TRUSTY: Yes, ma'am.

MRS HEIDEL: Well — Do you be sure now that everything is done in the most genteelest manner — and to the honour of the fammaly.

TRUSTY: Yes, ma'am.

MRS HEIDEL: Well — but mind what I say to you.

TRUSTY: Yes, ma'am.

MRS HEIDEL: His lordship is to lie in the chintz bedchamber — d'ye hear? — And Sir John in the blue damask room. — His lordship's valet-de-shamb in the opposite —

TRUSTY: But Mr Lovewell is come down — and you know that's his room, ma'am.

MRS HEIDEL: Well — well — Mr Lovewell may make shift — or get a bed at the George. — But hark ye, Trusty!

TRUSTY: Ma'am!

MRS HEIDEL: Get the great dining room in order as soon as possible. Unpaper the curtains, take the civers off the couch and the chairs, and put the china figures on the mantelpiece immediately.

TRUSTY: Yes ma'am.

MRS HEIDEL: Begone then! Fly, this instant! — Where's my brother Sterling —

TRUSTY: Talking to the butler, ma'am.

MRS HEIDEL: Very well. (*Exit* TRUSTY.) Miss Fanny! — I pertest I did not see you before. — Lord, child, what's the matter with you?

FANNY: With me? Nothing, ma'am.

MRS HEIDEL: Bless me! Why your face is as pale, and black, and yellow — of fifty colours, I pertest. And then you have dressed yourself as loose and as big — I declare there is not such a thing to be seen now as a young woman with a fine waist. You all make yourselves as round as Mrs Deputy Barter. Go, child! You know the qualaty will be here by and by. Go, and make yourself a little

---

Italian lutestring: glossy silk dress.

more fit to be seen. (*Exit* FANNY.) She is gone away in tears — absolutely crying, I vow and pertest. This ridicalous love! We must put a stop to it. It makes a perfect nataral of the girl.

MISS STERL: (*affectedly*) Poor soul! She can't help it.

MRS HEIDEL: Well, my dear! Now I shall have an opportunity of convincing you of the absurdity of what you was telling me concerning Sir John Melvil's behaviour.

MISS STERL: Oh, it gives me no manner of uneasiness. But, indeed, ma'am, I cannot be persuaded but that Sir John is an extremely cold lover. Such distant civility, grave looks, and lukewarm professions of esteem for me and the whole family! I have heard of flames and darts, but Sir John's is a passion of mere ice and snow.

MRS HEIDEL: Oh, fie, my dear! I am perfectly ashamed of you. That's so like the notions of your poor sister! What you complain of as coldness and indifference, is nothing but the extreme gentilaty of his address, an exact pictur of the manners of qualaty.

MISS STERL: Oh, he is the very mirror of complaisance! Full of formal bows and set speeches! I declare, if there was any violent passion on my side, I should be quite jealous of him.

MRS HEIDEL: I say jealus indeed. — Jealus of who, pray?

MISS STERL: My sister Fanny. She seems a much greater favourite than I am, and he pays her infinitely more attention, I assure you.

MRS HEIDEL: D'ye think a man of fashion, as he is, can't distinguish between the genteel and the wulgar part of the family? — Between you and your sister, for instance — or me and my brother? — Be advised by me, child! It is all politeness and good breeding. — Nobody knows the qualaty better than I do.

MISS STERL: In my mind the old lord, his uncle, has ten times more gallantry about him than Sir John. He is full of attentions to the ladies, and smiles, and grins, and leers, and ogles, and fills every wrinkle in his old wizen face with comical expressions of tenderness. I think he would make an admirable sweetheart.

　　　　　(*Enter* STERLING.)

STERL: (*at entering*) No fish? — Why the pond was dragged but yesterday morning. — There's carp and tench in the boat. — Pox on't, if that dog Lovewell had any thought, he would have brought down a turbot, or some of the land-carriage mackerel.

MRS HEIDEL: Lord, brother, I am afraid his lordship and Sir John will not arrive while it's light.

STERL: I warrant you. — But, pray, sister Heidelberg, let the turtle be dressed tomorrow, and some venison — and let the gardener cut some pineapples — and get out some ice. — I'll answer for wine, I warrant you; I'll give them such a glass of champagne as they never drank in their lives — no, not at a duke's table.

MRS HEIDEL: Pray now, brother, mind how you behave. I am always in a fright about you with people of qualaty. Take care that you don't fall asleep directly after supper, as you commonly do. Take a good deal of snuff; and that will keep you awake. And don't burst out with your horrible loud horse-laughs. It is monstrous wulgar.

STERL: Never fear, sister! — Who have we here?

MRS HEIDEL: It is Monsieur Cantoon, the Swish gentleman, that lives with his lordship, I vow and pertest.

(*Enter* CANTON.)

STERL: Ah, Mounseer! Your servant. — I am very glad to see you, Mounseer.

CANTON: Mosh oblige to Monsieur Sterling. — Ma'am, I am yours — Matemoiselle, I am yours (*bowing round*).

MRS HEIDEL: Your humble servant, Mr Cantoon!

CANTON: I kiss your hands, matam!

STERL: Well, Mounseer! And what news of your good family? When are we to see his lordship and Sir John?

CANTON: Monsieur Sterling! Milor Ogleby and Sir Jean Melvile will be here in one quarter-hour.

STERL: I am glad to hear it.

MRS HEIDEL: Oh, I am perdigious glad to hear it. Being so late I was afeared of some accident. — Will you please to have anything, Mr Cantoon, after your journey?

CANTON: No, I tank you, ma'am.

MRS HEIDEL: Shall I go and show you the apartments, sir?

CANTON: You do me great honeur, ma'am.

MRS HEIDEL: Come then! (*to* MISS STERLING) Come, my dear! (*Exeunt.*)

(*Manet* STERLING.)

STERL: Pox on't, it's almost dark. It will be too late to go round the garden this evening. However, I will carry them to take a peep at my fine canal at least, I am determined. (*Exit.*)

ACT II

SCENE 1.   *An ante-chamber to* LORD OGLEBY'*s bedchamber. Table with chocolate, and small case for medicines. Enter* BRUSH, *my lord's valet-de-chambre, and* STERLING'*s chambermaid.*

BRUSH: You shall stay, my dear, I insist upon it.

CHAMBER: Nay, pray, sir, don't be so positive; I can't stay indeed.

BRUSH: You shall take one cup to our better acquaintance.

CHAMBER: I seldom drinks chocolate; and if I did, one has no satisfaction, with such apprehensions about one — if my lord should wake, or the Swish gentle-man should see one, or Madam Heidelberg should know of it, I should be frighted to death — besides I have had my tea already this morning. — I'm sure I hear my lord (*in a fright*).

BRUSH: No, no, madam, don't flutter yourself — the moment my lord wakes, he rings his bell, which I answer sooner or later, as it suits my convenience.

CHAMBER: But should he come upon us without ringing —

BRUSH: I'll forgive him if he does. — This key (*Takes a phial out of the case.*) locks him up till I please to let him out.

CHAMBER: Law, sir! That's potecary's stuff.

BRUSH: It is so — but without this he can no more get out of bed — than he can read without spectacles (*Sips.*) What with qualms, age, rheumatism, and a few surfeits in his youth, he must have a great deal of brushing, oiling, screwing, and winding up to set him a-going for the day.

CHAMBER: (*Sips.*) That's prodigious indeed. (*Sips.*) My lord seems quite in a decay.

BRUSH: Yes, he's quite a spectacle (*Sips.*), a mere corpse, till he is revived and refreshed from our little magazine here. When the restorative pills and cordial waters warm his stomach, and get into his head, vanity frisks in his heart, and then he sets up for the lover, the rake, and the fine gentleman.

CHAMBER: (*Sips.*) Poor gentleman! — But should the Swish gentleman come upon us! (*frightened*)

BRUSH: Why then the English gentleman would be very angry. No foreigner must break in upon my privacy. (*Sips.*) But I can assure you Monsieur Canton is otherwise employed. He is obliged to skim the cream of half a score newspapers for my lord's breakfast — ha, ha, ha. Pray, madam, drink your cup peaceably. My lord's chocolate is remarkably good; he won't touch a drop but what comes from Italy.

CHAMBER: (*sipping*) 'Tis very fine indeed! (*Sips.*) And charmingly perfumed. It smells for all the world like our young ladies' dressing-boxes.

BRUSH: You have an excellent taste, madam, and I must beg of you to accept of a few cakes for your own drinking (*Takes them out of a drawer in the table.*), and in return I desire nothing but to taste the perfume of your lips. (*Kisses her.*) A small return of favours, madam, will make, I hope, this country and retirement agreeable to both. (*He bows, she curtsies.*) Your young ladies are fine girls, faith (*Sips.*): though upon my soul, I am quite of my old lord's mind about them; and were I inclined to matrimony, I should take the youngest. (*Sips.*)

CHAMBER: Miss Fanny's the most affablest and the most best-natered creter!

BRUSH: And the eldest a little haughty or so —

CHAMBER: More haughtier and prouder than Saturn himself — but this I say quite confidential to you, for one would not hurt a young lady's marriage, you know. (*Sips.*)

BRUSH: By no means; but you can't hurt it with us — we don't consider tempers — we want money, Mrs Nancy. Give us enough of that, we'll abate you a great deal in other particulars — ha, ha, ha.

CHAMBER: Bless me, here's somebody. (*Bell rings.* — Oh! 'tis my lord. — Well, your servant, Mr Brush — I'll clean the cups in the next room.

BRUSH: Do so — but never mind the bell — I shan't go this half-hour. Will you drink tea with me in the afternoon?

CHAMBER: Not for the world, Mr Brush — I'll be here to set all things to rights — but I must not drink tea indeed — and so your servant. (*Exit with tea-board.*)
    (*Bell rings again.*)

BRUSH: It is impossible to stupefy oneself in the country for a week without some little flirting with the Abigails: this is much the handsomest wench in the

---

Abigail: maid. Name of biblical King David's handmaid.

house, except the old citizen's youngest daughter, and I have not time enough to lay a plan for her. (*Bell rings.*) And now I'll go to my lord, for I have nothing else to do (*going*).

> (*Enter* CANTON *with newspapers in his hand.*)

CANTON: Monsieur Brush — Maistre Brush — My lor' stirra yet?

BRUSH: He has just rung his bell — I am going to him.

CANTON: Dépêchez-vous donc. (*Exit* BRUSH.) (*Puts on spectacles.*) I wish de deviel had all dese papiers — I forget as fast as I read. — De Advertise put out of my head de Gazette, de Gazette de Chronique, and so dey all go l'un après l'autre — I must get some nouvelle for my lor', or he'll be enragé contre moi — Voyons! (*Reads in the papers.*) Here is noting but Anti-Sejanus and advertise — (*Enter* MAID *with chocolate things.*) Vat you vant, child?

CHAMBER: Only the chocolate things, sir.

CANTON: O ver well — dat is good girl — and ver prit too!

> (*Exit* MAID.)

LORD OGLEBY: (*within*) Canton, he, he — (*Coughs.*) — Canton!

CANTON: I come, my lor'. — Vat shall I do? — I have no news. — He vill make great tintamarre! —

LORD OGLEBY: (*within*) Canton, I say, Canton! Where are you?

> (*Enter* LORD OGLEBY *leaning on* BRUSH.)

CANTON: Here, my lor'. I ask pardon, my lor', I have not finish de papiers —

LORD OGLEBY: Dem your pardon, and your papers — I want you here, Canton.

CANTON: Den I run, dat is all. (*Shuffles along.* LORD OGLEBY *leans upon* CANTON *too, and comes forward.*)

LORD OGLEBY: You Swiss are the most unaccountable mixture — you have the language and the impertinence of the French, with the laziness of Dutchmen.

CANTON: 'Tis very true, my lor' — I can't help —

LORD OGLEBY: (*cries out*) O Diavolo!

CANTON: You are not in pain, I hope, my lor'.

LORD OGLEBY: Indeed but I am, my lor'. That vulgar fellow Sterling, with his city politeness, would force me down his slope last night to see a clay-coloured ditch, which he calls a canal; and what with the dew, and the east wind, my hips and shoulders are absolutely screwed to my body.

CANTON: A littel véritable eau d'arquibusade vil set all to right again. (*My lord sits down,* BRUSH *gives chocolate.*)

LORD OGLEBY: Where are the palsy-drops, Brush?

BRUSH: Here, my lord! (*pouring out*)

LORD OGLEBY: Quelle nouvelle avez vous, Canton?

CANTON: A great deal of papier, but no news at all.

LORD OGLEBY: What! Nothing at all, you stupid fellow?

CANTON: Yes, my lor', I have littel advertise here vil give you more plaisir den all de lies about noting at all. La voilà! (*Puts on his spectacles.*)

LORD OGLEBY: Come read it, Canton, with good emphasis, and good discretion.

CANTON: I vil, my lor'. (CANTON *reads.*) 'Dere is no question, but dat de Cos-

---

Anti-Sejanus: pen-name of James Scott, political writer against Pitt.

metique Royale vil utterlie take away all heats, pimps, frecks and oder
eruptions of de skin, and likewise de wrinque of old age, etc.' — A great deal
more, my lor' — 'be sure to ask for de Cosmetique Royale, signed by de
docteur own hand. — Dere is more raison for dis caution dan good men vil
tink.' — Eh bien, my lor'!

LORD OGLEBY: Eh bien, Canton! Will you purchase any?

CANTON: For you, my lor'?

LORD OGLEBY: For me, you old puppy! For what?

CANTON: My lor'?

LORD OGLEBY: Do I want cosmetics?

CANTON: My lor'!

LORD OGLEBY: Look in my face. Come, be sincere. Does it want the assistance of
art?

CANTON: (*with his spectacles*) En vérité, non. 'Tis very smoose and brillian' — but
I tote dat you might take a little by way of prevention.

LORD OGLEBY: You thought like an old fool, monsieur, as you generally do —
The surfeit-water, Brush! (BRUSH *pours out.*) What do you think, Brush, of
this family we are going to be connected with? — Eh!

BRUSH: Very well to marry in, my lord; but it would not do to live with.

LORD OGLEBY: You are right, Brush. There is no washing the Blackamoor white.
Mr Sterling will never get rid of Blackfriars, always taste of the Borachio —
and the poor woman his sister is so busy and so notable, to make one welcome, that I have not yet got over her first reception; it almost amounted to
suffocation! I think the daughters are tolerable. — Where's my cephalic snuff?
(BRUSH *gives him a box.*)

CANTON: Dey tink so of you, my lor', for dey look at noting else, ma foi.

LORD OGLEBY: Did they? — Why, I think they did a little. — Where's my glass?
(BRUSH *puts one on the table.*) The youngest is delectable. (*Takes snuff.*)

CANTON: O, oui, my lor' — very delect, inteed; she made doux yeux at you, my
lor'.

LORD OGLEBY: She was particular — the eldest, my nephew's lady, will be a most
valuable wife; she has all the vulgar spirits of her father and aunt, happily
blended with the termagant qualities of her deceased mother. — Some pepper-
mint water, Brush! — How happy is it, Cant, for young ladies in general, that
people of quality overlook everything in a marriage contract but their fortune.

CANTON: C'est bien heureux, et commode aussi.

LORD OGLEBY: Brush, give me that pamphlet by my bedside. — (BRUSH *goes for
it.*) Canton, do you wait in the ante-chamber, and let nobody interrupt me
till I call you.

CANTON: Mush goot may do your lordship!

LORD OGLEBY: (*to* BRUSH, *who brings the pamphlet*) And now Brush, leave me
a little to my studies. (*Exit* BRUSH.) What can I possibly do among these
women here, with this confounded rheumatism? It is a most grievous enemy
to gallantry and address. (*Gets off his chair.*) He! Courage, my lor'! By

---

taste of the Borachio: betray his origins (*Borachio*: wineskin).

heavens, I'm another creature! (*Hums and dances a little.*) It will do, faith. Bravo, my lor'! These girls have absolutely inspired me. If they are for a game of romps — me voilà prêt! (*Sings and dances.*) Oh! that's an ugly twinge — but it's gone. — I have rather too much of the lily this morning in my complexion; a faint tincture of the rose will give a delicate spirit to my eyes for the day. (*Unlocks a drawer at the bottom of the glass, and takes out rouge: while he's painting himself, a knocking at the door.*) Who's there? I won't be disturbed.

CANTON: (*without*) My lor', my lor', here is Monsieur Sterling to pay his devoir to you this morn in your chambre.

LORD OGLEBY: (*softly*) What a fellow! (*aloud*) I am extremely honoured by Mr Sterling. Why don't you see him in, monsieur? — I wish he was at the bottom of his stinking canal. (*Door opens.*) Oh, my dear Mr Sterling, you do me a great deal of honour.

(*Enter* STERLING *and* LOVEWELL.)

STERL: I hope, my lord, that your lordship slept well in the night. — I believe there are no better beds in Europe than I have — I spare no pains to get 'em, nor money to buy 'em. — His Majesty — God bless him — don't sleep upon a better out of his palace; and if I had said in too, I hope no treason, my lord.

LORD OGLEBY: Your beds are like everything else about you, incomparable! They not only make one rest well, but give one spirits, Mr Sterling.

STERL: What say you then, my lord, to another walk in the garden? You must see my water by daylight, and my walks, and my slopes, and my clumps, and my bridge, and my flowering trees, and my bed of Dutch tulips. — Matters looked but dim last night, my lord; I feel the dew in my great toe — but I would put on a cut shoe that I might be able to walk you about — I may be laid up tomorrow.

LORD OGLEBY: (*aside*) I pray Heaven you may!

STERL: What say you, my lord?

LORD OGLEBY: I was saying, sir, that I was in hopes of seeing the young ladies at breakfast. Mr Sterling, they are, in my mind, the finest tulips in this part of the world — he, he.

CANTON: Bravissimo, my lor'! — ha, ha, he!

STERL: They shall meet your lordship in the garden — we won't lose our walk for them; I'll take you a little round before breakfast, and a larger before dinner, and in the evening you shall go to the Grand Tower, as I call it, ha, ha, ha!

LORD OGLEBY: Not a foot, I hope, Mr Sterling. Consider your gout, my good friend. You'll certainly be laid by the heels for your politeness — he, he, he.

CANTON: Ha, ha, ha — 'tis admirable! en vérité — (*laughing very heartily*).

STERL: If my young man (*to* LOVEWELL) here, would but laugh at my jokes, which he ought to do, as Mounseer does at yours, my lord, we should be all life and mirth.

LORD OGLEBY: What say you, Cant? Will you take my kinsman under your tuition? You have certainly the most companionable laugh I ever met with, and never out of tune.

CANTON: But when your lordship is out of spirits.

LORD OGLEBY: Well said, Cant! — But here comes my nephew, to play his part.

(*Enter* SIR JOHN MELVIL.) Well, Sir John, what news from the island of love? Have you been sighing and serenading this morning?

SIR JOHN: I am glad to see your lordship in such spirits this morning.

LORD OGLEBY: I'm sorry to see you so dull, sir. What poor things, Mr Sterling, these *very* young fellows are! They make love with faces as if they were burying the dead — though, indeed, a marriage sometimes may be properly called a burying of the living — eh, Mr Sterling?

STERL: Not if they have enough to live upon, my lord. Ha, ha, ha!

CANTON: Dat is all Monsieur Sterling tink of.

SIR JOHN: Prithee, Lovewell, come with me into the garden; I have something of consequence for you, and I must communicate it directly. *(aside)*

LOVE: We'll go together —

If your lordship and Mr Sterling please, we'll prepare the ladies to attend you in the garden. (*Exeunt* SIR JOHN *and* LOVEWELL.)

STERL: My girls are always ready, I make 'em rise soon, and to bed early; their husbands shall have 'em with good constitutions, and good fortunes, if they have nothing else, my lord.

LORD OGLEBY: Fine things, Mr Sterling!

STERL: Fine things indeed, my lord! Ah, my lord, had not you run off your speed in your youth, you had not been so crippled in your age, my lord.

LORD OGLEBY: Very pleasant, I protest — He, he, he — (*half-laughing*).

STERL: Here's Mounseer now, I suppose, is pretty near your lordship's standing; but having little to eat, and little to spend, in his own country, he'll wear three of your lordship out. Eating and drinking kills us all.

LORD OGLEBY: Very pleasant, I protest. — (*aside*) What a vulgar dog!

CANTON: My lor' so old as me! He is shicken to me — and look like a boy to pauvre me.

STERL: Ha, ha, ha! Well said, Mounseer — keep to that, and you'll live in any country of the world. Ha, ha, ha! — But, my lord, I will wait upon you into the garden: we have but a little time to breakfast. I'll go for my hat and cane, fetch a little walk with you, my lord, and then for the hot rolls and butter! (*Exit.*)

LORD OGLEBY: I shall attend you with pleasure. Hot rolls and butter in July! I sweat with the thoughts of it. What a strange beast it is!

CANTON: C'est un barbare.

LORD OGLEBY: He is a vulgar dog, and if there was not so much money in the family, which I can't do without, I would leave him and his hot rolls and butter directly. Come along, monsieur! (*Exeunt.*)

SCENE 2.   *The garden. Enter* SIR JOHN MELVIL *and* LOVEWELL.

LOVE: In my room this morning? Impossible!

SIR JOHN: Before five this morning, I promise you.

LOVE: On what occasion?

SIR JOHN: I was so anxious to disclose my mind to you, that I could not sleep in my bed. But I found that you could not sleep neither — the bird was flown, and the nest long since cold. Where was you, Lovewell?

LOVE: Pooh! prithee! ridiculous!

SIR JOHN: Come now! Which was it? Miss Sterling's maid? — a pretty little rogue! — or Miss Fanny's Abigail? — a sweet soul too! — or —

LOVE: Nay, nay, leave trifling, and tell me your business.

SIR JOHN: Well, but where was you, Lovewell?

LOVE: Walking — writing — what signifies where I was?

SIR JOHN: Walking! Yes, I dare say. It rained as hard as it could pour. Sweet refreshing showers to walk in! No, no, Lovewell. Now would I give twenty pounds to know which of the maids —

LOVE: But your business! Your business, Sir John!

SIR JOHN: Let me a little into the secrets of the family.

LOVE: Psha!

SIR JOHN: Poor Lovewell! He can't bear it, I see. She charged you not to kiss and tell. Eh, Lovewell! However, though you will not honour me with your confidence, I'll venture to trust you with mine. — What do you think of Miss Sterling?

LOVE: What do I think of Miss Sterling?

SIR JOHN: Ay; what d'ye think of her?

LOVE: An odd question! — But I think her a smart, lively girl, full of mirth and sprightliness.

SIR JOHN: All mischief and malice, I doubt.

LOVE: How?

SIR JOHN: But her person — what d'ye think of that?

LOVE: Pretty and agreeable.

SIR JOHN: A little grisette thing.

LOVE: What is the meaning of all this?

SIR JOHN: I'll tell you. You must know, Lovewell, that notwithstanding all appearances — (*seeing* LORD OGLEBY, *etc.*) We are interrupted. When they are gone, I'll explain.

> (*Enter* LORD OGLEBY, STERLING, MRS HEIDELBERG, MISS STERLING, *and* FANNY.)

LORD OGLEBY: Great improvements indeed, Mr Sterling! Wonderful improvements! The four Seasons in lead, the flying Mercury, and the basin with Neptune in the middle, are all in the very extreme of fine taste. You have as many rich figures as the man at Hyde Park Corner.

STERL: The chief pleasure of a country house is to make improvements, you know, my lord. I spare no expense, not I. This is quite another-guess sort of place than it was when I first took it, my lord. We were surrounded with trees. I cut down above fifty to make the lawn before the house, and let in the wind and the sun — smack-smooth, as you see. Then I made a greenhouse out of the old laundry, and turned the brew-house into a pinery. The high octagon summer-house, you see yonder, is raised on the mast of a ship, given me by an East India captain who has turned many a thousand of my money.

---

man at Hyde Park Corner: a dealer in plaster statuary.
pinery: place for growing pineapples.

It commands the whole road. All the coaches and chariots, and chaises, pass and repass under your eye. I'll mount you up there in the afternoon, my lord. 'Tis the pleasantest place in the world to take a pipe and a bottle — and so you shall say, my lord.

LORD OGLEBY: Ay — or a bowl of punch, or a can of flip, Mr Sterling; for it looks like a cabin in the air. If flying chairs were in use, the captain might make a voyage to the Indies in it still, if he had but a fair wind.

CANTON: Ha! ha! ha! ha!

MRS HEIDEL: My brother's a little comical in his ideas, my lord! But you'll excuse him. I have a little gothic dairy, fitted up entirely in my own taste. — In the evening I shall hope for the honour of your lordship's company to take a dish of tea there, or a sullabub warm from the cow.

LORD OGLEBY: I have every moment a fresh opportunity of admiring the elegance of Mrs Heidelberg — the very flower of delicacy and cream of politeness.

MRS HEIDEL: Oh my lord! } (leering at each other)
LORD OGLEBY: Oh madam! }

STERL: How d'ye like these close walks, my lord?

LORD OGLEBY: A most excellent serpentine! It forms a perfect maze, and winds like a true-lover's knot.

STERL: Ay — here's none of your straight lines here — but all taste — zigzag — crinkum-crankum — in and out — right and left — to and again — twisting and turning like a worm, my lord!

LORD OGLEBY: Admirably laid out indeed, Mr Sterling! One can hardly see an inch beyond one's nose anywhere in these walks. You are a most excellent economist of your land, and make a little go a great way. It lies together in as small parcels as if it was placed in pots out at your window in Gracechurch Street.

CANTON: Ha! ha! ha! ha!

LORD OGLEBY: What d'ye laugh at, Canton?

CANTON: Ah! Que cette similitude est drôle! So clever what you say, mi lor'.

LORD OGLEBY: (to FANNY) You seem mightily engaged, madam. What are those pretty hands so busily employed about?

FANNY: Only making up a nosegay, my lord! Will your lordship do me the honour of accepting it? (presenting it)

LORD OGLEBY: I'll wear it next my heart, madam! — (aside) I see the young creature dotes on me.

MISS STERL: Lord, sister, you've loaded his lordship with a bunch of flowers as big as the cook or nurse carry to town on Monday morning for a beaupot. — Will your lordship give me leave to present you with this rose and a sprig of sweet brier?

LORD OGLEBY: The truest emblems of yourself, madam! All sweetness and poignancy. — (aside) A little jealous, poor soul!

---

flip: spiced ale warmed by hot poker.
beaupot: ornamented vase for cut flowers.

STERL: Now, my lord, if you please, I'll carry you to see my ruins.

MRS HEIDEL: You'll absolutely fatigue his lordship with overwalking, brother!

LORD OGLEBY: Not at all, madam! We're in the Garden of Eden, you know; in the region of perpetual spring, youth, and beauty (*leering at the women*).

MRS HEIDEL: (*apart*) Quite the man of qualaty, I pertest.

CANTON: Take a my arm, mi lor'! (LORD OGLEBY *leans on him.*)

STERL: I'll only show his lordship my ruins, and the cascade, and the Chinese bridge, and then we'll go in to breakfast.

LORD OGLEBY: Ruins, did you say, Mr Sterling?

STERL: Ay, ruins, my lord! And they are reckoned very fine ones too. You would think them ready to tumble on your head. It has just cost me a hundred and fifty pounds to put my ruins in thorough repair. — This way, if your lordship pleases.

LORD OGLEBY: (*Going, stops.*) What steeple's that we see yonder? The parish church, I suppose.

STERL: Ha! ha! ha! That's admirable. It is no church at all, my lord! It is a spire that I have built against a tree, a field or two off, to terminate the prospect. One must always have a church, or an obelisk, or a something, to terminate the prospect, you know. That's a rule in taste, my lord!

LORD OGLEBY: Very ingenious, indeed! For my part, I desire no finer prospect than this I see before me (*leering at the women*). — Simple, yet varied; bounded, yet extensive. — Get away. Canton! (*pushing away* CANTON) I want no assistance. — I'll walk with the ladies.

STERL: This way, my lord!

LORD OGLEBY: Lead on, sir! We young folks here will follow you. — Madam! — Miss Sterling! — Miss Fanny! I attend you. (*Exit after* STERLING, *gallanting the ladies.*)

CANTON: (*following*) He is cock o'de game, ma foi! — (*Exit.*)

(*Manent* SIR JOHN MELVIL *and* LOVEWELL.)

SIR JOHN: At length, thank heaven, I have an opportunity to unbosom — I know you are faithful, Lovewell, and flatter myself you would rejoice to serve me.

LOVE: Be assured, you may depend on me.

SIR JOHN: You must know then, notwithstanding all appearances, that this treaty of marriage between Miss Sterling and me will come to nothing.

LOVE: How!

SIR JOHN: It will be no match, Lovewell.

LOVE: No match!

SIR JOHN: No.

LOVE: You amaze me. What should prevent it?

SIR JOHN: I.

LOVE: You! Wherefore?

SIR JOHN: I don't like her.

LOVE: Very plain indeed! I never supposed that you was extremely devoted to her from inclination, but thought you always considered it as a matter of convenience, rather than affection.

SIR JOHN: Very true. I came into the family without any impressions on my mind — with an unimpassioned indifference ready to receive one woman as soon as another. I looked upon love, serious, sober love, as a chimaera, and marriage as a thing of course, as you know most people do. But I, who was lately so great an infidel in love, am now one of its sincerest votaries. – In short, my defection from Miss Sterling proceeds from the violence of my attachment to another.

LOVE: Another! So! so! Here will be fine work. And pray who is she?

SIR JOHN: Who is she! Who can she be? but Fanny, the tender, amiable, engaging Fanny.

LOVE: Fanny! What Fanny?

SIR JOHN: Fanny Sterling. Her sister. – Is not she an angel, Lovewell?

LOVE: Her sister? Confusion! – You must not think of it, Sir John.

SIR JOHN: Not think of it? I can think of nothing else. Nay, tell me, Lovewell, was it possible for me to be indulged in a perpetual intercourse with two such objects as Fanny and her sister, and not find my heart led by insensible attraction towards her? – You seem confounded. – Why don't you answer me?

LOVE: Indeed, Sir John, this event gives me infinite concern.

SIR JOHN: Why so? – Is not she an angel, Lovewell?

LOVE: I foresee that it must produce the worst consequences. Consider the confusion it must unavoidably create. Let me persuade you to drop these thoughts in time.

SIR JOHN: Never – never, Lovewell!

LOVE: You have gone too far to recede. A negotiation so nearly concluded cannot be broken off with any grace. The lawyers, you know, are hourly expected; the preliminaries almost finally settled between Lord Ogleby and Mr Sterling; and Miss Sterling herself ready to receive you as a husband.

SIR JOHN: Why the banns have been published, and nobody has forbidden them, 'tis true. But you know either of the parties may change their minds even after they enter the church.

LOVE: You think too lightly of this matter. To carry your addresses so far – and then to desert her – and for her sister too! It will be such an affront to the family, that they can never put up with it.

SIR JOHN: I don't think so: for as to my transferring my passion from her to her sister, so much the better! For then, you know, I don't carry my affections out of the family.

LOVE: Nay, but prithee be serious, and think better of it.

SIR JOHN: I have thought better of it already, you see. Tell me honestly, Lovewell! Can you blame me? Is there any comparison between them?

LOVE: As to that now – why that – that is just – just as it may strike different people. There are many admirers of Miss Sterling's vivacity.

SIR JOHN: Vivacity! A medley of Cheapside pertness, and Whitechapel pride. – No – no – if I do go so far into the city for a wedding-dinner, it shall be upon turtle at least.

LOVE: But I see no probability of success; for granting that Mr Sterling would have consented to it at first, he cannot listen to it now. Why did not you break this affair to the family before?

SIR JOHN: Under such embarrassed circumstances as I have been, can you wonder at my irresolution or perplexity! Nothing but despair, the fear of losing my dear Fanny, could bring me to a declaration even now: and yet, I think I know Mr Sterling so well, that, strange as my proposal may appear, if I can make it advantageous to him as a money transaction as I am sure I can, he will certainly come into it.

LOVE: But even suppose he should, which I very much doubt, I don't think Fanny herself would listen to your addresses.

SIR JOHN: You are deceived a little in that particular.

LOVE: You'll find I am in the right.

SIR JOHN: I have some little reason to think otherwise.

LOVE: You have not declared your passion to her already?

SIR JOHN: Yes, I have.

LOVE: Indeed! — And — and — and how did she receive it?

SIR JOHN: I think it is not very easy for me to make my addresses to any woman without receiving some little encouragement.

LOVE: Encouragement! Did she give you any encouragement?

SIR JOHN: I don't know what you call encouragement! — But she blushed — and cried — and desired me not to think of it any more; upon which I pressed her hand — kissed it — swore she was an angel — and I could see it tickled her to the soul.

LOVE: And did she express no surprise at your declaration?

SIR JOHN: Why, faith, to say the truth, she was a little surprised — and she got away from me too, before I could thoroughly explain myself. If I should not meet with an opportunity of speaking to her, I must get you to deliver a letter from me.

LOVE: I? — A letter! — I had rather have nothing —

SIR JOHN: Nay, you promised me your assistance — and I am sure you cannot scruple to make yourself useful on such an occasion. — You may, without suspicion, acquaint her verbally of my determined affection for her, and that I am resolved to ask her father's consent.

LOVE: As to that, I — your commands, you know — that is, if she — Indeed, Sir John, I think you are in the wrong.

SIR JOHN: Well — well — that's my concern. — Ha! There she goes, by heaven! along that walk yonder, d'ye see? I'll go to her immediately.

LOVE: You are too precipitate. Consider what you are doing.

SIR JOHN: I would not lose this opportunity for the universe.

LOVE: Nay, pray don't go! Your violence and eagerness may overcome her spirits. — The shock will be too much for her (*detaining him*).

SIR JOHN: Nothing shall prevent me. — Ha! Now she turns into another walk. — Let me go! (*Breaks from him.*) I shall lose her. — (*Going, turns back.*) Be sure now to keep out of the way! If you interrupt us, I shall never forgive you. (*Exit hastily.*)

LOVE: (*alone*) 'Sdeath! I can't bear this. In love with my wife! Acquaint me with his passion for her! Make his addresses before my face! — I shall break out before my time. — This was the meaning of Fanny's uneasiness. She could not encourage him — I am sure she could not. — Ha! They are turning into the walk, and coming this way. Shall I leave the place? — Leave him to solicit my wife! I can't submit to it. — They come nearer and nearer. If I stay it will look suspicious — it may betray us, and incense him. — They are here — I must go — I am the most unfortunate fellow in the world. (*Exit.*)

(*Enter* FANNY *and* SIR JOHN.)

FANNY: Leave me, Sir John, I beseech you leave me! — Nay, why will you persist to follow me with idle solicitations, which are an affront to my character, and an injury to your own honour?

SIR JOHN: I know your delicacy, and tremble to offend it: but let the urgency of the occasion be my excuse! Consider, madam, that the future happiness of my life depends on my present application to you; consider that this day must determine my fate; and these are perhaps the only moments left me to incline you to warrant my passion, and to entreat you not to oppose the proposals I mean to open to your father.

FANNY: For shame, Sir John! Think of your previous engagements! Think of your own situation, and think of mine! — What have you discovered in my conduct that might encourage you to so bold a declaration? I am shocked that you should venture to say so much, and blush that I should even dare to give it a hearing. — Let me be gone!

SIR JOHN: Nay, stay, madam! But one moment! — Your sensibility is too great. — Engagements! What engagements have even been pretended on either side than those of family convenience? I went on in the trammels of matrimonial negotiation with a blind submission to your father and Lord Ogleby; but my heart soon claimed a right to be consulted. It has devoted itself to you, and obliges me to plead earnestly for the same tender interest in yours.

FANNY: Have a care, Sir John! Do not mistake a depraved will for a virtuous inclination. By these common pretences of the heart, half of our sex are made fools, and a greater part of yours despise them for it.

SIR JOHN: Affection, you will allow, is involuntary. We cannot always direct it to the object on which it should fix; but when it is once inviolably attached, inviolably as mine is to you, it often creates reciprocal affection. — When I last urged you on this subject, you heard me with more temper, and I hoped with some compassion.

FANNY: You deceived yourself. If I forbore to exert a proper spirit, nay if I did not even express the quickest resentment of your behaviour, it was only in consideration of that respect I wish to pay you, in honour to my sister: and be assured, sir, woman as I am, that my vanity could reap no pleasure from a triumph that must result from the blackest treachery to her (*going*).

SIR JOHN: One word, and I have done. (*stopping her*) — Your impatience and anxiety, and the urgency of the occasion, oblige me to be brief and explicit with you. — I appeal therefore from your delicacy to your justice. — Your sister, I verily believe, neither entertains any real affection for me, or tenderness for you. — Your father, I am inclined to think, is not much concerned by means of which of his daughters the families are united. — Now as they cannot, shall not be connected, otherwise than by my union with you, why will

---

temper: restraint, temperateness.

you, from a false delicacy, oppose a measure so conducive to my happiness, and, I hope, your own? I love you, most passionately and sincerely love you — and hope to propose terms agreeable to Mr Sterling. If then you don't absolutely loathe, abhor, and scorn me — if there is no other happier man —

FANNY: Hear me, sir! Hear my final determination. — Were my father and sister as insensible as you are pleased to represent them; were my heart for ever to remain disengaged to any other — I could not listen to your proposals. — What! You on the very eve of a marriage with my sister; I living under the same roof with her, bound not only by the laws of friendship and hospitality, but even the ties of blood, to contribute to her happiness, — and not to conspire against her peace — the peace of a whole family — and that my own too! — Away! away, Sir John! — At such a time, and in such circumstances, your addresses only inspire me with horror. — Nay, you must detain me no longer. — I will go.

SIR JOHN: Do not leave me in absolute despair! — Give me a glimpse of hope! (*falling on his knees*)

FANNY: I cannot. Pray, Sir John! (*struggling to go*)

SIR JOHN: Shall this hand be given to another? (*kissing her hand*) No — I cannot endure it. — My whole soul is yours, and the whole happiness of my life is in your power.

    (*Enter* MISS STERLING.)

FANNY: Ha! My sister is here. Rise for shame, Sir John!

SIR JOHN: Miss Sterling! (*rising*)

MISS STERL: I beg pardon, sir! — You'll excuse me, madam! — I have broke in upon you a little unopportunely, I believe; but I did not mean to interrupt you. — I only came, sir, to let you know that breakfast waits, if you have finished your morning's devotions.

SIR JOHN: I am very sensible, Miss Sterling, that this may appear particular, but —

MISS STERL: Oh dear, Sir John, don't put yourself to the trouble of an apology. The thing explains itself.

SIR JOHN: It will soon, madam! — In the meantime I can only assure you of my profound respect and esteem for you, and make no doubt of convincing Mr Sterling of the honour and integrity of my intentions. And — and — your humble servant, madam! (*Exit in confusion.*)

    (*Manent* FANNY *and* MISS STERLING.)

MISS STERL: Respect? — Insolence! — Esteem? — Very fine truly! — And you, madam! My sweet, delicate, innocent, sentimental sister! Will you convince my papa too of the integrity of your intentions?

FANNY: Do not upbraid me, my dear sister! Indeed, I don't deserve it. Believe me, you can't be more offended at his behaviour than I am, and I am sure it cannot make you half so miserable.

MISS STERL: Make me miserable! You are mightily deceived, madam! It gives me no sort of uneasiness, I assure you. — A base fellow! — As for you, miss! The pretended softness of your disposition, your artful good nature, never imposed upon me. I always knew you to be sly, and envious, and deceitful.

FANNY: Indeed you wrong me.

MISS STERL: Oh, you are all goodness, to be sure! — Did not I find him on his

knees before you? Did not I see him kiss your sweet hand? Did not I hear his
protestations? Was not I witness of your dissembled modesty? – No – no,
my dear! Don't imagine that you can make a fool of your elder sister so
easily.

FANNY: Sir John, I own, is to blame; but I am above the thoughts of doing you
the least injury.

MISS STERL: We shall try that, madam! – I hope, miss, you'll be able to give a
better account to my papa and my aunt – for they shall both know of this
matter, I promise you. (*Exit.*)

FANNY: (*alone*) How unhappy I am! My distresses multiply upon me. – Mr Lovewell must now become acquainted with Sir John's behaviour to me – and in
a manner that may add to his uneasiness. – My father, instead of being disposed by fortunate circumstances to forgive any transgression, will be
previously incensed against me. – My sister and my aunt will become irrecon-
cilably my enemies, and rejoice in my disgrace. – Yet, at all events, I am
determined on a discovery. I dread it, and am resolved to hasten it. It is surrounded with more horrors every instant, as it appears every instant more
necessary. (*Exit.*)

ACT III

SCENE 1.   *A hall. Enter a* SERVANT *leading in* SERJEANT FLOWER, *and*
COUNSELLORS TRAVERSE *and* TRUEMAN – *all booted.*

SERVANT: This way, if you please, gentlemen! My master is at breakfast with the
family at present – but I'll let him know, and he will wait on you immediately.

FLOWER: Mighty well, young man, mighty well.

SERVANT: Please to favour me with your names, gentlemen.

FLOWER: Let Mr Sterling know that Mr Serjeant Flower, and two other gentlemen
of the Bar, are come to wait on him according to his appointment.

SERVANT: I will, sir (*going*).

FLOWER: And harkee, young man! (SERVANT *returns*.) Desire my servant – Mr
Serjeant Flower's servant – to bring in my green and gold saddle-cloth and
pistols, and lay them down here in the hall with my portmanteau.

SERVANT: I will, sir. (*Exit.*)
                         (*Manent lawyers.*)

FLOWER: Well, gentlemen! The settling these marriage articles falls conveniently
enough, almost just on the eve of the circuits. – Let me see – the Home,
the Midland, Oxford and Western, – ay, we can all cross the country well
enough to our several destinations. – Traverse, when do you begin at
Abingdon?

TRAVERSE: The day after tomorrow.

FLOWER: That is commission-day with us at Warwick too. But my clerk has
retainers for every cause in the paper, so it will be time enough if I am there
the next morning. Besides, I have about half a dozen cases that have lain by
me ever since the Spring Assizes, and I must tack opinions to them before I

see my country clients again — so I will take the evening before me — and then *currente calamo*, as I say — eh, Traverse!

TRAVERSE: True, Mr Serjeant — and the easiest thing in the world too — for those country attorneys are such ignorant dogs, that in case of the devise of an estate to A and his heirs for ever, they'll make a query whether he takes in fee or in tail.

FLOWER: Do you expect to have much to do in the Home circuit these assizes?

TRAVERSE: Not much *nisi prius* business, but a good deal on the Crown side, I believe. The jails are brimful — and some of the felons in good circumstances, and likely to be tolerable clients. — Let me see! I'm engaged for three highway robberies, two murders, one forgery, and half a dozen larcenies, at Kingston.

FLOWER: A pretty decent jail-delivery! Do you expect to bring off Darkin for the robbery on Putney Common? Can you make out your alibi?

TRAVERSE: Oh, no! The Crown witnesses are sure to prove our identity. We shall certainly be hanged: but that don't signify. — But, Mr Serjeant, have you much to do? Any remarkable cause on the Midland this circuit?

FLOWER: Nothing very remarkable — except two rapes, and Rider and Western at Nottingham, for *crim. con.* — but, on the whole, I believe a good deal of business. Our associate tells me there are above thirty *venires* for Warwick.

TRAVERSE: Pray, Mr Serjeant, are you concerned in Jones and Thomas at Lincoln?

FLOWER: I am — for the plaintiff.

TRAVERSE: And what do you think on't?

FLOWER: A non-suit.

TRAVERSE: I thought so.

FLOWER: Oh, no manner of doubt on't — *luce clarius* — we have no right in us — we have but one chance.

TRAVERSE: What's that?

FLOWER: Why, my Lord Chief does not go the circuit this time, and my brother Puzzle being in the commission, the cause will come on before him.

TRUE: Ay, that may do, indeed, if you can but throw dust in the eyes of the defendant's counsel.

FLOWER: (*to* TRUEMAN) Mr Trueman, I think you are concerned for Lord Ogleby in this affair?

TRUE: I am, sir — I have the honour to be related to his lordship, and hold some courts for him in Somersetshire — go the Western circuit, and attend the session at Exeter, merely because his lordship's interest and property lie in that part of the kingdom.

FLOWER: Ha! — and pray, Mr Trueman, how long have you been called to the Bar?

---

currente calamo: with a flowing pen.
in fee or in tail: in absolute ownership or limited to the issue of a particular person.
nisi prius business: civil actions brought before a judge and jury at assizes.
crim. con.: adultery (abbr. of *criminal conversation*).
venires: writs summoning juries.
luce clarius: it is clear.

TRUE: About nine years and three-quarters.

FLOWER: Ha! I don't know that I ever had the pleasure of seeing you before. I wish you success, young gentleman!

(*Enter* STERLING.)

STERL: Oh, Mr Serjeant Flower, I am glad to see you. Your servant, Mr Serjeant! Gentlemen, your servant! — Well, are all matters concluded? Has that snail-paced conveyancer, old Ferret of Gray's Inn, settled the articles at last? Do you approve of what he has done? Will his tackle hold? Tight and strong? — Eh, Master Serjeant?

FLOWER: My friend Ferret's slow and sure, sir. — But then, *serius aut citius*, as we say, sooner or later, Mr Sterling, he is sure to put his business out of hand as he should do. — My clerk has brought the writings and all other instruments along with him, and the settlement is, I believe, as good a settlement as any settlement on the face of the earth!

STERL: But that damn'd mortgage of sixty thousand pounds. — There don't appear to be any other incumbrances, I hope?

TRAVERSE: I can answer for that, sir — and that will be cleared off immediately on the payment of the first part of Miss Sterling's portion. You agree, on your part, to come down with eighty thousand pounds. —

STERL: Down on the nail. Ay, ay, my money is ready tomorrow if he pleases — he shall have it in India-bonds, or notes, or how he chooses. Your lords, and your dukes, and your people at the Court end of the town stick at payments sometimes — debts unpaid, no credit lost with them — but no fear of us substantial fellows — eh, Mr Serjeant!

FLOWER: Sir John having last term, according to agreement, levied a fine, and suffered a recovery, has thereby cut off the entail of the Ogleby estate for the better effecting the purposes of the present intended marriage; on which above-mentioned Ogleby estate, a jointure of two thousand pounds per ann. is secured to your eldest daughter, now Elizabeth Sterling, spinster, and the whole estate, after the death of the aforesaid earl, descends to the heirs male of Sir John Melvil on the body of the aforesaid Elizabeth Sterling lawfully to be begotten.

TRAVERSE: Very true — and Sir John is to be put in immediate possession of as much of his lordship's Somersetshire estate as lies in the manors of Hogmore and Cranford, amounting to between two and three thousands per ann., and at the death of Mr Sterling, a further sum of seventy thousand —

(*Enter* SIR JOHN MELVIL.)

STERL: Ah, Sir John! Here we are — hard at it — paving the road to matrimony. We'll have no jolts; all upon the nail, as easy as the new pavement. — First the lawyers, then comes the doctor. — Let us but dispatch the long-robe, we shall soon set Pudding-sleeves to work, I warrant you.

SIR JOHN: I am sorry to interrupt you, sir — but I hope that both you and these gentlemen will excuse me. Having something very particular for your private

---

serius aut citius: sooner or later.
long-robe: lawyer.
Pudding-sleeves: parson.

ear, I took the liberty of following you, and beg you will oblige me with an audience immediately.

STERL: Ay, with all my heart. — Gentlemen, Mr Serjeant, you'll excuse it — business must be done, you know. — The writings will keep cold till tomorrow morning.

FLOWER: I must be at Warwick, Mr Sterling, the day after.

STERL: Nay, nay, I shan't part with you tonight, gentlemen, I promise you. — My house is very full, but I have beds for you all, beds for your servants, and stabling for all your horses. — Will you take a turn in the garden, and view some of my improvements before dinner? Or will you amuse yourselves on the green with a game of bowls and a cool tankard? — My servants shall attend you. Do you choose any other refreshment? — Call for what you please; do as you please; make yourselves quite at home, I beg of you. — Here, — Thomas, Henry, William, wait on these gentlemen! (*Follows the lawyers out, bawling and talking, and then returns to* SIR JOHN.) And now, sir, I am entirely at your service. What are your commands with me, Sir John?

SIR JOHN: After having carried the negotiation between our families to so great a length, after having assented so readily to all your proposals, as well as received so many instances of your cheerful compliance with the demands made on our part, I am extremely concerned, Mr Sterling, to be the involuntary cause of any uneasiness.

STERL: Uneasiness! What uneasiness? Where business is transacted as it ought to be, and the parties understand one another, there can be no uneasiness. You agree, on such and such conditions, to receive my daughter for a wife; on the same conditions I agree to receive you as a son-in-law; and as to all the rest, it follows of course, you know, as regularly as the payment of a bill after acceptance.

SIR JOHN: Pardon me, sir; more uneasiness has arisen than you are aware of. I am myself, at this instant, in a state of inexpressible embarrassment; Miss Sterling, I know, is extremely disconcerted too; and unless you will oblige me with the assistance of your friendship, I foresee the speedy progress of discontent and animosity through the whole family.

STERL: What the deuce is all this? I don't understand a single syllable.

SIR JOHN: In one word then — it will be absolutely impossible for me to fulfil my engagements in regard to Miss Sterling.

STERL: How, Sir John? Do you mean to put an affront upon my family? What! Refuse to —

SIR JOHN: Be assured, sir, that I neither mean to affront nor forsake your family. — My only fear is, that you should desert me; for the whole happiness of my life depends on my being connected with your family by the nearest and tenderest ties in the world.

STERL: Why, did you not tell me, but a moment ago, that it was absolutely impossible for you to marry my daughter?

SIR JOHN: True. — But you have another daughter, sir —

STERL: Well?

SIR JOHN: Who has obtained the most absolute domination over my heart. I have already declared my passion to her; nay, Miss Sterling herself is also apprised of it, and if you will but give a sanction to my present address, the uncommon merit of Miss Sterling will no doubt recommend her to a person of equal, if not superior rank to myself, and our families may still be allied by my union with Miss Fanny.

STERL: Mighty fine, truly! Why, what the plague do you make of us, Sir John? Do you come to market for my daughters, like servants at a statute fair? Do you think that I will suffer you, or any man in the world, to come into my house, like the Grand Signior, and throw the handkerchief first to one, and then to t'other, just as he pleases? Do you think I drive a kind of African slave-trade with them? And —

SIR JOHN: A moment's patience, sir! Nothing but the excess of my passion for Miss Fanny should have induced me to take any step that had the least appearance of disrespect to any part of your family; and even now I am desirous to atone for my transgression, by making the most adequate compensation that lies in my power.

STERL: Compensation! What compensation can you possibly make in such a case as this, Sir John?

SIR JOHN: Come, come, Mr Sterling; I know you to be a man of sense, a man of business, a man of the world. I'll deal frankly with you; and you shall see that I do not desire a change of measures for my own gratification, without endeavouring to make it advantageous to you.

STERL: What advantage can your inconstancy be to me, Sir John?

SIR JOHN: I'll tell you, sir. — You know that by the articles at present subsisting between us, on the day of my marriage with Miss Sterling you agree to pay down the gross sum of eighty thousand pounds.

STERL: Well!

SIR JOHN: Now if you will but consent to my waiving that marriage —

STERL: I agree to your waiving that marriage? Impossible, Sir John!

SIR JOHN: I hope not, sir; as on my part, I will agree to waive my right to thirty thousand pounds of the fortune I was to receive with her.

STERL: Thirty thousand, d'ye say?

SIR JOHN: Yes, sir; and accept of Miss Fanny with fifty thousand, instead of fourscore.

STERL: Fifty thousand — (*pausing*)

SIR JOHN: Instead of fourscore.

STERL: Why, — why, — there may be something in that. — Let me see; Fanny with fifty thousand instead of Betsey with fourscore. — But how can this be, Sir John? — For you know I am to pay this money into the hands of my Lord Ogleby; who, I believe — between you and me, Sir John, — is not overstocked with ready money at present; and threescore thousand of it, you know, is to go to pay off the present incumbrances on the estate, Sir John.

SIR JOHN: That objection is easily obviated. — Ten of the twenty thousand which would remain as a surplus of the fourscore, after paying off the mortgage, was intended by his lordship for my use, that we might set off with some little

---

Grand Signior: Sultan of Turkey.

éclat on our marriage; and the other ten for his own. – Ten thousand pounds, therefore, I shall be able to pay you immediately; and for the remaining twenty thousand you shall have a mortgage on that part of the estate which is to be made over to me, with whatever security you shall require for the regular payment of the interest, till the principal is fully discharged.

STERL: Why – to do you justice, Sir John, there is something fair and open in your proposal; and since I find you do not mean to put an affront upon the family –

SIR JOHN: Nothing was ever farther from my thoughts, Mr Sterling. – And after all, the whole affair is nothing extraordinary – such things happen every day – and as the world has only heard generally of a treaty between the families, when the marriage takes place, nobody will be the wiser, if we have but discretion enough to keep our own counsel.

STERL: True, true; and since you only transfer from one girl to another, it is no more than transferring so much stock, you know.

SIR JOHN: The very thing.

STERL: Odso! I had quite forgot. We are reckoning without our host here. There is another difficulty –

SIR JOHN: You alarm me. What can that be?

STERL: I can't stir a step in this business without consulting my sister Heidelberg. The family has very great expectations from her, and we must not give her any offence.

SIR JOHN: But if you come into this measure, surely she will be so kind as to consent –

STERL: I don't know that – Betsey is her darling, and I can't tell how far she may resent any slight that seems to be offered to her favourite niece. – However, I'll do the best I can for you. – You shall go and break the matter to her first, and by that time that I may suppose that your rhetoric has prevailed on her to listen to reason, I will step in to reinforce your arguments.

SIR JOHN: I'll fly to her immediately: you promise me your assistance?

STERL: I do.

SIR JOHN: Ten thousand thanks for it! And now success attend me! (*going*)

STERL: Harkee, Sir John! (SIR JOHN *returns.*) Not a word of the thirty thousand to my sister, Sir John.

SIR JOHN: Oh, I am dumb, I am dumb, sir (*going*).

STERL: You remember it is thirty thousand.

SIR JOHN: To be sure I do.

STERL: But, Sir John! – One thing more. (SIR JOHN *returns.*) My lord must know nothing of this stroke of friendship between us.

SIR JOHN: Not for the world. – Let me alone! Let me alone! (*offering to go*)

STERL: (*holding him*) And when everything is agreed, we must give each other a bond to be held fast to the bargain.

SIR JOHN: To be sure. A bond by all means! A bond, or whatever you please. (*Exit hastily.*)

STERL: (*alone*) I should have thought of more conditions – he's in a humour to give me everything. – Why, what mere children are your fellows of quality; that cry for a plaything one minute, and throw it by the next! As changeable

as the weather, and as uncertain as the stocks. — Special fellows to drive a
bargain! And yet they are to take care of the interest of the nation truly! —
Here does this whirligig man of fashion offer to give up thirty thousand
pounds in hard money, with as much indifference as if it was a china orange.
— By this mortgage I shall have a hold on his *terra firma*, and if he wants
more money, as he certainly will, — let him have children by my daughter or
no, I shall have his whole estate in a net for the benefit of my family. — Well,
thus it is that the children of citizens, who have acquired fortunes, prove
persons of fashion; and thus it is, that persons of fashion, who have ruined
their fortunes, reduce the next generation to cits. (*Exit.*)

SCENE 2.   *Another apartment. Enter* MRS HEIDELBERG *and* MISS
STERLING.

MISS STERL: This is your gentle-looking, soft-speaking, sweet-smiling, affable Miss
    Fanny for you!

MRS HEIDEL: My Miss Fanny! I disclaim her. With all her arts she could never
    insinuat herself into my good graces — and yet she has a way with her that
    deceives man, woman, and child, except you and me, niece.

MISS STERL: Oh ay; she wants nothing but a crook in her hand, and a lamb under
    her arm, to be a perfect picture of innocence and simplicity.

MRS HEIDEL: Just as I was drawn at Amsterdam, when I went over to visit my
    husband's relations.

MISS STERL: And then she's so mighty good to servants — *pray, John, do this* —
    pray, Tom, do that — *thank you, Jenny* — and then so humble to her
    relations — *to be sure, papa!* — *as my aunt pleases* — *my sister knows best.*
    — But with all her demureness and humility she has no objection to be Lady
    Melvil, it seems, nor to any wickedness that can make her so.

MRS HEIDEL: She Lady Melvil? Compose yourself, niece! I'll ladyship her indeed!
    A little creepin, cantin — She shan't be the better for a farden of my money.
    But tell me, child, how does this intriguing with Sir John correspond with her
    partiality to Lovewell? I don't see a concatunation here.

MISS STERL: There I was deceived, madam. I took all their whisperings and
    stealing into corners to be the mere attraction of vulgar minds; but, behold!
    their private meetings were not to contrive their own insipid happiness, but to
    conspire against mine. — But I know whence proceeds Mr Lovewell's resent-
    ment to me. I could not stoop to be familiar with my father's clerk, and so I
    have lost his interest.

MRS HEIDEL: My spurrit to a T — My dear child — (*kissing her*) Mr Heidelberg lost
    his election for member of parliament because I would not demean myself to
    be slobbered about by drunken shoemakers, beastly cheesemongers, and
    greasy butchers and tallow-chandlers. However, niece, I can't help diffuring a
    little in opinion from you in this matter. My experunce and sagucity makes
    me still suspect that there is something more between her and that Lovewell,
    notwithstanding this affair of Sir John — I had my eye upon them the whole
    time of breakfast. — Sir John, I observed, looked a little confounded, indeed,
    though I knew nothing of what had passed in the garden. You seemed to sit
    upon thorns too: but Fanny and Mr Lovewell made quite another-guess sort

of a figur; and were as perfet a pictur of two distressed lovers, as if it had been drawn by Raphael Angelo. – As to Sir John and Fanny, I want a matter of fact.

MISS STERL: Matter of fact, madam! Did not I come unexpectedly upon them? Was not Sir John kneeling at her feet and kissing her hand? Did not he look all love, and she all confusion? Is not that matter of fact? And did not Sir John, the moment that papa was called out of the room to the lawyermen, get up from breakfast and follow him immediately? And I warrant you that by this time he has made proposals to him to marry my sister. – Oh, that some other person, an earl, or a duke, would make his addresses to me, that I might be revenged on this monster!

MRS HEIDEL: Be cool, child! You *shall* be Lady Melvil, in spite of all their caballins, if it costs me ten thousand pounds to turn the scale. Sir John may apply to my brother, indeed; but I'll make them all know who governs this fammaly.

MISS STERL: As I live, madam, yonder comes Sir John. A base man! I can't endure the sight of him. I'll leave the room this instant (*disordered*).

MRS HEIDEL: Poor thing! Well, retire to your own chamber, child; I'll give it him, I warrant you; and by and by I'll come and let you know all that has passed between us.

MISS STERL: Pray do, madam! – (*looking back*) A vile wretch! (*Exit in a rage.*)
        (*Enter* SIR JOHN MELVIL.)

SIR JOHN: Your most obedient humble servant, madam! (*bowing very respectfully*)

MRS HEIDEL: Your servant, Sir John! (*dropping a half-curtsy, and pouting*)

SIR JOHN: Miss Sterling's manner of quitting the room on my approach, and the visible coolness of your behaviour to me, madam, convince me that she has acquainted you with what passed this morning.

MRS HEIDEL: I am very sorry, Sir John, to be made acquainted with anything that should induce me to change the opinion which I could always wish to entertain of a person of quallaty (*pouting*).

SIR JOHN: It has always been my ambition to merit the best opinion from Mrs Heidelberg; and when she comes to weigh all circumstances, I flatter myself –

MRS HEIDEL: You do flatter yourself, if you imagine that I can approve of your behaviour to my niece, Sir John. – And give me leave to tell you, Sir John, that you have been drawn into an action much beneath you, Sir John; and that I look upon every injury offered to Miss Betty Sterling as an affront to myself, Sir John (*warmly*).

SIR JOHN: I would not offend you for the world, madam! But when I am influenced by a partiality for another, however ill-founded, I hope your discernment and good sense will think it rather a point of honour to renounce engagements which I could not fulfil so strictly as I ought; and that you will excuse the change in my inclinations, since the new object, as well as the first, has the honour of being your niece, madam.

MRS HEIDEL: I disclaim her as a niece, Sir John; Miss Sterling disclaims her as a sister, and the whole fammaly must disclaim her for her monstrous baseness and treachery.

SIR JOHN: Indeed she has been guilty of none, madam. Her hand and heart are, I am sure, entirely at the disposal of yourself and Mr Sterling. (*Enter* STERLING *behind.*) And if you should not oppose my inclinations, I am sure of Mr Sterling's consent, madam.

MRS HEIDEL: Indeed!

SIR JOHN: Quite certain, madam.

STERL: (*behind*) So! They seem to be coming to terms already. I may venture to make my appearance.

MRS HEIDEL: To marry Fanny?

                 (STERLING *advances by degrees.*)

SIR JOHN: Yes, madam.

MRS HEIDEL: My brother has given his consent, you say?

SIR JOHN: In the most ample manner, with no other restriction than the failure of your concurrence, madam. (*Sees* STERLING.) Oh, here's Mr Sterling, who will confirm what I have told you.

MRS HEIDEL: What! have you consented to give up your own daughter in this manner, brother?

STERL: Give her up! No, not give her up, sister; only in case that you — (*aside to* SIR JOHN) Zounds, I am afraid you have said too much, Sir John.

MRS HEIDEL: Yes, yes, I see now that it is true enough what my niece told me. You are all plottin and caballin against her. — Pray, does Lord Ogleby know of this affair?

SIR JOHN: I have not yet made him acquainted with it, madam.

MRS HEIDEL: No, I warrant you. I thought so. — And so his lordship and myself truly, are not to be consulted till the last.

STERL: What! Did not you consult my lord? Oh, fie for shame, Sir John!

SIR JOHN: Nay, but, Mr Sterling —

MRS HEIDEL: We, who are the persons of most consequence and experunce in the two fammalies, are to know nothing of the matter till the whole is as good as concluded upon. But his lordship, I am sure, will have more generosaty than to countenance such a perceeding. — And I could not have expected such behaviour from a person of your quallaty, Sir John. — And as for you, brother —

STERL: Nay, nay, but hear me, sister!

MRS HEIDEL: I am perfetly ashamed of you. — Have you no spurrit? No more concern for the honour of our fammaly than to consent —

STERL: Consent? — I consent? — As I hope for mercy, I never gave my consent. Did I consent, Sir John?

SIR JOHN: Not absolutely, without Mrs Heidelberg's concurrence. But in case of her approbation —

STERL: Ay, I grant you, if my sister approved. — (*to* MRS HEIDELBERG) But that's quite another thing, you know.

MRS HEIDEL: Your sister approve, indeed! — I thought you knew her better, brother Sterling! — What! Approve of having your eldest daughter returned upon your hands, and exchanged for the younger? — I am surprised how you could listen to such a scandalus proposal.

STERL: I tell you, I never did listen to it. — Did not I say that I would be governed

entirely by my sister, Sir John? — And unless she agreed to your marrying
Fanny —

MRS HEIDEL: I agree to his marrying Fanny? Abominable! The man is absolutely
out of his senses. — Can't that wise head of yours foresee the consequences of
all this, brother Sterling? Will Sir John take Fanny without a fortune? No. —
After you have settled the largest part of your property on your youngest
daughter, can there be an equal portion left for the eldest? No. — Does not
this overturn the whole systum of the fammaly? Yes, yes, yes. You know I
was always for my niece Betsey's marrying a person of the very first quallaty.
That was my maxum. And, therefore, much the largest settlement was of
course to be made upon her. — As for Fanny, if she could, with a fortune of
twenty or thirty thousand pounds, get a knight, or a member of parliament,
or a rich common-council man for a husband, I thought it might do very well.

SIR JOHN: But if a better match should offer itself, why should not it be accepted,
madam?

MRS HEIDEL: What! At the expense of her elder sister? Oh, fie, Sir John! — How
could you bear to hear of such an indignaty, brother Sterling?

STERL: I! Nay, I shan't hear of it, I promise you. — I can't hear of it indeed, Sir
John.

MRS HEIDEL:.But you *have* heard of it, brother Sterling. You know you have; and
sent Sir John to propose it to me. But if you can give up your daughter, I
shan't forsake my niece, I assure you. Ah! If my poor dear Mr Heidelberg and
our sweet babes had been alive, he would not have behaved so.

STERL: Did I, Sir John? Nay, speak! (*apart to* SIR JOHN) Bring me off, or we are
ruined.

SIR JOHN: Why, to be sure, to speak the truth —

MRS HEIDEL: To speak the truth, I'm ashamed of you both. But have a care what
you are about, brother! Have a care, I say. The lawyers are in the house, I
hear; and if everything is not settled to my liking I'll have nothing more to
say to you, if I live these hundred years. — I'll go over to Holland, and settle
with Mr Vanderspracken, my poor husband's first cousin; and my own
fammaly shall never be the better for a farden of my money, I promise you.
(*Exit.*)

(*Manent* SIR JOHN *and* STERLING.)

STERL: I thought so. I knew she never would agree to it.

SIR JOHN: 'Sdeath, how unfortunate! What can we do, Mr Sterling?

STERL: Nothing.

SIR JOHN: What! Must our agreement break off the moment it is made then?

STERL: It can't be helped, Sir John. The family, as I told you before, have great
expectations from my sister; and if this matter proceeds, you hear yourself
that she threatens to leave us. — My brother Heidelberg was a warm man; a
very warm man; and died worth a plum at least; a plum! ay, I warrant you,
he died worth a plum and a half.

SIR JOHN: Well; but if I —

---

plum: £100,000 sterling.

STERL: And then, my sister has three or four very good mortgages, a deal of
 money in the three per cents and old South Sea annuities, besides large concerns in the Dutch and French funds. — The greatest part of all this she means
 to leave to our family.

SIR JOHN: I can only say, sir —

STERL: Why, your offer of the difference of thirty thousand was very fair and
 handsome to be sure, Sir John.

SIR JOHN: Nay, but I am even willing to —

STERL: Ay, but if I was to accept it against her will, I might lose above a hundred
 thousand; so, you see, the balance is against you, Sir John.

SIR JOHN: But is there no way, do you think, of prevailing on Mrs Heidelberg to
 grant her consent?

STERL: I am afraid not. — However, when her passion is a little abated — for she's
 very passionate — you may try what can be done: but you must not use my
 name any more, Sir John.

SIR JOHN: Suppose I was to prevail on Lord Ogleby to apply to her, do you think
 that would have any influence over her?

STERL: I think he would be more likely to persuade her to it than any other person in the family. She has a great respect for Lord Ogleby. She loves a lord.

SIR JOHN: I'll apply to him this very day. — And if he should prevail on Mrs
 Heidelberg, I may depend on your friendship, Mr Sterling?

STERL: Ay, ay, I shall be glad to oblige you, when it is in my power; but as the
 account stands now, you see it is not upon the figures. And so your servant,
 Sir John. (*Exit.*)

SIR JOHN: (*alone*) What a situation am I in! — Breaking off with her whom I was
 bound by treaty to marry; rejected by the object of my affections; and
 embroiled with this turbulent woman, who governs the whole family. — And
 yet opposition, instead of smothering, increases my inclination. I must have
 her. I'll apply immediately to Lord Ogleby; and if he can but bring over the
 aunt to our party, her influence will overcome the scruples and delicacy of
 my dear Fanny, and I shall be the happiest of mankind. (*Exit.*)

ACT IV

SCENE 1.   *A room. Enter* STERLING, MRS HEIDELBERG, *and* MISS
STERLING.

STERL: What! Will you send Fanny to town, sister?

MRS HEIDEL: Tomorrow morning. I've given orders about it already.

STERL: Indeed?

MRS HEIDEL: Positively.

STERL: But consider, sister, at such a time as this, what an odd appearance it will
 have.

MRS HEIDEL: Not half so odd as her behaviour, brother. — This time was intended
 for happiness, and I'll keep no incendaries here to destroy it. I insist on her
 going off tomorrow morning.

STERL: I'm afraid this is all your doing, Betsey.

MISS STERL: No, indeed, papa. My aunt knows that it is not. — For all Fanny's baseness to me, I am sure I would not do or say anything to hurt her with you or my aunt for the world.

MRS HEIDEL: Hold your tongue, Betsey! — I will have my way. — When she is packed off, everything will go on as it should do. — Since they are at their intrigues, I'll let them see that we can act with vigur on our part; and the sending her out of the way shall be the purlimunary step to all the rest of my perceedings.

STERL: Well, but, sister —

MRS HEIDEL: It does not signify talking, brother Sterling, for I'm resolved to be rid of her, and I will. — (*to* MISS STERLING) Come along, child! The post-shay shall be at the door by six o'clock in the morning; and if Miss Fanny does not get into it, why *I* will, and so there's an end of the matter. (*Bounces out with* MISS STERLING. *Returns.*) One word more, brother Sterling! — I expect that you will take your eldest daughter in your hand, and make a formal complaint to Lord Ogleby of Sir John Melvil's behaviour. — Do this, brother; show a proper regard for the honour of your fammaly yourself, and I shall throw in my mite to the raising of it. If not — but now you know my mind. So act as you please, and take the consequences. (*Exit.*)

STERL: (*alone*) The devil's in the woman for tyranny — mothers, wives, mistresses, or sisters, they always will govern us. — As to my sister Heidelberg, she knows the strength of her purse, and domineers upon the credit of it. — (*mimicking*) 'I will do this' — and — 'you shall do that' — and 'you must do t'other, or else the fammaly shan't have a farden of —' So absolute with her money! — But to say the truth, nothing but money *can* make us absolute, and so we must e'en make the best of her.

SCENE 2.   *The garden. Enter* LORD OGLEBY *and* CANTON.

LORD OGLEBY: What! Mademoiselle Fanny to be sent away! — Why? — Wherefore? — What's the meaning of all this?

CANTON: Je ne sais pas. — I know noting of it.

LORD OGLEBY: It can't be; it shan't be. I protest against the measure. She's a fine girl, and I had much rather that the rest of the family were annihilated than that she should leave us. — Her vulgar father, that's the very abstract of 'Change Alley — the aunt, that's always endeavouring to be a fine lady — and the pert sister, forever showing that she is one, are horrid company indeed, and without her would be intolerable. Ah, la petite Fanchon! She's the thing. Isn't she, Cant?

CANTON: Dere is very good sympatie entre vous and dat young lady, mi lor'.

LORD OGLEBY: I'll not be left among these Goths and Vandals, your Sterlings, your Heidelbergs, and Devilbergs. — If she goes, I'll positively go too.

CANTON: In de same post-shay, mi lor'? You have no object to dat I believe, nor Mademoiselle neider too — ha, ha, ha!

LORD OGLEBY: Prithee hold thy foolish tongue, Cant. Does thy Swiss stupidity imagine that I can see and talk with a fine girl without desires? — My eyes are involuntarily attracted by beautiful objects — I fly as naturally to a fine girl —

CANTON: As de fine girl to you, my lor', ha, ha, ha! you alway fly togedre like un pair de pigeons. —

LORD OGLEBY: Like un pair de pigeons. (*Mocks him.*) — Vous êtes un sot,
    Monsieur Canton — Thou art always dreaming of my intrigues, and never
    seest me *badiner*, but you suspect mischief, you old fool, you.
CANTON: I am fool, I confess, but not always fool in dat, my lor', he, he, he!
LORD OGLEBY: He, he, he! — Thou art incorrigible, but thy absurdities amuse
    one. Thou art like my rappee here (*Takes out his box.*), a most ridiculous
    superfluity, but a pinch of thee now and then is a most delicious treat.
CANTON: You do me great honour, my lor'.
LORD OGLEBY: 'Tis fact, upon my soul. Thou art properly my cephalic snuff,
    and art no bad medicine against megrims, vertigoes, and profound thinking —
    ha, ha, ha!
CANTON: Your flatterie, my lor', vil make me too prode.
LORD OGLEBY: The girl has some little partiality for me, to be sure. But prithee,
    Cant, is not that Miss Fanny yonder?
CANTON: (*looking with a glass*) En vérité, 'tis she, my lor' — 'tis one of de pigeons,
    — de pigeons d'amour.
LORD OGLEBY: (*smiling*) Don't be ridiculous, you old monkey.
CANTON: I am monkee, I am ole, but I have eye, I have ear, and a little under-
    stand, now and den. —
LORD OGLEBY: Taisez-vous bête!
CANTON: Elle vous attend, my lor'. — She vil make a love to you.
LORD OGLEBY: Will she? Have at her then! A fine girl can't oblige me more. —
    Egad, I find myself a little enjoué. Come along, Cant! She is but in the next
    walk — but there is such a deal of this damned crinkum-crankum, as Sterling
    calls it, that one sees people for half an hour before one can get to them. —
    Allons, Monsieur Canton, allons donc! (*Exeunt, singing in French.*)

SCENE 3.   *Another part of the garden.* LOVEWELL *and* FANNY.
LOVE: My dear Fanny, I cannot bear your distress; it overcomes all my resolutions,
    and I am prepared for the discovery.
FANNY: But how can it be effected before my departure?
LOVE: I'll tell you. Lord Ogleby seems to entertain a visible partiality for you; and
    notwithstanding the peculiarities of his behaviour, I am sure that he is humane
    at the bottom. He is vain to an excess; but withal extremely good-natured,
    and would do anything to recommend himself to a lady. — Do you open the
    whole affair of our marriage to him immediately. It will come with more
    irresistible persuasion from you than from myself; and I doubt not but you'll
    gain his friendship and protection at once. — His influence and authority will
    put an end to Sir John's solicitations, remove your aunt's and sister's unkind-
    ness and suspicions, and, I hope, reconcile your father and the whole family
    to our marriage.
FANNY: Heaven grant it! Where is my lord?
LOVE: I have heard him and Canton since dinner singing French songs under the
    great walnut-tree by the parlour door. If you meet with him in the garden,
    you may disclose the whole immediately.
FANNY: Dreadful as the task is, I'll do it. — Anything is better than this continual
    anxiety.

LOVE: By that time the discovery is made, I will appear to second you. — Ha! Here comes my lord. — Now, my dear Fanny, summon up all your spirits, plead our cause powerfully, and be sure of success — (*going*).

FANNY: Ah, don't leave me!

LOVE: Nay, you must let me.

FANNY: Well, since it must be so, I'll obey you, if I have the power. Oh, Lovewell!

LOVE: Consider, our situation is very critical. Tomorrow morning is fixed for your departure, and if we lose this opportunity, we may wish in vain for another. — He approaches — I must retire. — Speak, my dear Fanny, speak, and make us happy! (*Exit.*)

FANNY: (*alone*) Good heaven, what a situation am I in! What shall I do? What shall I say to him? I am all confusion.

(*Enter* LORD OGLEBY *and* CANTON.)

LORD OGLEBY: To see so much beauty so solitary, madam, is a satire upon mankind, and 'tis fortunate that one man has broke in upon your reverie for the credit of our sex. — I say *one*, madam, for poor Canton here, from age and infirmities, stands for nothing.

CANTON: Noting at all, inteed.

FANNY: Your lordship does me great honour. — I had a favour to request, my lord!

LORD OGLEBY: A favour, madam! — To be honoured with your command is an inexpressible favour done to me, madam.

FANNY: If your lordship could indulge me with the honour of a moment's — (*aside*) What is the matter with me?

LORD OGLEBY: The girl's confused — he! — here's something in the wind, faith — I'll have a tête-à-tête with her — (*to* CANTON) Allez vous en!

CANTON: I go — ah, pauvre Mademoiselle! My lor', have pitié upon de poor pigeone!

LORD OGLEBY: I'll knock you down, Cant, if you're impertinent (*smiling*).

CANTON: Den I mus avay. (*Shuffles along.*) — You are mosh please, for all dat. (*Aside, and exit.*)

FANNY: (*aside*) I shall sink with apprehension.

LORD OGLEBY: What a sweet girl! — She's a civilised being, and atones for the barbarism of the rest of the family.

FANNY: My lord! I — (*She curtsies, and blushes.*)

LORD OGLEBY: (*addressing her*) I look upon it, madam, to be one of the luckiest circumstances of my life that I have this moment the honour of receiving your commands, and the satisfaction of confirming with my tongue what my eyes perhaps have but too weakly expressed — that I am literally — the humblest of your servants.

FANNY: I think myself greatly honoured by your lordship's partiality to me; but it distresses me that I am obliged in my present situation to apply to it for protection.

LORD OGLEBY: I am happy in your distress, madam, because it gives me an opportunity to show my zeal. Beauty to me is a religion, in which I was born and bred a bigot, and would die a martyr. — (*aside*) I'm in tolerable spirits, faith!

FANNY: There is not perhaps at this moment a more distressed creature than
myself. Affection, duty, hope, despair, and a thousand different sentiments,
are struggling in my bosom; and even the presence of your lordship, to whom
I have flown for protection, adds to my perplexity.

LORD OGLEBY: Does it, madam? — Venus forbid! — My old fault; the devil's in
me, I think, for perplexing young women (*aside and smiling*). Take courage,
madam! Dear Miss Fanny, explain. — You have a powerful advocate in my
breast, I assure you — my heart, madam — I am attached to you by all the
laws of sympathy and delicacy. — By my honour, I am.

FANNY: Then I will venture to unburthen my mind. — Sir John Melvil, my lord,
by the most misplaced and mistimed declaration of affection for me, has
made me the unhappiest of women.

LORD OGLEBY: How, madam! Has Sir John made his addresses to you?

FANNY: He has, my lord, in the strongest terms. But I hope it is needless to say,
that my duty to my father, love to my sister, and regard to the whole family,
as well as the great respect I entertain for your lordship (*curtsying*), made me
shudder at his addresses.

LORD OGLEBY: Charming girl! — Proceed, my dear Miss Fanny, proceed!

FANNY: In a moment — give me leave, my lord! — But if what I have to disclose
should be received with anger or displeasure —

LORD OGLEBY: Impossible, by all the tender powers! — Speak, I beseech you, or
I shall divine the cause before you utter it.

FANNY: Then, my lord, Sir John's addresses are not only shocking to me in themselves, but are more particularly disagreeable to me at this time, as — as —
(*hesitating*)

LORD OGLEBY: As what, madam?

FANNY: As — pardon my confusion — I am entirely devoted to another.

LORD OGLEBY: (*aside*) If this is not plain, the devil's in it. — But tell me, my dear
Miss Fanny, for I must know; tell me the how, the when, and the where. Tell
me —

> (*Enter* CANTON *hastily.*)

CANTON: My lor', my lor', my lor'! —

LORD OGLEBY: Damn your Swiss impertinence! How durst you interrupt me in
the most critical melting moment that ever love and beauty honoured me with?

CANTON: I demande pardonne, my lor'! Sir John Melvil, my lor', send me to beg
you to do him the honour to speak a little to your lordship.

LORD OGLEBY: I'm not at leisure. — I'm busy. — Get away, you stupid old dog,
you Swiss rascal, or I'll —

CANTON: Fort bien, my lor'. (*Goes out on tiptoe.*)

LORD OGLEBY: By the laws of gallantry, madam, this interruption should be
death; but as no punishment ought to disturb the triumph of the softer
passions, the criminal is pardoned and dismissed. — Let us return, madam, to
the highest luxury of exalted minds — a declaration of love from the lips of
beauty.

FANNY: The entrance of a third person has a little relieved me, but I cannot go
through with it — and yet I must open my heart with a discovery, or it will
break with its burthen.

LORD OGLEBY: (*aside*) What passion in her eyes! I am alarmed to agitation. I presume, madam (and as you have flattered me by making me a party concerned, I hope you'll excuse the presumption), that —

FANNY: Do you excuse my making you a party concerned, my lord, and let me interest your heart in my behalf, as my future happiness or misery in a great measure depend —

LORD OGLEBY: Upon me, madam?

FANNY: Upon you, my lord! (*Sighs.*)

LORD OGLEBY: There's no standing this: I have caught the infection — her tenderness dissolves me. (*Sighs.*)

FANNY: And should you too severely judge of a rash action which passion prompted, and modesty has long concealed —

LORD OGLEBY: (*taking her hand*) Thou amiable creature — command my heart, for it is vanquished. — Speak but thy virtuous wishes, and enjoy them.

FANNY: I cannot, my lord — indeed, I cannot. — Mr Lovewell must tell you my distresses — and when you know them — pity and protect me! — (*Exit, in tears.*)

LORD OGLEBY: (*alone*) How the devil could I bring her to this? It is too much — too much — I can't bear it. — I must give way to this amiable weakness. (*Wipes his eyes.*) My heart overflows with sympathy, and I feel every tenderness I have inspired. (*Stifles the tear.*) How blind have I been to the desolation I have made! — How could I possibly imagine that a little partial attention and tender civilities to this young creature should have gathered to this burst of passion! Can I be a man and withstand it? No — I'll sacrifice the whole sex to her. — But here comes the father, quite apropos. I'll open the matter immediately, settle the business with him and take the sweet girl down to Ogleby House tomorrow morning. — But what the devil! Miss Sterling too! What mischief's in the wind now?

(*Enter* STERLING *and* MISS STERLING.)

STERL: My lord, your servant! I am attending my daughter here upon rather a disagreeable affair. Speak to his lordship, Betsey!

LORD OGLEBY: Your eyes, Miss Sterling — for I always read the eyes of a young lady — betray some little emotion. What are your commands, madam?

MISS STERL: I have but too much cause for my emotion, my lord!

LORD OGLEBY: I cannot commend my kinsman's behaviour, madam. He has behaved like a false knight, I must confess. I have heard of his apostasy. Miss Fanny has informed me of it.

MISS STERL: Miss Fanny's baseness has been the cause of Sir John's inconstancy.

LORD OGLEBY: Nay, now, my dear Miss Sterling, your passion transports you too far. Sir John may have entertained a passion for Miss Fanny, but believe me, my dear Miss Sterling, believe me, Miss Fanny has no passion for Sir John. She has a passion, indeed, a most tender passion. She has opened her whole soul to me, and I know where her affections are placed (*conceitedly*).

MISS STERL: Not upon Mr Lovewell, my lord; for I have great reason to think that her seeming attachment to him is, by his consent, made use of as a blind to cover her designs upon Sir John.

LORD OGLEBY: Lovewell! No, poor lad! She does not think of him (*smiling*).

MISS STERL: Have a care, my lord, that both the families are not made the dupes
of Sir John's artifice and my sister's dissimulation! You don't know her —
indeed, my lord, you don't know her — a base, insinuating, perfidious! — It is
too much — She has been beforehand with me, I perceive. Such unnatural
behaviour to me! — But since I see I can have no redress, I am resolved that
some way or other I will have revenge. (*Exit.*)

STERL: This is foolish work, my lord!

LORD OGLEBY: I have too much sensibility to bear the tears of beauty.

STERL: It is touching indeed, my lord — and very moving for a father.

LORD OGLEBY: To be sure, sir! — You must be distressed beyond measure! —
Wherefore, to divert your too exquisite feelings, suppose we change the subject, and proceed to business.

STERL: With all my heart, my lord!

LORD OGLEBY: You see, Mr Sterling, we can make no union in our families by
the proposed marriage.

STERL: And very sorry I am to see it, my lord.

LORD OGLEBY: Have you set your heart upon being allied to our house, Mr
Sterling?

STERL: 'Tis my only wish, at present, my omnium, as I may call it.

LORD OGLEBY: Your wishes shall be fulfilled.

STERL: Shall they, my lord! — But how — how?

LORD OGLEBY: I'll marry in your family.

STERL: What! My sister Heidelberg?

LORD OGLEBY: You throw me into a cold sweat, Mr Sterling. No, not your sister
— but your daughter.

STERL: My daughter!

LORD OGLEBY: Fanny! — Now the murder's out!

STERL: What *you*, my lord? —

LORD OGLEBY: Yes — I, I, Mr Sterling!

STERL: No, no, my lord — that's too much (*smiling*).

LORD OGLEBY: Too much? — I don't comprehend you.

STERL: What, you, my lord, marry my Fanny! — Bless me, what will the folks say?

LORD OGLEBY: Why, what will they say?

STERL: That you're a bold man, my lord — that's all.

LORD OGLEBY: Mr Sterling, this may be city wit for aught I know. Do you court
my alliance?

STERL: To be sure, my lord.

LORD OGLEBY: Then I'll explain. — My nephew won't marry your eldest daughter
— nor I neither. — Your youngest daughter won't marry him — I will marry
your youngest daughter —

STERL: What! With a younger daughter's fortune, my lord?

LORD OGLEBY: With any fortune, or no fortune at all, sir. Love is the idol of my
heart, and the demon Interest sinks before him. So, sir, as I said before, I will
marry your youngest daughter; your youngest daughter will marry me —

STERL: Who told you so, my lord?

LORD OGLEBY: Her own sweet self, sir.

STERL: Indeed?

LORD OGLEBY: Yes, sir; our affection is mutual; your advantage double and treble — your daughter will be a countess directly — I shall be the happiest of beings — and you'll be father to an earl instead of a baronet.

STERL: But what will my sister say? — And my daughter?

LORD OGLEBY: I'll manage that matter — nay, if they won't consent, I'll run away with your daughter in spite of you.

STERL: Well said, my lord! — Your spirit's good — I wish you had my constitution! — But if you'll venture, I have no objection, if my sister has none.

LORD OGLEBY: I'll answer for your sister, sir. Apropos! The lawyers are in the house — I'll have articles drawn, and the whole affair concluded tomorrow morning.

STERL: Very well: and I'll dispatch Lovewell to London immediately for some fresh papers I shall want, and I shall leave you to manage matters with my sister. You must excuse me, my lord, but I can't help laughing at the match — He! he! he! What will the folks say? (*Exit.*)

LORD OGLEBY: What a fellow am I going to make a father of? — He has no more feeling than the post in his warehouse — But Fanny's virtues tune me to rapture again, and I won't think of the rest of the family.

(*Enter* LOVEWELL *hastily.*)

LOVE: I beg your lordship's pardon, my lord; are you alone, my lord?

LORD OGLEBY: No, my lord, I am not alone! I am in company, the best company.

LOVE: My lord!

LORD OGLEBY: I never was in such exquisite enchanting company since my heart first conceived, or my senses tasted pleasure.

LOVE: Where are they, my lord? (*looking about*)

LORD OGLEBY: In my mind, sir.

LOVE: What company have you there, my lord? (*smiling*)

LORD OGLEBY: My own ideas, sir, which so crowd upon my imagination, and kindle it to such a delirium of ecstasy, that wit, wine, music, poetry, all combined, and each perfection, are but mere mortal shadows of my felicity.

LOVE: I see that your lordship is happy, and I rejoice at it.

LORD OGLEBY: You *shall* rejoice at it, sir; my felicity shall not selfishly be confined, but shall spread its influence to the whole circle of my friends. I need not say, Lovewell, that you shall have your share of it.

LOVE: Shall I, my lord? — Then I understand you — you have heard — Miss Fanny has informed you —

LORD OGLEBY: She has — I have heard, and she shall be happy — 'tis determined.

LOVE: Then I have reached the summit of my wishes. And will your lordship pardon the folly?

LORD OGLEBY: Oh yes. Poor creature, how could she help it? 'Twas unavoidable — fate and necessity.

LORD: It was indeed, my lord. Your kindness distracts me.

LORD OGLEBY: And so it did the poor girl, faith.

LOVE: She trembled to disclose the secret, and declare her affections?

LORD OGLEBY: The world, I believe, will not think her affections ill-placed.

LOVE: (*bowing*) You are too good, my lord. And do you really excuse the rashness of the action?

LORD OGLEBY: From my very soul, Lovewell.

LOVE: Your generosity overpowers me (*bowing*). I was afraid of her meeting with a cold reception.

LORD OGLEBY: More fool you then.

> Who pleads her cause with never-failing beauty,
> Here finds a full redress. (*Strikes his breast.*)

She's a fine girl, Lovewell.

LOVE: Her beauty, my lord, is her least merit. She has an understanding —

LORD OGLEBY: Her choice convinces me of that.

LOVE: (*bowing*) That's your lordship's goodness. Her choice was a disinterested one.

LORD OGLEBY: No — no — not altogether — it began with interest, and ended in passion.

LOVE: Indeed, my lord, if you were acquainted with her goodness of heart, and generosity of mind, as well as you are with the inferior beauties of her face and person —

LORD OGLEBY: I am so perfectly convinced of their existence, and so totally of your mind touching every amiable particular of that sweet girl, that were it not for the cold unfeeling impediments of the law, I would marry her tomorrow morning.

LOVE: My lord!

LORD OGLEBY: I would, by all that's honourable in man, and amiable in woman.

LOVE: Marry her! — Who do you mean, my lord?

LORD OGLEBY: Miss Fanny Sterling, that is — the Countess of Ogleby that shall be.

LOVE: I am astonished.

LORD OGLEBY: Why, could you expect less from me?

LOVE: I did not expect this, my lord.

LOVE OGLEBY: Trade and accounts have destroyed your feeling.

LOVE: No, indeed, my lord. (*Sighs.*)

LORD OGLEBY: The moment that love and pity entered my breast, I was resolved to plunge into matrimony, and shorten the girl's tortures — I never do anything by halves; do I, Lovewell?

LOVE: No, indeed, my lord. (*Sighs.*) What an accident!

LORD OGLEBY: What's the matter, Lovewell? Thou seemest to have lost thy faculties. Why don't you wish me joy, man?

LOVE: Oh, I do, my lord. (*Sighs.*)

LORD OGLEBY: She said that you would explain what she had not power to utter — but I wanted no interpreter for the language of love.

LOVE: But has your lordship considered the consequences of your resolution?

LORD OGLEBY: No, sir; I am above consideration when my desires are kindled.

LOVE: But consider the consequences, my lord, to your nephew, Sir John.

LORD OGLEBY: Sir John has considered no consequences himself, Mr Lovewell.

LOVE: Mr Sterling, my lord, will certainly refuse his daughter to Sir John.

LORD OGLEBY: Sir John has already refused Mr Sterling's daughter.

LOVE: But what will become of Miss Sterling, my lord?

LORD OGLEBY: What's that to you? — You may have her, if you will. — I depend upon Mr Sterling's city-philosophy, to be reconciled to Lord Ogleby's being his son-in-law, instead of Sir John Melvil, Baronet. Don't you think that your master may be brought to that, without having recourse to his calculations? Eh, Lovewell!

LOVE: But, my lord, that is not the question.

LORD OGLEBY: Whatever is the question, I'll tell you my answer. — I am in love with a fine girl, whom I resolve to marry.

> (*Enter* SIR JOHN MELVIL.)

What news with you, Sir John? — You look all hurry and impatience — like a messenger after a battle.

SIR JOHN: After a battle, indeed, my lord. — I have this day had a severe engagement, and wanting your lordship as an auxiliary, I have at last mustered up resolution to declare what my duty to you and to myself have demanded from me some time.

LORD OGLEBY: To the business then, and be as concise as possible; for I am upon the wing — eh, Lovewell? (*He smiles, and* LOVEWELL *bows.*)

SIR JOHN: I find 'tis in vain, my lord, to struggle against the force of inclination.

LORD OGLEBY: Very true, nephew — I am your witness, and will second the motion — shan't I, Lovewell? (*Smiles, and* LOVEWELL *bows.*)

SIR JOHN: Your lordship's generosity encourages me to tell you — that I cannot marry Miss Sterling.

LORD OGLEBY: I am not at all surprised at it — she's a bitter potion, that's the truth of it; but as you were to swallow it, and not I, it was your business, and not mine. — Anything more?

SIR JOHN: But this, my lord — that I may be permitted to make my addresses to the other sister.

LORD OGLEBY: Oh yes — by all means — have you any hopes there, nephew? — Do you think he'll succeed, Lovewell? (*Smiles, and winks at* LOVEWELL.)

LOVE: (*gravely*) I think not, my lord.

LORD OGLEBY: I think so too, but let the fool try.

SIR JOHN: Will your lordship favour me with your good offices to remove the chief obstacle to the match, the repugnance of Mrs Heidelberg?

LORD OGLEBY: Mrs Heidelberg! — Had you not better begin with the young lady first? It will save you a great deal of trouble; won't it, Lovewell? (*Smiles.*) But do what you please, it will be the same thing to me — won't it, Lovewell? (*conceitedly*) — Why don't you laugh at him?

LOVE: I do, my lord. (*Forces a smile.*)

SIR JOHN: And your lordship will endeavour to prevail on Mrs Heidelberg to consent to my marriage with Miss Fanny?

LORD OGLEBY: I'll go and speak to Mrs Heidelberg about the adorable Fanny as soon as possible.

SIR JOHN: Your generosity transports me.

LORD OGLEBY: (*aside*) Poor fellow, what a dupe! He little thinks who's in possession of the town.

SIR JOHN. And your lordship is not offended at this seeming inconstancy?

LORD OGLEBY: Not in the least. Miss Fanny's charms will even excuse infidelity — I look upon women as the *ferae naturae*, — lawful game — and every man

who is qualified, has a natural right to pursue them; Lovewell as well as you,
and I as well as either of you. – Every man shall do his best, without offence
to any – what say you, kinsmen?

SIR JOHN: You have made me happy, my lord.

LOVE: And me, I assure you, my lord.

LORD OGLEBY: And I am superlatively so. – *Allons donc* – to horse and away,
boys! – You to your affairs, and I to mine – (*Sings.*) *suivons l'amour!*
(*Exeunt severally.*)

ACT V

SCENE 1.   *Fanny's apartment. Enter* LOVEWELL *and* FANNY, *followed by*
BETTY.

FANNY: Why did you come so soon, Mr Lovewell? The family is not yet in bed,
and Betty certainly heard somebody listening near the chamber-door.

BETTY: My mistress is right, sir! Evil spirits are abroad; and I am sure you are both
too good not to expect mischief from them.

LOVE: But who can be so curious, or so wicked?

BETTY: I think we have wickedness, and curiosity enough in this family, sir, to
expect the worst.

FANNY: I do expect the worst. – Prithee, Betty, return to the outward door, and
listen if you hear anybody in the gallery; and let us know directly.

BETTY: I warrant you, madam – the Lord bless you both! (*Exit.*)

FANNY: What did my father want with you this evening?

LOVE: He gave me the key of his closet, with orders to bring from London some
papers relating to Lord Ogleby.

FANNY: And why did you not obey him?

LOVE: Because I am certain that his lordship has opened his heart to him about
you, and those papers are wanted merely on that account – but as we shall
discover all tomorrow, there will be no occasion for them, and it would be
idle in me to go.

FANNY: Hark! – hark! Bless me, how I tremble! – I feel the terrors of guilt –
indeed, Mr Lovewell, this is too much for me.

LOVE: And for me too, my sweet Fanny. Your apprehensions make a coward of
me. – But what can alarm you? Your aunt and sister are in their chambers,
and you have nothing to fear from the rest of the family.

FANNY: I fear everybody, and everything, and every moment. – My mind is in
continual agitation and dread; – indeed, Mr Lovewell, this situation may
have very unhappy consequences. (*Weeps.*)

LOVE: But it shan't – I would rather tell our story this moment to all the house,
and run the risk of maintaining you by the hardest labour, than suffer you to
remain in this dangerous perplexity. – What! Shall I sacrifice all my best
hopes and affections, in your dear health and safety, for the mean, and in
such a case, the meanest consideration – of our fortune! Were we to be
abandoned by all our relations, we have that in our hearts and minds, will
weigh against the most affluent circumstances. – I should not have proposed
the secrecy of our marriage but for your sake; and with hopes that the most

generous sacrifice you have made to love and me, might be less injurious to you by waiting a lucky moment of reconciliation.

FANNY: Hush! hush! For heaven's sake, my dear Lovewell, don't be so warm! — Your generosity gets the better of your prudence; you will be heard, and we shall be discovered. — I am satisfied, indeed I am. — Excuse this weakness, this delicacy — this what you will. — My mind's at peace — indeed it is. — Think no more of it, if you love me!

LOVE: That one word has charmed me, as it always does, to the most implicit obedience; it would be the worst of ingratitude in me to distress you a moment. (*Kisses her.*)

>   (*Re-enter* BETTY.)

BETTY: (*in a low voice*) I'm sorry to disturb you.

FANNY: Ha! What's the matter?

LOVE: Have you heard anybody?

BETTY: Yes, yes, I have, and they have heard *you* too, or I am mistaken. If they had *seen* you too, we should have been in a fine quandary.

FANNY: Prithee don't prate now, Betty!

LOVE: What did you hear?

BETTY: I was preparing myself, as usual, to take me a little nap.

LOVE: A nap!

BETTY: Yes, sir, a nap; for I watch much better so than wide awake; and when I had wrapped this handkerchief round my head, for fear of the earache, from the keyhole I thought I heard a kind of a sort of a buzzing, which I first took for a gnat, and shook my head two or three times, and went so with my hand —

FANNY: Well — well — and so —

BETTY: And so, madam, when I heard Mr Lovewell a little loud, I heard the buzzing louder too — and pulling off my handkerchief softly — I could hear this sort of noise. (*Makes an indistinct noise like speaking.*)

FANNY: Well, and what did they say?

BETTY: Oh! I could not understand a word of what was said.

LOVE: The outward door is locked?

BETTY: Yes; and I bolted it too, for fear of the worst.

FANNY: Why did you? They must have heard you, if they were near.

BETTY: And I did it on purpose, madam, and coughed a little too, that they might not hear Mr Lovewell's voice. When I was silent, they were silent, and so I came to tell you.

FANNY: What shall we do?

LOVE: Fear nothing; we know the worst; it will only bring on our catastrophe a little too soon. But Betty might fancy this noise — she's in the conspiracy, and can make a man of a mouse at any time.

BETTY: I can distinguish a man from a mouse, as well as my betters. I am sorry you think so ill of me, sir.

FANNY: He compliments you: don't be a fool! — (*to* LOVEWELL) Now you have set her tongue a-running, she'll mutter for an hour. I'll go and hearken myself. (*Exit.*)

BETTY: I'll turn my back upon no girl, for sincerity and service (*half aside, and muttering*).

LOVE: Thou art the first in the world for both; and I will reward you soon, Betty, for one and the other.

BETTY: I'm not marcenary neither — I can live on a little, with a good carreter.
        (*Re-enter* FANNY.)

FANNY: All seems quiet. — Suppose, my dear, you go to your own room. — I shall be much easier then — and tomorrow we will be prepared for the discovery.

BETTY: You may discover, if you please; but for my part, I shall still be secret (*half aside, and muttering*).

LOVE: Should I leave you now, if they still are upon the watch, we shall lose the advantage of our delay. — Besides, we should consult upon tomorrow's business. — Let Betty go to her own room, and lock the outward door after her; we can fasten this; and when she thinks all safe, she may return and let me out as usual.

BETTY: Shall I, madam?

FANNY: Do let me have my way tonight, and you shall command me ever after. — I would not have you surprised here for the world. — Pray leave me! I shall be quite myself again, if you will oblige me.

LOVE: I live only to oblige you, my sweet Fanny! I'll be gone this moment (*going*).

FANNY: Let us listen first at the door, that you may not be intercepted. — Betty shall go first, and if they lay hold of her —

BETTY: They'll have the wrong sow by the ear, I can tell them that (*going hastily*).

FANNY: Softly — softly — Betty! Don't venture out, if you hear a noise. — Softly, I beg of you! — See, Mr Lovewell, the effects of indiscretion!

LOVE: But love, Fanny, makes amends for all.
        (*Exeunt all softly.*)

SCENE 2.   *A gallery, which leads to several bedchambers. Enter* MISS STERLING, *leading* MRS HEIDELBERG *in a night-cap.*

MISS STERL: This way, dear madam, and then I'll tell you all.

MRS HEIDEL: Nay, but, niece — consider a little — don't drag me out in this figur. — Let me put on my fly-cap! — If any of my lord's fammaly, or the counsellors at law, should be stirring, I should be perdigus disconcarted.

MISS STERL: But, my dear madam, a moment is an age, in my situation. I am sure my sister has been plotting my disgrace and ruin in that chamber. — Oh she's all craft and wickedness!

MRS HEIDEL: Well, but softly, Betsey! — You are all in emotion — your mind is too much flustrated — you can neither eat nor drink, nor take your natural rest. — Compose yourself, child; for if we are not as warysome as they are wicked, we shall disgrace ourselves and the whole fammaly.

MISS STERL: We are disgraced already, madam — Sir John Melvil has forsaken me; my lord cares for nobody but himself; or, if for anybody, it is my sister; my father, for the sake of a better bargain, would marry me to a 'Change-broker; so that if you, madam, don't continue my friend — if you forsake me — if I am to lose my best hopes and consolation — in your tenderness — and

---

fly-cap: headdress worn by elderly ladies, with raised-up side flaps.

affections – I had better – at once – give up the matter – and let my sister enjoy – the fruits of her treachery – trample with scorn upon the rights of her elder sister, the will of the best of aunts, and the weakness of a too interested father. (*She pretends to be bursting into tears all this speech.*)

MRS HEIDEL: Don't, Betsey – keep up your spurrit – I hate whimpering – I am your friend. – Depend upon me in every partickler – but be composed, and tell me what new mischief you have discovered.

MISS STERL: I had no desire to sleep, and would not undress myself, knowing that my Machiavel sister would not rest till she had broke my heart – I was so uneasy that I could not stay in my room, but when I thought that all the house was quiet, I sent my maid to discover what was going forward; she immediately came back and told me that they were in high consultation; that she had heard only, for it was in the dark, my sister's maid conduct Sir John Melvil to her mistress, and then lock the door.

MRS HEIDEL: And how did you conduct yourself in this dalimma?

MISS STERL: I returned with her, and could hear a man's voice, though nothing that they said distinctly; and you may depend upon it, that Sir John is now in that room, that they have settled the matter, and will run away together before morning, if we don't prevent them.

MRS HEIDEL: Why the brazen slut! Has she got her sister's husband (that is to be) locked up in her chamber! at night too? – I tremble at the thoughts!

MISS STERL: Hush, madam! I hear something.

MRS HEIDEL: You frighten me. – Let me put on my fly-cap – I would not be seen in this figur for the world.

MISS STERL: 'Tis dark, madam, you can't be seen.

MRS HEIDEL: I protest there's a candle coming, and a man too.

MISS STERL: Nothing but servants; let us retire a moment! (*They retire.*)
   (*Enter* BRUSH, *half drunk, laying hold of the* CHAMBERMAID, *who has a candle in her hand.*)

CHAMBER: Be quiet, Mr Brush: I shall drop down with terror!

BRUSH: But, my sweet and most amiable Chambermaid, if you have no love, you may hearken to a little reason; that cannot possibly do your virtue any harm.

CHAMBER: But you will do me harm, Mr Brush, and a great deal of harm too. – Pray let me go – I am ruined if they hear you – I tremble like an asp.

BRUSH: But they shan't hear us – and if you have a mind to be ruined, it shall be the making of your fortune, you little slut, you! – Therefore I say it again, if you have no love – hear a little reason!

CHAMBER: I wonder at your impurence, Mr Brush, to use me in this manner; this is not the way to keep me company, I assure you. – You are a town rake I see, and now you are a little in liquor, you fear nothing.

BRUSH: Nothing, by heavens, but your frowns, most amiable Chambermaid; I am a little electrified, that's the truth on't; I am not used to drink port, and your master's is so heady, that a pint of it oversets a claret-drinker.

CHAMBER: Don't be rude! Bless me! – I shall be ruined – what will become of me?

---

asp: she means aspen.

BRUSH: I'll take care of you, by all that's honourable.

CHAMBER: You are a base man to use me so — I'll cry out, if you don't let me go. — That is Miss Sterling's chamber, that Miss Fanny's and that Madam Heidelberg's (*pointing*).

BRUSH: And that my Lord Ogleby's, and that my Lady What-d'ye-call-'em's: I don't mind such folks when I'm sober, much less when I am whimsical — rather above that too.

CHAMBER: More shame for you, Mr Brush! — You terrify me. — You have no modesty.

BRUSH: Oh but I have, my sweet spider-brusher! — For instance, I reverence Miss Fanny. — She's a most delicious morsel and fit for a prince. — With all my horrors of matrimony, I could marry her myself; but for her sister —

MISS STERL: There, there, madam, all in a story!

CHAMBER: Bless me, Mr Brush! — I heard something!

BRUSH: Rats, I suppose, that are gnawing the old timbers of this execrable old dungeon. — If it was mine, I would pull it down, and fill your fine canal up with the rubbish; and then I should get rid of two damned things at once.

CHAMBER: Law! law! How you blaspheme! — We shall have the house upon our heads for it.

BRUSH: No, no, it will last our time — but as I was saying, the eldest sister — Miss Jezabel —

CHAMBER: Is a fine young lady for all your evil tongue.

BRUSH: No — we have smoked her already; and unless she marries our old Swiss, she can have none of us. — No, no, she won't do. — We are a little too nice.

CHAMBER: You're a monstrous rake, Mr Brush, and don't care what you say.

BRUSH: Why, for that matter, my dear, I am a little inclined to mischief; and if you won't have pity upon me, I will break open that door and ravish Mrs Heidelberg.

MRS HEIDEL: (*coming forward*) There's no bearing this — you profligate monster!

CHAMBER: Ha! I am undone!

BRUSH: Zounds! Here she is, by all that's monstrous. (*Runs off.*)

MISS STERL: A fine discourse you have had with that fellow!

MRS HEIDEL: And a fine time of night it is to be here with that drunken monster.

MISS STERL: What have you to say for yourself?

CHAMBER: I can say nothing — I am so frightened, and so ashamed — but indeed I am vartuous — I am vartuous indeed.

MRS HEIDEL: Well, well — don't tremble so; but tell us what you know of this horrable plot here.

MISS STERL: We'll forgive you, if you'll discover all.

CHAMBER: Why, madam — don't let me betray my fellow-servants — I shan't sleep in my bed, if I do.

MRS HEIDEL: Then you shall sleep somewhere else tomorrow night.

CHAMBER: Oh dear! — What shall I do?

MRS HEIDEL: Tell us this moment — or I'll turn you out of doors directly.

CHAMBER: Why our butler has been treating us below in his pantry — Mr Brush forced us to make a kind of a holiday night of it.

MISS STERL: Holiday! For what?

CHAMBER: Nay, I only made one.

MISS STERL: Well, well; but upon what account?

CHAMBER: Because as how, madam, there was a change in the family they said — that his honour, Sir John — was to marry Miss Fanny instead of your lady-ship.

MISS STERL: And so you made a holiday for that. — Very fine!

CHAMBER: I did not make it, ma'am.

MRS HEIDEL: But do you know nothing of Sir John's being to run away with Miss Fanny tonight?

CHAMBER: No, indeed, ma'am!

MISS STERL: Nor of his being now locked up in my sister's chamber?

CHAMBER: No, as I hope for marcy, ma'am.

MRS HEIDEL: Well, I'll put an end to all this directly. — Do you run to my brother Sterling —

CHAMBER: Now, ma'am? — 'Tis very late, ma'am —

MRS HEIDEL: I don't care how late it is. Tell him there are thieves in the house — that the house is o' fire — tell him to come here immediately — go, I say!

CHAMBER: I will, I will, though I'm frightened out of my wits. (*Exit.*)

MRS HEIDEL: Do you watch here, my dear; and I'll put myself in order, to face them. We'll plot 'em, and counter-plot 'em too. (*Exit into her chamber.*)

MISS STERL: I have as much pleasure in this revenge, as in being made a countess! — Ha! They are unlocking the door. — Now for it! (*Retires.*)

> (FANNY*'s door is unlocked and* BETTY *comes out with a candle.*
> MISS STERLING *approaches her.*)

BETTY: (*calling within*) Sir, sir! — Now's your time — all's clear. (*seeing* MISS STERLING) Stay, stay — not yet — we are watched.

MISS STERL: And so you are, Madam Betty!

> (MISS STERLING *lays hold of her, while* BETTY *locks the door,*
> *and puts the key in her pocket.*)

BETTY: (*turning round*) What's the matter, madam?

MISS STERL: Nay, that you shall tell my father and aunt, madam.

BETTY: I am no tell-tale, madam, and no thief; they'll get nothing from me.

MISS STERL: You have a great deal of courage, Betty; and considering the secrets you have to keep, you have occasion for it.

BETTY: My mistress shall never repent her good opinion of me, ma'am.

> (*Enter* STERLING.)

STERL: What is all this? What's the matter? Why am I disturbed in this manner?

MISS STERL: This creature, and my distresses, sir, will explain the matter.

> (*Re-enter* MRS HEIDELBERG, *with another headdress.*)

MRS HEIDEL: Now I'm prepared for the rancounter. — Well, brother, have you heard of this scene of wickedness?

STERL: Not I — but what is it? Speak! I was got into my little closet — all the lawyers were in bed, and I had almost lost my senses in the confusion of Lord Ogleby's mortgages, when I was alarmed with a foolish girl, who could hardly speak; and whether it's fire, or thieves, or murder, or a rape, I am quite in the dark.

MRS HEIDEL: No, no, there's no rape, brother! — All parties are willing, I believe.

MISS STERL: Who's in that chamber? (*detaining* BETTY, *who seemed to be stealing away*)

BETTY: My mistress.

MISS STERL: And who is with your mistress?

BETTY: Why, who should there be?

MISS STERL: Open the door then, and let us see!

BETTY: The door is open, madam. (MISS STERLING *goes to the door.*) I'll sooner die than peach! (*Exit hastily.*)

MISS STERL: The door's locked; and she has got the key in her pocket.

MRS HEIDEL: There's impudence, brother! Piping hot from your daughter Fanny's school!

STERL: But, zounds! What is all this about? You tell me of a sum total, and you don't produce the particulars.

MRS HEIDEL: Sir John Melvil is locked up in your daughter's bedchamber. – There is the particular!

STERL: The devil he is? – That's bad!

MISS STERL: And he has been there some time too.

STERL: Ditto!

MRS HEIDEL: Ditto! Worse and worse, I say. I'll raise the house, and expose him to my lord and the whole family.

STERL: By no means! We shall expose ourselves, sister! – The best way is to insure privately – let me alone! – I'll make him marry her tomorrow morning.

MISS STERL: Make him marry her! This is beyond all patience! – You have thrown away all your affection; and I shall do as much by my obedience: unnatural fathers make unnatural children. – My revenge is in my own power, and I'll indulge it. – Had they made their escape, I should have been exposed to the derision of the world: – but the deriders shall be derided; and so: Help! help, there! Thieves! thieves!

MRS HEIDEL: Tit for tat, Betsey! – You are right, my girl.

STERL: Zounds! You'll spoil all – you'll raise the whole family. – The devil's in the girl.

MRS HEIDEL: No, no; the devil's in *you*, brother. I am ashamed of your principles. – What! Would you connive at your daughter's being locked up with her sister's husband? Help! thieves! thieves! I say. (*Cries out.*)

STERL: Sister, I beg you! – Daughter, I command you. – If you have no regard for me, consider yourselves! – We shall lose this opportunity of ennobling our blood, and getting above twenty per cent for our money.

MISS STERL: What, by my disgrace and my sister's triumph! I have a spirit above such mean considerations; and to show you that it is not a low-bred, vulgar 'Change-alley spirit – Help! help! thieves! thieves! thieves! I say.

STERL: Ay, ay, you may save your lungs – the house is in an uproar! – Women at best have no discretion; but in a passion they'll fire a house, or burn themselves in it, rather than not be revenged.

(*Enter* CANTON, *in a night-gown and slippers.*)

CANTON: Eh, diable! Vat is de raison of dis great noise, dis tintamarre?

STERL: Ask those ladies, sir; 'tis of their making.

LORD OGLEBY: (*Calls within.*) Brush! — Canton! Where are you? — What's the matter? (*Rings a bell.*) Where are you?

STERL: 'Tis my lord calls, Mr Canton.

CANTON: I com, mi lor'! (*Exit,* LORD OGLEBY *still rings.*)

SERJEANT FLOWER: (*Calls within.*) A light! A light here! — Where are the servants? Bring a light for me and my brothers.

STERL: Lights here! Lights for the gentlemen! (*Exit.*)

MRS HEIDEL: My brother feels, I see — your sister's turn will come next.

MISS STERL: Ay, ay, let it go round, madam! It is the only comfort I have left.

(*Re-enter* STERLING, *with lights, before* SERJEANT FLOWER, *with one boot and a slipper, and* TRAVERSE.)

STERL: This way, sir! This way, gentlemen!

FLOWER: Well, but, Mr Sterling, no danger I hope. — Have they made a burglarious entry? — Are you prepared to repulse them? — I am very much alarmed about thieves at circuit-time. — They would be particularly severe with us gentlemen of the Bar.

TRAVERSE: No danger, Mr Sterling? — No trespass, I hope?

STERL: None, gentlemen, but of those ladies' making.

MRS HEIDEL: You'll be ashamed to know, gentlemen, that all your labours and studies about this young lady are thrown away — Sir John Melvil is at this moment locked up with this lady's younger sister.

FLOWER: The thing is a little extraordinary, to be sure — but, why were we to be frightened out of our beds for this? Could not we have tried this cause tomorrow morning?

MISS STERL: But, sir, by tomorrow morning, perhaps, even your assistance would not have been of any service. — The birds now in that cage would have flown away.

(*Enter* LORD OGLEBY *in his robe-de-chambre, night-cap, etc. — leaning on* CANTON.)

LORD OGLEBY: I had rather lose a limb than my night's rest. — What's the matter with you all?

STERL: Ay, ay, 'tis all over! — Here's my lord too.

LORD OGLEBY: What is all this shrieking and screaming? — Where's my angelic Fanny? She's safe, I hope!

MRS HEIDEL: Your angelic Fanny, my lord, is locked up with your angelic nephew in that chamber.

LORD OGLEBY: My nephew! Then will I be excommunicated.

MRS HEIDEL: Your nephew, my lord, has been plotting to run away with the younger sister; and the younger sister has been plotting to run away with your nephew; and if we had not watched them and called up the fammaly, they had been upon the scamper to Scotland by this time.

LORD OGLEBY: Look'ee, ladies! — I know that Sir John has conceived a violent passion for Miss Fanny; and I know too that Miss Fanny has conceived a violent passion for another person; and I am so well convinced of the rectitude of her affections, that I will support them with my fortune, my honour, and my life. — Eh, shan't I, Mr Sterling? (*smiling*) What say you? —

STERL: (*sulkily*) To be sure, my lord. — (*aside*) These bawling women have been
    the ruin of everything.

LORD OGLEBY: But come, I'll end this business in a trice — if you, ladies, will
    compose yourselves, and Mr Sterling will ensure Miss Fanny from violence,
    I will engage to draw her from her pillow with a whisper through the key-
    hole.

MRS HEIDEL: The horrid creatures! — I say, my lord, break the door open.

LORD OGLEBY: Let me beg of your delicacy not to be too precipitate! — Now to
    our experiment! (*advancing towards the door*)

MISS STERL: Now, what will they do? — My heart will beat through my bosom.
        (*Enter* BETTY, *with the key.*)

BETTY: There's no occasion for breaking open doors, my lord; we have done
    nothing that we ought to be ashamed of, and my mistress shall face her
    enemies (*going to unlock the door*).

MRS HEIDEL: There's impudence.

LORD OGLEBY: The mystery thickens. Lady of the Bedchamber! (*to* BETTY)
    Open the door, and entreat Sir John Melvil (for these ladies will have it that
    he is there) to appear and answer to high crimes and misdemeanours. — Call
    Sir John Melvil into the court!
        (*Enter* SIR JOHN MELVIL, *on the other side.*)

SIR JOHN: I am here, my lord.

MRS HEIDEL: Heyday!

MISS STERL: Astonishment!

SIR JOHN: What is all this alarm and confusion? There is nothing but hurry in the
    house; what is the reason of it?

LORD OGLEBY: Because you have been in that chamber; — *have* been! Nay
    you *are* there at this moment, as these ladies have protested, so don't deny
    it —

TRAVERSE: This is the clearest *alibi* I ever knew, Mr Serjeant.

FLOWER: *Luce clarius*.

LORD OGLEBY: Upon my word, ladies, if you have often these frolics, it would
    be really entertaining to pass a whole summer with you. But come (*to*
    BETTY), open the door, and entreat your amiable mistress to come forth,
    and dispel all our doubts with her smiles.

BETTY: (*opening the door*) Madam, you are wanted in this room (*pertly*).
        (*Enter* FANNY, *in great confusion.*)

MISS STERL: You see she's ready dressed — and what confusion she's in?

MRS HEIDEL: Ready to pack off, bag and baggage! — Her guilt confounds her!

FLOWER: Silence in the court, ladies!

FANNY: I *am* confounded, indeed, madam!

LORD OGLEBY: Don't droop, my beauteous lily! But with your own peculiar
    modesty declare your state of mind. — Pour conviction into their ears, and
    raptures into mine (*smiling*).

FANNY: I am at this moment the most unhappy — most distressed — the tumult is
    too much for my heart — and I want the power to reveal a secret, which to
    conceal has been the misfortune and misery of my — my — (*Faints away.*)

LORD OGLEBY: She faints! Help, help! for the fairest
and best of women.

BETTY: (*running to her*) Oh my dear mistress! — help,
help, there! —

SIR JOHN: Ha! Let me fly to her assistance.

(speaking all at once)

        (LOVEWELL *rushes out from the chamber.*)

LOVE: My Fanny in danger! I can contain no longer. — Prudence were now a crime;
all other cares are lost in this! — Speak, speak to me, my dearest Fanny! —
Let me but hear thy voice, open your eyes, and bless me with the smallest
sign of life! (*During this speech they are all in amazement.*)

MISS STERL: Lovewell! — I am easy —

MRS HEIDEL: I am thunderstruck!

LORD OGLEBY: I am petrified!

SIR JOHN: And I undone!

FANNY: (*recovering*) Oh Lovewell! — Even supported by thee, I dare not look my
father nor his lordship in the face.

STERL: What now! Did not I send you to London, sir?

LORD OGLEBY: Eh! — What! — How's this? — By what right and title have you
been half the night in that lady's bedchamber?

LOVE: By that right that makes me the happiest of men; and by a title which I
would not forgo, for any the best of kings could give me.

BETTY: I could cry my eyes out to hear his magnimity.

LORD OGLEBY: I am annihilated!

STERL: I have been choked with rage and wonder; but now I can speak. — Zounds,
what have you to say to me? — Lovewell, you are a villain. — You have broke
your word with me.

FANNY: Indeed, sir, he has not. — You forbade him to think of me, when it was
out of his power to obey you; we have been married these four months.

STERL: And he shan't stay in my house four hours. What baseness and treachery!
As for you, you shall repent this step as long as you live, madam.

FANNY: Indeed, sir, it is impossible to conceive the tortures I have already endured
in consequence of my disobedience. My heart has continually upbraided me
for it; and though I was too weak to struggle with affection, I feel that I must
be miserable for ever without your forgiveness.

STERL: Lovewell, you shall leave my house directly; — (*to* FANNY) and you shall
follow him, madam.

LORD OGLEBY: And if they do, I will receive them into mine. Look ye, Mr
Sterling, there have been some mistakes, which we had all better forget for
our own sakes; and the best way to forget them is to forgive the cause of
them; which I do from my soul. — Poor girl! I swore to support her affection
with my life and fortune — 'tis a debt of honour, and must be paid; — you
swore as much too, Mr Sterling; but your laws in the city will excuse you, I
suppose; for you never strike a balance without errors excepted.

STERL: I am a father, my lord; but for the sake of all other fathers, I think I
ought not to forgive her, for fear of encouraging other silly girls like herself
to throw themselves away without the consent of their parents.

LOVE: I hope there will be no danger of that, sir. Young ladies with minds like my

Fanny's would startle at the very shadow of vice; and when they know to what uneasiness only an indiscretion has exposed her, her example, instead of encouraging, will rather serve to deter them.

MRS HEIDEL: Indiscretion, quoth a! A mighty pretty delicat word to express disobedience!

LORD OGLEBY: For my part, I indulge my own passions too much to tyrannise over those of other people. Poor souls, I pity them. And you must forgive them too. Come, come, melt a little of your flint, Mr Sterling!

STERL: Why, why — as to that, my lord — to be sure he is a relation of yours, my lord. — What say you, sister Heidelberg?

MRS HEIDEL: The girl's ruined, and I forgive her.

STERL: Well — so do I then. — Nay, no thanks. (*to* LOVEWELL *and* FANNY, *who seem preparing to speak*) There's an end of the matter.

LORD OGLEBY: But, Lovewell, what makes you dumb all this while?

LOVE: Your kindness, my lord — I can scarce believe my own senses — they are all in a tumult of fear, joy, love, expectation, and gratitude; I ever was, and am now more bound in duty to your lordship. For you, Mr Sterling, if every moment of my life, spent gratefully in your service, will in some measure compensate the want of fortune, you perhaps will not repent your goodness to me. And you, ladies, I flatter myself, will not for the future suspect me of artifice and intrigue — I shall be happy to oblige and serve you. — As for you, Sir John —

SIR JOHN: No apologies to me, Lovewell. I do not deserve any. All I have to offer in excuse for what has happened, is my total ignorance of your situation. Had you dealt a little more openly with me, you would have saved me, and yourself, and that lady (who I hope will pardon my behaviour) a great deal of uneasiness. Give me leave, however, to assure you, that light and capricious as I may have appeared, now my infatuation is over, I have sensibility enough to be ashamed of the part I have acted, and honour enough to rejoice at your happiness.

LOVE: And now, my dearest Fanny, though we are seemingly the happiest of beings, yet all our joys will be damped, if his lordship's generosity and Mr Sterling's forgiveness should not be succeeded by the indulgence, approbation, and consent of these our best benefactors (*to the audience*).

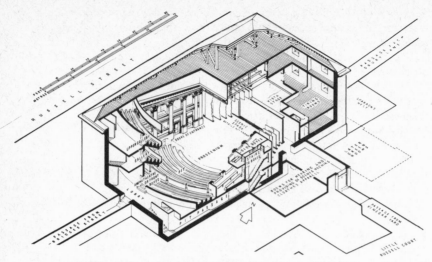

5a. Wren's Drury Lane. Isometric reconstruction by Richard Leacroft from *The Development of the English Playhouse*

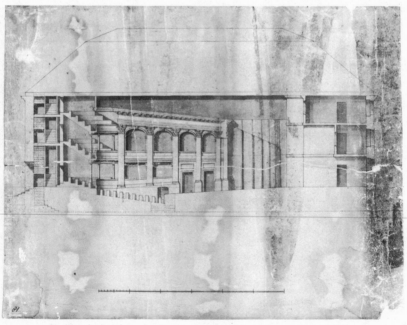

5b. Wren's drawing of a theatre, presumed to be Drury Lane, 1674

THE IRISH WIDOW

by David Garrick

First performed at Drury Lane on 23 October 1772,
with the following cast:

SIR PATRICK O'NEALE	Mr Moody
WHITTLE	Mr Parsons
NEPHEW	Mr Cautherley
BATES	Mr Baddeley
KECKSY	Mr Dodd
THOMAS	Mr Weston
FOOTMAN	Mr Griffiths
WIDOW BRADY	Mrs Barry

(*Not included in printed cast list:*
POMPEY, black boy attending Widow Brady
SERVANT to Whittle)

ACT I

SCENE 1.   *Whittle's house. Enter* BATES *and* SERVANT.

BATES: Is he gone out? His card tells me to come directly. I did but lock up some papers, take my hat and cane, and away I hurried.

SERVANT: My master desires you will sit down; he will return immediately. He had some business with his lawyer, and went out in great haste, leaving the message I have delivered. Here is my young master. (*Exit.*)

                    (*Enter* NEPHEW.)

BATES: What, lively Billy! — Hold, I beg your pardon — melancholy William, I think! — Here's fine revolution! I hear your uncle, who was last month all gravity, and you all mirth, have changed characters; he is now all spirit, and you are in the dumps, young man.

NEPHEW: And for the same reason. This journey to Scarborough will unfold the riddle.

BATES: Come, come, in plain English, and before your uncle comes, explain the matter.

NEPHEW: In the first place, I am undone.

BATES: In love, I know. I hope your uncle is not undone too! That would be the devil!

NEPHEW: He has taken possession of him in every sense. In short, he came to Scarborough to see the lady I had fallen in love with —

BATES: And fell in love himself?

NEPHEW: Yes, and with the same lady.

BATES: That is the devil indeed!

NEPHEW: Oh, Mr Bates, when I thought my happiness complete, and wanted only my uncle's consent to give me the independence he so often has promised me, he came to Scarborough for that purpose, and wished me joy of my choice; but in less than a week his approbation turned into a passion for her; he now hates the sight of me, and is resolved with the consent of the father to make her his wife directly.

BATES: So he keeps you out of your fortune, won't give his consent, which his brother's foolish will requires, and he would marry himself the same woman, because right, title, conscience, nature, justice, and every law, divine and human, are against it.

NEPHEW: Thus he tricks me at once both of wife and fortune, without the least want of either.

BATES: Well said, friend Whittle! But it can't be, it shan't be, and it must not be. This is murder and robbery in the strongest sense, and he shan't be hanged in chains to be laughed at by the whole town, if I can help it.

NEPHEW: I am distracted, the widow is distressed, and we shall both run mad.

BATES: A widow too! Gad a mercy, three score and five!

NEPHEW: But such a widow! She is now in town with her father, who wants to get her off his hands; 'tis equal to him who has her, so she is provided for. — I hear somebody coming. — I must away to her lodgings, where she waits for me to execute a scheme directly for our delivery.

BATES: What is her name, Billy?

NEPHEW: Brady.

BATES: Brady! Is not she daughter to Sir Patrick O'Neale?

NEPHEW: The same. She was sacrificed to the most senseless, drunken profligate in the whole country. He lived to run out his fortune, and the only advantage she got from the union was he broke that and his neck, before he had broke her heart.

BATES: The affair of marriage is in this country put upon the easiest footing; there is neither love or hate in the matter; necessity brings them together; they are united at first for their mutual convenience, and separated ever after for their particular pleasures. O rare matrimony! Where does she lodge?

NEPHEW: In Pall Mall, near the Hotel.

BATES: I'll call in my way and assist at the consultation. I am for a bold stroke, if gentle methods should fail.

NEPHEW: We have a plan, and a spirited one, if my sweet widow is able to go through it. Pray let us have your friendly assistance. Ours is the cause of love and reason.

BATES: Get you gone with your love and reason; they seldom pull together nowadays. I'll give your uncle a dose first, and then I'll meet you at the widow's. What says your uncle's privy counsellor, Mr Thomas, to this?

NEPHEW: He is greatly our friend, and will enter sincerely into our service. He is honest, sensible, ignorant and particular — a kind of half coxcomb, with a thorough good heart. But he's here.

BATES: Do you go about your business, and leave the rest to me. (*Exit* NEPHEW. *Enter* THOMAS.) Mr Thomas, I am glad to see you; upon my word, you look charmingly. You wear well, Mr Thomas.

THOMAS: Which is a wonder, considering how the times go, Mr Bates. They'll wear and tear me too, if I don't take care of myself. My old master has taken the nearest way to wear himself out, and all that belong to him.

BATES: Why, surely this strange tale about town is not true, that the old gentleman is fallen in love?

THOMAS: Ten times worse than that!

BATES: The devil!

THOMAS: And his horns! — going to be married! —

BATES: Not if I can help it.

THOMAS: You never saw such an altered man in your born days! He's grown young again; he frisks, and prances, and runs about as if he had a new pair of legs. He has left off his brown camlet surtout which he wore all summer, and now with his hat under his arm he goes open-breasted, and he dresses, and powders, and smirks so that you would take him for the mad Frenchman in Bedlam — something wrong in his upper storey! Would you think it, he wants me to have a pig-tail?

BATES: Then he is far gone indeed!

THOMAS: As sure as you are there, Mr Bates, a pig-tail! We have had sad work

---

camlet surtout: overcoat of plain material such as goat's hair.
pig-tail: hair-style that had replaced shoulder-length wig about twenty years earlier.

about it. I made a compromise with him, to wear these ruffled shirts which he gave me — but they stand in my way — I am not so listless with them. Though I have tied up my hands for him, I won't tie up my head, that I am resolute.

BATES: This it is to be in love, Thomas!

THOMAS: He may make free with himself; he shan't make a fool of me. He has got his head into a bag but I won't have a pig-tail tied to mine — and so I told him —

BATES: What did you tell him?

THOMAS: That as I and my father and his father before him had wore their own hair as heaven had sent it, I thought myself rather too old to set up for a monkey at my time of life, and wear a pig-tail. He! he! he! — he took it.

BATES: With a wry face, for it was wormwood.

THOMAS: Yes, he was frumped, and called me old block-head, and would not speak to me for the rest of the day — but the next day he was at it again. He then put me into a passion, and I could not help telling him that I was an Englishman born and had my prerogative as well as he, and that as long as I had breath in my body I was for liberty and a straight head of hair!

BATES: Well said, Thomas. He could not answer that.

THOMAS: The poorest man in England is a match for the greatest, if he will but stick to the laws of the land, and the statute books, as they are delivered down to us from our forefathers.

BATES: You are right. We must lay our wits together, and drive the widow out of your old master's head, and put her into your young master's hands.

THOMAS: With all my heart — nothing can be more meritorious. Marry at his years! What a terrible account would he make of it, Mr Bates! Let me see — on the debtor side of sixty-five — and per contra creditor a buxom widow of twenty-three. He'll be bankrupt in a fortnight — he! he! he!

BATES: And so he would, Mr Thomas. What have you got in your hand?

THOMAS: A pamphlet my old gentleman takes in. He has left off buying histories and religious pieces by numbers, as he used to do, and since he has got this widow in his head he reads nothing but Amorous Repository, Cupid's Revels, Call to Marriage, Hymen's Delights, Love Lies a Bleeding, Love in the Suds, and such like tender compositions —

BATES: Here he comes with his folly about him —

THOMAS: Yes, and the first fool from vanity-fair. Heaven help us! Love turns man and woman topsy-turvy! (*Exit.*)

WHITTLE: (*without*) Where is he? Where is my good friend?
      (*Enter* WHITTLE.)

WHITTLE: Ha! Here he is — give me your hand.

BATES: I am glad to see you in such spirits, my old gentleman.

WHITTLE: Not so old neither. No man ought to be called old, friend Bates, if he is in health, spirits, and —

BATES: In his senses — which I should rather doubt, as I never saw you half so frolicsome in my life.

---

listless: careless, at ease.

WHITTLE: Never too old to learn, friend, and if I don't make use of my philosophy now, I may wear it out in twenty years. I have been always bantered as of too grave a cast. You know when I studied at Lincoln's Inn, they used to call me Young Wisdom.

BATES: And if they should now call you Old Folly, it will be a much worse name.

WHITTLE: No young jackanapes dares call me so, while I have this friend at my side — (*Touches his sword.*)

BATES: A hero too! What in the name of common sense is come to you, my friend? High spirits, quick honour, a long sword and a bag. You want nothing but to be terribly in love and sally forth Knight of the Woeful Countenance, ha! ha! ha!

WHITTLE: Mr Bates — the ladies, who are best judges of countenances, are not of your opinion; and unless you'll be a little serious, I must beg pardon for giving you this trouble, and I'll open my mind to some more attentive friend.

BATES: Well, come, unlock then, you wild, handsome, vigorous young dog you — I will please you if I can.

WHITTLE: I believe you never saw me look better, Frank, did you?

BATES: Oh yes, rather better forty years ago.

WHITTLE: What, when I was at Merchant Taylors' School?

BATES: At Lincoln's Inn, Tom.

WHITTLE: It can't be — I never disguise my age, and next February I shall be fifty-four.

BATES: Fifty-four! Why, I am sixty, and you always licked me at school — though I believe I could do as much for you now, and ecod I believe you deserve it too.

WHITTLE: I tell you I am in my fifty-fifth year.

BATES: Oh, you are? — Let me see, we were together at Cambridge, Anno Domini 25, which is near fifty years ago. You came to college indeed surprisingly young, and what is more surprising, by this calculation you went to school before you was born! You was always a forward child.

WHITTLE: I see there is no talking or consulting with you in this humour, and so, Mr Bates, when you are in temper to show less of your wit, and more of your friendship, I shall consult with you.

BATES: Fare you well, my old boy — young fellow, I mean. When you have done sowing your wild oats, and have been blistered into your right senses; when you have half killed yourself with being a beau, and return to your woollen caps, flannel waistcoats, worsted stockings, cork soles and galloshes, I am at your service again; so bonjour to you, Monsieur Fifty-four, ha! ha! (*Exit.*)

WHITTLE: He has certainly heard of my affair — but he is old and peevish. He wants spirit, and strength of constitution to conceive my happiness. I am in love with the widow, and must have her. Every man knows his own wants. — Let the world laugh, and my friends stare; let them call me imprudent and mad if they please — I live in good times, and among people of fashion, so none of my neighbours, thank heaven, can have the assurance to laugh at me.
(*Enter* OLD KECKSY.)

KECKSY: What, my friend Whittle, joy! Joy to you, old boy. You are going, a-going! a-going! A fine widow has bid for you, and will have you, hah, friend?

All for the best — there is nothing like it, hugh! hugh! hugh! A good wife is a good thing, and a young one is better — hah! Who's afraid? If I had not lately married one, I should have been at death's door by this time — hugh! hugh! hugh! (*Coughs.*)

WHITTLE: Thank, thank you, friend! I was coming to advise with you. I am got into the pound again — in love up to the ears — a fine woman, faith — and there's no love lost between us! Am I right, friend?

KECKSY: Right! Aye, right as my leg, Tom. Life's nothing without love — hugh! hugh! I'm as happy as the day's long! My wife loves gadding, and I can't stay at home, so we are both of a mind. She's every night at one or other of the garden places; but among friends, I am a little afraid of the damp — hugh! hugh! hugh! She has got an Irish gentleman, a kind of cousin of hers, to take care of her; a fine fellow, and so good-natured. It is a vast comfort to have such a friend in a family! hugh! hugh! hugh!

WHITTLE: You are a bold man, cousin Kecksy.

KECKSY: Bold! Ay, to be sure, none but the brave deserve the fair. Hugh! hugh! hugh! Who's afraid?

WHITTLE: Why, your wife is five feet ten.

KECKSY: Without her shoes. I hate your little shrimps; none of your lean meagre French frogs for me. I was always fond of the majestic; give me a slice of a good English sirloin — cut and come again, hugh! hugh! hugh! That's my taste.

WHITTLE: I'm glad you have so good a stomach. And so you would advise me to marry the widow directly?

KECKSY: To be sure — you have not a moment to lose. I always mind what the poet says:

> 'Tis folly to lose time,
> When man is in his prime.
> Hugh! hugh! hugh!

WHITTLE: You have an ugly cough, cousin.

KECKSY: Marriage is the best lozenge for it.

WHITTLE: You have raised me from the dead — I am glad you came. Frank Bates had almost killed me with his jokes — but you have comforted me, and we will walk through the Park; and I will carry you to the widow in Pall Mall.

KECKSY: With all my heart — I'll raise her spirits, and yours too. — Courage, Tom. — Come along. — Who's afraid?
(*Exeunt.*)

SCENE 2.   *The* WIDOW's *lodgings. Enter* WIDOW, NEPHEW *and* BATES.

BATES: Indeed, madam, there is no other way but to cast off your real character and assume a feigned one; it is an extraordinary occasion, and requires extraordinary measures. Pluck up a spirit and do it for the honour of your sex.

NEPHEW: Only consider, my sweet widow, that our all is at stake!

---

pound: enclosure for stray animals.

WIDOW: Could I bring my heart to act contrary to its feelings, would not you hate
me for being a hypocrite, though it is done for your sake?

NEPHEW: Could I think myself capable of such ingratitude —

WIDOW: Don't make fine speeches; you men are strange creatures — you turn our
heads to your purposes and then despise us for the folly you teach us. 'Tis
hard to assume a character contrary to my disposition. I cannot get rid of my
unfashionable prejudices till I have been married in England some time, and
lived among my betters.

NEPHEW: Thou charming adorable woman! What shall we do, then? I never wished
for a fortune till this moment.

WIDOW: Could we live upon affection, I would give your fortune to your uncle,
and thank him for taking it; and then —

NEPHEW: What then, my sweet widow?

WIDOW: I would desire you to run away with me as fast as you can. What a pity it
is that this money, which my heart despises, should hinder its happiness, or
that for the want of a few dirty acres a poor woman must be made miserable,
and sacrificed twice to those who have them.

NEPHEW: Heaven forbid! These exquisite sentiments endear you more to me, and
distract me with the dread of losing you.

BATES: Young folks, let an old man who is not quite in love, and yet will admire a
fine woman to the day of his death, throw in a little advice among your
flames and darts.

WIDOW: Though a woman, a widow, and in love too, I can hear reason, Mr Bates.

BATES: And that's a wonder. You have no time to lose; for want of a jointure you
are still your father's slave; he is obstinate, and has promised you to the old
man. Now, madam, if you will not rise superior to your sex's weakness to
secure a young fellow instead of an old one, your eyes are a couple of hypo-
crites.

WIDOW: They are a couple of traitors, I'm sure, and have led their mistress into a
toil from which all her wit cannot release her.

NEPHEW: But it can, if you will but exert it. My uncle adored and fell in love with
you for your beauty, softness and almost speechless reserve. Now, if amidst
all his rapturous ideas of your delicacy, you would bounce upon him a wild,
ranting, buxom widow, he will grow sick of his bargain, and give me a fortune
to take you off his hands.

WIDOW: I shall make a very bad actress.

NEPHEW: You are an excellent mimic. Assume but the character of your Irish
female neighbour in the country, with which you astonished us so agreeably
at Scarborough, you will frighten my uncle into terms, and do that for us
which neither my love nor your virtue can accomplish without it.

WIDOW: Now for a trial — (*mimicking a strong brogue*) — fait and trot, if you will
be after bringing me before the old jontleman, if he loves music, I will trate
his ears with a little of the brogue, and some dancing too into the bargain,

---

fait and trot: faith and troth.

if he loves capering — Oh bless me! My heart fails me, and I am frightened out of my wits. I can never go through it.

(NEPHEW *and* BATES *both laugh.*)

NEPHEW: (*kneeling and kissing her hand*) Oh 'tis admirable! Love himself inspires you, and we shall conquer. What say you, Mr Bates?

BATES: I'll ensure you success. I can scarce believe my own ears; such a tongue and a brogue would make Hercules tremble at five-and-twenty. But away, away, and give him the first broadside in the Park. There you'll find him hobbling with that old cuckold Kecksy.

WIDOW: But will my dress suit the character I play?

NEPHEW: The very thing. Is your retinue ready and your part got by heart?

WIDOW: All is ready; 'tis an act of despair to punish folly and reward merit; 'tis the last effort of pure honourable love; and if every woman would exert the same spirit for the same out-of-fashion rarity, there would be less business for Doctors Commons. Now let the critics laugh at me if they dare. (*Exit with spirit.*)

NEPHEW: Brava! bravissima! sweet widow! (*Exit after her.*)

BATES: Huzza! huzza! (*Exit.*)

SCENE 3.   *The park. Enter* WHITTLE *and* KECKSY.

WHITTLE: Yes, yes, she is Irish, but so modest, so mild, and so tender, and just enough of the accent to give a peculiar sweetness to her words, which drop from her in monosyllables, with such a delicate reserve that I shall have all the comfort, without the impertinence, of a wife.

KECKSY: There our taste differs, friend: I am for a lively smart girl in my house — hugh! hugh! — to keep up my spirits and make me merry. I don't admire dumb waiters, not I — no still-life for me! I love their prittle prattle; it sets me to sleep, and I can take a sound nap while my Sally and her cousin are running and playing about the house like young cats.

WHITTLE: I am for no cats in my house. I cannot sleep with a noise. The widow was made on purpose for me; she is so bashful, has no acquaintance, and she never would stir out of doors if her friends were not afraid of a consumption, and so force her into the air. Such a delicate creature! You shall see her. You were always for a tall, chattering, frisky wench: now for my part I am with the old saying:

> Wife a mouse,
> Quiet house:
> Wife a cat —
> Dreadful that!

KECKSY: I don't care for your sayings. Who's afraid?

WHITTLE: There goes Bates. Let us avoid him; he will only be joking with us. When I have a serious thing in my head, I can't bear to have it laughed out again. This way, friend Kecksy. What have we got here?

KECKSY: Some fine prancing wench, with her lovers and footman about her. She's a gay one by her motions!

WHITTLE: Were she not so flaunting, I should take it for — No, it is impossible! — and yet is not that my nephew with her? I forbade him speaking to her. It can't be the widow! I hope it is not.

(*Enter* WIDOW, *followed by* NEPHEW, *three* FOOTMEN *and a*
BLACK BOY.)

WIDOW: Don't bother me, young man, with your darts, your cupids and your
pangs; if you had half of 'em about you that you swear you have, they would
have cured you, by killing you long ago. Would you have me faitless to your
uncle, ha! young man? Was not I faitful to you, till I was ordered to be faitful
to him? But I must know more of your English ways, and live more among
English ladies, to learn how to be faitful to two at a time — and so there's my
answer for you.

NEPHEW: Then I know my relief, for I cannot live without you. (*Exit.*)

WIDOW: Take what relief you plase, young jontleman. What have I to do with
that? He is certainly mad, or out of his sinses, for he swears he can't *live* without me, and yet he talks of *killing* himself. How does he make out dat? If a
countryman of mine had made such a blunder, they would have put it into
all the newspapers, and *Falkner's Journal* besides. But an Englishman may
look over the hedge, while an Irishman must not stale a horse.

KECKSY: Is this the widow, friend Whittle?

WHITTLE: I don't know. (*half sighing*) It is — and it is not.

WIDOW: Your servant, Mr Whittol. I wish you would spake to your nephew not to
be whining and dangling after me all day in his green coat like a parrot. It is
not for my reputation that he should follow me about like a beggar-man, and
ask me for what I had given him long ago but have since bestowed upon you,
Mr Whittol.

WHITTLE: He is an impudent beggar, and shall be really so for his disobedience.

WIDOW: As he can't live without me, you know, it will be charity to starve him. I
wish the poor young man dead with all my heart, as he thinks it will do him a
grate dale of good.

KECKSY: (*to* WHITTLE) She is tender indeed! And I think she has the brogue a
little — hugh! hugh!

WHITTLE: 'Tis stronger today than ever I heard it (*staring*).

WIDOW: And are you now talking of my brogue? It is always the most fullest when
the wind is easterly; it has the same effect upon me as upon stammering
people — they can't spake for their impediment, and my tongue is fixed so
loose in my mouth I can't stop it for the life of me.

WHITTLE: What a terrible misfortune, friend Kecksy!

KECKSY: Not at all: the more tongue the better, say I.

WIDOW: When the wind changes I have no brogue at all, at all. But come, Mr
Whittol, don't let us be vulgar, and talk of our poor relations. It is impossible
to be in the metropolis of London and have any thought but of operas,

<hr />

Falkner's Journal: George Falkner (d. 1775) was a Dublin printer and bookseller who edited a
journal. He was an associate of Swift and a correspondent of Garrick.
An Englishman . . . a horse: an Englishman may relieve himself by the wayside, but an Irishman
must not even let his horse do so.
Whittol: pun (no doubt intended) on *wittol*, a fool or cuckold.

plays, masquerades and pantaons, to keep up one's spirits in the winter; and Ranelagh, Vauxhall and Marybone fireworks to cool and refresh one in the summer. (*Sings.*) La! la! la!

WHITTLE: I protest she puts me into a sweat. I shall have a mob about us!

KECKSY: The more the merrier, I say. Who's afraid?

WIDOW: How the people stare, as if they never saw a woman's voice before! But my vivacity has got the better of my good manners. This, I suppose, this strange gentleman, is a near friend and relation, and as such, notwithstanding his apparence, I shall always trate him, though I might dislike him upon a nearer acquaintence.

KECKSY: Madam, you do me honour. I like your frankness and I like your person, and I envy my friend Whittle; and if you were not engaged, and I were not married, I would endeavour to make myself agreeable to you, that I would – hugh! hugh!

WIDOW: And indeed, sir, it would be very *agreeable* to *me*, for if I should hate you as much as I did my first dare husband, I should always have the comfort that in all human probability my tormants would not last long.

KECKSY: She utters something more than monosyllables, friend. This is better than bargain. She has a fine bold way of talking.

WHITTLE: More bold than welcome! I am struck all of a heap!

WIDOW: What, are you low-spirited, my dare Mr Whittol? When you were at Scarborough, and winning my affections, you were all mirth and gaiety; and now you have won me, you are as thoughtful about it as if we had been married some time.

WHITTLE: Indeed, madam, I can't but say I am a little thoughtful. We take it by turns; you were very sorrowful a month ago for the loss of your husband, and that you could dry up your tears so soon naturally makes me a little thoughtful.

WIDOW: Indeed, I could dry up my tears for a dozen husbands when I were sure of having a tirteenth like Mr Whittol. That's very natural sure, both in England and Dublin too.

KECKSY: She won't die of a consumption; she has a fine full-toned voice, and you'll be very happy, Tom – Hugh! hugh!

WHITTLE: (*aside*) Oh yes, very happy.

WIDOW: But come, don't let us be melancholy before the time. I am sure I have been moped up for a year and a half; I was obliged to mourn for my first husband, that I might be sure of a second; and my father kept my spirits in subjection as the best receipt (he said) for changing a widow into a wife. But now I have my arms and legs at liberty I must and will have my swing; now I am out of my cage I could dance two nights togeder, and a day too, like any singing bird; and I'm in such spirits that I have got rid of my father, I could fly over the moon without wings, and back again before dinner. Bless my eyes, and don't I see there Miss Nancy O'Flarty, and her brother Captain O'Flarty?

---

pantaons: Irish pronunciation of *Pantheon*, a neo-Grecian building in Oxford Street, London, opened in 1772 for musical promenades.

He was one of my dying Strephons at Scarborough. I have a very grate regard for him and must make him a little miserable with my happiness. (*Curtsies.*) Come along, Skips, (*to the servants*) don't you be gostring there; show your liveries and bow to your master that is to be, and to his friend; and hold up your heads and trip after me as lightly as if you had no legs to your feet. I shall be with you again, jontlemen, in the crack of a fan. Oh, I'll have a husband, ay marry. (*Exit singing.*)

KECKSY: A fine buxom widow, faith! No acquaintance! — Delicate reserve! — Mopes at home — forced into the air — inclined to a consumption. — What a description you gave of your wife! Why, she beats my Sally, Tom.

WHITTLE: Yes, and she'll beat me if I don't take care! What a change is here! I must turn about, or this will turn my head. Dance for two nights together, and leap over the moon! You shall dance and leap by yourself — that I'm resolved.

KECKSY: Here she comes again; it does my heart good to see her. You are in luck, Tom.

WHITTLE: I'd give a finger to be out of such luck.
                    (*Enter* WIDOW *and the rest.*)

WIDOW: Ha! ha! ha! the poor captain is marched off in a fury. He can't bear to hear that the town has capitulated to you, Mr Whittol. I have promised to introduce him to you. He will make one of my danglers to take a little exercise with me when you take your nap in the afternoon.

WHITTLE: You shan't catch me napping, I assure you. What a discovery and escape I have made! I am in a sweat with the thoughts of my danger!

KECKSY: I protest, cousin, there goes my wife, and her friend Mr MacBrawn. What a fine stately couple they are! I must after 'em and have a laugh with them. Now they giggle, and walk quick, that I mayn't overtake them. Madam, your servant. You're a happy man, Tom — Hugh! hugh! Who's afraid? (*Exit.*)

WIDOW: I know Mr MacBrawn extremely well. He was very intimate at our house in my first husband's time; a great comfort he was to me, to be sure! He would very often leave his claret and companions for a little conversation with me. He was bred at the Dublin Univarsity, and being a very deep scholar, has fine talents for a tate a tate.

WHITTLE: She knows him too! I shall have my house overrun with the *MacBrawns*, *O'Shoulders* and the blood of the *Backwells*; lord have mercy upon me!

WIDOW: Pray, Mr Whittol, is that poor spindle-legged crater of a cousin of yours lately married? Ha! ha! ha! I don't pity the poor crater his wife, for that agrayable cough of his will soon reward her for all her sufferings.

WHITTLE: (*aside*) What a delivery! A reprieve before the knot was tied!

WIDOW: Are you unwell, Mr Whittol? I should be sorry you would fall sick before the happy day. Your being in danger afterwards would be a great consolation to me, because I should have the pleasure of nursing you myself.

Skips: 'skip' (sing.) was Dublin University slang for a college servant. Johnson's dictionary has *skipjack*: a lackey.
gostring: to gauster or goster: to swagger.

WHITTLE: I hope never to give you that trouble, madam.

WIDOW: No trouble at all, at all. I assure you, sir, from my soul, that I shall take great delight in the occasion.

WHITTLE: Indeed, madam, I believe it.

WIDOW: I don't care how soon, the sooner the better; and the more danger, the more honour. I spake from my heart.

WHITTLE: (*Sighs.*) And so do I from mine.

WIDOW: But don't let us think of future pleasure, and neglect the present satisfaction. My mantua-maker is waiting for me to choose my clothes, in which I shall forget the sorrows of Mrs Brady in the joys of Mrs Whittol. Though I have a fortune myself, I shall bring a tolerable one to you — in debts, Mr Whittol; and which I will pay you tinfold in tinderness. Your deep purse and my open heart will make us the envy of the little great ones and great little ones — the people of quality with no souls and the great souls with no cash at all. I hope you'll meet me at the Pantaon this evening. Lady Rantiton and her daughter Miss Nettledown, and Nancy Tittup, with half a dozen Maccaroonies, and two savoury vivers, are to take me there, and we propose a great dale of chat and merriment, and dancing all night and all other kind of recreations. I am quite another kind of a crater now I am a bird in the fields; I can junket about a week together; I have a fine constitution and am never molested with your nasty vapours. Are you ever troubled with vapours, Mr Whittol?

WHITTLE: A little now and then, madam.

WIDOW: I'll rattle 'em away like smoke! There are no vapours where I come. I hate your dumps and your nerves and your megrims; and I had much rather break your rest with a little racketing than let anything get into your head that should not be there, Mr Whittol.

WHITTLE: I will take care that nothing shall be in my head but what ought to be there. (*aside*) What a deliverance!

WIDOW: (*looking at her watch*) Bless me! How the hours of the clock creep away when we are plased with our company! But I must lave you; for there are half a hundred people waiting for me to pick your pocket, Mr Whittol; and there is my own brother, Lieutenant O'Neale, is to arrive this morning, and he is so like me you would not know us asunder when we are together. You will be very fond of him, poor lad! He lives by his wits, as you do by fortune, and so you may assist one another. Mr Whittol, your obadient, till we meet at the Pantaon. Follow me. Pompey; and Skips, do you follow him.

POMPEY: The Baccararo whiteman no let blacky boy go first after you, missis; they pull and pinch me.

FOOTMAN: It is a shame, your ladyship, that a black negro should take place of English Christians. We can't follow him indeed.

Tittup: a minx (see *Bon Ton*).

Maccaroonies: same as *maccaroons*, *maccaronis*. Originally members of the Maccaroni Club, for dandies who affected foreign dress and behaviour. Later applied to fops in general.

savoury vivers: tasty titbits. As with *maccaroons*, there is a suggestion of sweetmeats, but the reference is to female exquisites.

Baccararo: perhaps a gambler at baccarat.

WIDOW: Then you may follow one another out of my sarvice; if you follow me you shall follow him, for he shall go before me. Can't I make him your superior, as the laws of the land have made him your aqual? Therefore resign as fast as you plase; you shan't oppose government and keep your places too; that is not good politics in England or Ireland either. So come along, Pompey; be after going before me. — Mr Whittol, most tinderly yours. (*Exit.*)

WHITTLE: (*mimicking her*) *Most tinderly yours*! Ecod I believe you are, and anybody else's. Oh what an escape I have had! But how shall I clear myself of this business? I'll serve her as I would bad money — put her off into other hands. My nephew is fool enough to be in love with her, and if I give him a fortune he'll take the good and the bad together. He shall do so or starve. I'll send for Bates directly, confess my folly, ask his pardon, send him to my nephew, write and declare off with the widow, and so get rid of her *tinderness* as fast as I can. (*Exit.*)

ACT II

A room in WHITTLE*'s house. Enter* BATES *and* NEPHEW.

NEPHEW: (*taking him by the hand*) We are bound to you for ever, Mr Bates; I can say no more; words but ill express the real feelings of the heart.

BATES: I know you are a good lad, or I would not have meddled in the matter; but the business is not yet completed until *signatum et sigillatum.*

NEPHEW: Let me fly to the widow and tell her how prosperously we go on.

BATES: Don't be in a hurry, young man: she is not in the dark I assure you, nor has she yet finished her part. So capital an actress should not be idle in the last act.

NEPHEW: I could wish that you would let me come into my uncle's proposal at once, without vexing him farther.

BATES: Then I declare off. Thou silly young man, are you to be duped by your own weak good nature and his worldly craft? This does not arise from his love and justice to you, but from his own miserable situation. He must be tortured into justice; he shall not only give up your whole estate, which he is loth to part with, but you must now have a premium for agreeing to your own happiness. What, shall your widow, with wit and spirit that would do the greatest honour to our sex, go through her talk cheerfully, and shall your courage give way, and be outdone by a woman's? Fie! for shame!

NEPHEW: I beg your pardon, Mr Bates; I will follow your directions; be as hardhearted as my uncle, and vex his body and mind for the good of his soul.

BATES: That's a good child, and remember your own and your widow's future happiness depends upon your both going through this business with spirit. Make your uncle feel for himself, that he may do justice to other people. Is the widow ready for the last experiment?

NEPHEW: She is; but think what anxiety I shall feel while she is in danger!

BATES: Ha! ha! ha! She'll be in no danger; besides, shan't we be at hand to assist

---

signatum et sigillatum: signed and sealed.

her? Hark! I hear him coming. I'll probe his callous heart to the quick; and if we are not paid for our trouble, say I am no politician. Fly! Now we shall do! (*Exit* NEPHEW. *Enter* WHITTLE.)

WHITTLE: Well, Mr Bates, have you talked with my nephew? Is he not overjoyed at the proposal?

BATES: The demon of discord has been among you and has untuned the whole family. You have screwed him too high. The young man is out of his senses, I think; he stares and mopes about and sighs; looks at me indeed, but gives very absurd answers. I don't like him.

WHITTLE: What is the matter, think you?

BATES: What I have always expected; there is a crack in your family, and you take it by turns! You have had it, and now transfer it to your nephew — which, to your shame be it spoken, is the only transfer you have ever made him.

WHITTLE: But am I not going to do him more than justice?

BATES: As you have done him much less than justice hitherto, you can't begin too soon.

WHITTLE: Am I not going to give him the lady he likes, and which I was going to marry myself?

BATES: Yes, that is, you are taking a perpetual blister off your own back, to clap it upon him. What a tender uncle you are!

WHITTLE: But you don't consider the whole estate which I shall give him.

BATES: *Restore* to him, you mean — 'tis his own, and you should have given it up long ago. You must do more, or Old Nick will have you. Your nephew won't take the widow off your hands without a fortune. Throw him ten thousand into the bargain.

WHITTLE: Indeed but I shan't; he shall run mad, and I'll marry her myself, rather than do that. Mr Bates, be a true friend and sooth my nephew to consent to my proposal.

BATES: You have raised the fiend; and ought to lay him. However, I'll do my best for you. When the head is turned, nothing can bring it right again so soon as ten thousand pounds. Shall I promise for you?

WHITTLE: I'd sooner go to Bedlam myself. (*Exit* BATES.) Why, I am in a worse condition than I was before! If this widow's father will not let me be off without providing for his daughter, I may lose a great sum of money, and none of us be the better for it: my nephew half mad; myself half married; and no remedy for either of us.
(*Enter* SERVANT.)

SERVANT: Sir Patrick O'Neale is come to wait upon you. Would you please to see him?

WHITTLE: By all means, the very person I wanted. Don't let him wait. (*Exit* SERVANT.) I wonder if he has seen my letter to the widow. I will sound him by degrees, that I may be sure of my mark before I strike the blow.
(*Enter* SIR PATRICK.)

SIR PATRICK: Mr Whizzle, your humble sarvant. It gives me great pleasure that an old jontleman of your property will have the honour of being united with the family of the O'Nales. We have been too much jontlemen not to spend our estate, as you have made yourself a kind of jontleman by getting one. One runs out one way and t'other runs in another, which makes them both meet at last, and keeps up the balance of Europe.

WHITTLE: I am much obliged to you, Sir Patrick. I am an old gentleman, you say true; and I was thinking —

SIR PATRICK: And I was thinking if you were ever so old, my daughter can't make you young again. She has as fine rich tick blood in her veins as any in all Ireland. I wish you had a swate crater of a daughter like mine, that we might make a double cross of it.

WHITTLE: That would be a double cross indeed! (*aside*)

SIR PATRICK: Tho' I was miserable enough with my first wife, who had the devil of a spirit, and the very moddel of her daughter, yet a brave man never shrinks from danger, and I may have better luck another time.

WHITTLE: Yes, but I am no brave man, Sir Patrick, and I begin to shrink already.

SIR PATRICK: I have bred her up in great subjiction; she is tame as a young colt and as tinder as a sucking chicken. You will find her a true jontlewoman, and so knowing that you can tache her nothing. She brings everything but money, and you have enough of that, if you have nothing else, and that is what I call the balance of things.

WHITTLE: But I have been considering your daughter's great deserts, and my great age —

SIR PATRICK: She is a charming crater. I would venture to say that, if I was not her father.

WHITTLE: I say, sir, as I have been considering your daughter's great deserts, and as I own I have great demerits —

SIR PATRICK: To be sure you have, but you can't help that; and if my daughter was to mention anything of a fleering at your age, or your stinginess — by the balance of power but I would make her repate it a hundred times to your face, to make her ashamed of it. But mum, old gentleman, the devil a word of your informities will she touch upon. I have brought her up to softness and to gentleness, as a kitten to new milk. She will spake nothing but no, and yes, as if she were dumb; and no tame rabbit or pigeon will keep house or be more inganious with her needle and tambourine.

WHITTLE: She is vastly altered then since I saw her last, or I have lost my senses; and in either case we had much better — since I must speak plain — not come together —

SIR PATRICK: Till you are married, you mean. With all my heart; it is the more gentale for that, and like our family. I never saw Lady O'Nale, your mother-in-law — who, poor crater, is dead, and can never be a mother-in-law again — till the week before I married her; and I did not care if I had never seen her then — which is a comfort too in case of death, or other accidents in life.

WHITTLE: But you don't understand me, Sir Patrick, I say —

SIR PATRICK: I say, how can that be, when we both spake English?

WHITTLE: But you mistake my meaning, and don't comprehend me.

SIR PATRICK: Then you don't comprehend yourself, Mr Whizzle, and I have not the gift of prophecy, to find out after you have spoke what never was in you.

WHITTLE: Let me entreat you to attend to me a little. Your daughter —

SIR PATRICK: Your wife that is to be —

WHITTLE: My wife that is *not* to be — Zounds! man, will you hear me?

SIR PATRICK: To be or not to be, that is the question. I can swear too, if it wants a little of that.

WHITTLE: Dear Sir Patrick, hear me. I confess myself unworthy of her; I have the greatest regard for you, Sir Patrick; I should think myself honoured by being in your family; but there are many reasons —

SIR PATRICK: To be sure there are many reasons why an old man should not marry a young woman; but as that was your business and not mine —

WHITTLE: I have wrote a letter to your daughter, which I was in hopes you had seen, and had brought me an answer to it.

SIR PATRICK: What the devil, Mr Whizzle, do you make a letter porter of me? Do you imagine, you dirty fellow with your cash, that Sir Patrick O'Nale would carry your letters? I would have you know that I despise letters and all that belong to 'em, nor would I carry a letter to the king, heaven bless him, unless it came from myself.

WHITTLE: But, dear Sir Patrick, don't be in a passion for nothing.

SIR PATRICK: What? Is it nothing to make a penny postman of me? But I'll go to my daughter directly, for I have not seen her today, and if I find that you have written anything that I won't understand, I shall take it as an affront to my family, and you shall either let out the noble blood of the O'Nales, or we will spill the last drop of the red puddle of the Whizzles. (*Goes and returns.*) Harkee, old Mr Whizzle, Wheesle, Whistle — what's your name? You must not stir till I come back. If you offer to ate, drink or sleep, till my honour is satisfied, 'twill be the worst male you ever took in your life. You had better fast a year, and die at the end of six months, than dare to lave your house. So now, Mr Weezle, you are to do as you plase. (*Exit.*)

WHITTLE: Now the devil is at work indeed! If some miracle don't save me, I shall run mad like my nephew, and have a long Irish sword through me into the bargain. While I am in my senses I won't have the woman, and therefore he that is out of them shall have her, if I give half my fortune to make the match. Thomas! (*Enter* THOMAS.) Sad work, Thomas!

THOMAS: Sad work indeed! Why would you think of marrying? I knew what it would come to.

WHITTLE: Why, what is it come to?

THOMAS: It is in all the papers.

WHITTLE: So much the better; then nobody will believe it.

THOMAS: But they come to me to enquire.

WHITTLE: And you contradict it.

THOMAS: What signifies that? I was telling Lady Gabble's footman at the door just now that it was all a lie, and your nephew looks out of the two-pair-of-stairs window, with eyes all on fire, and tells the whole story. Upon that, there gathered such a mob!

WHITTLE: I shall be murdered — and have my house pulled down into the bargain!

THOMAS: It is all quiet again. I told them the young man was out of his senses, and that you were out of town, so they went away quietly, and said they would come and mob you another day.

WHITTLE: Thomas, what shall I do?

THOMAS: Nothing you have done, if you will have matters mend.

WHITTLE: I am out of my depth, and you won't lend me your hand to draw me out.

THOMAS: You were out of your depth to fall in love. Swim away as fast as you can. You'll be drowned if you marry.

WHITTLE: I'm frightened out of my wits. Yes, yes, 'tis all over with me. I must not stir out of my house; but am ordered to stay to be murdered in it for aught I know. What are you muttering, Thomas? Prithee speak out and comfort me.

THOMAS: It is all a judgement on you. Because your brother's foolish will says the young man must have your consent, you won't let him have her, but will marry the widow yourself. That's the dog in the manger; you can't eat the oats and won't let those who can.

WHITTLE: But I consent he shall have both the widow and the fortune, if we can get him into his right senses.

THOMAS: For fear I should lose mine, I'll get out of Bedlam as soon as possible. You must provide yourself with another servant.

WHITTLE: The whole earth conspires against me! You shall stay with me till I die, and then you shall have a good legacy; and I won't live long, I promise you. (knocking at the door)

THOMAS: Here are the undertakers already. (Exit.)

WHITTLE: What shall I do? My head can't bear it. I will hang myself for fear of being run through the body.

                    (THOMAS returns with bills.)

THOMAS: Half a score people I never saw before with these bills and drafts upon you for payment, signed Martha Brady.

WHITTLE: I wish Martha Brady was at the bottom of the Thames! What an impudent extravagant baggage to begin her tricks already! Send them to the devil, and say I won't pay a farthing.

THOMAS: (going) You'll have another mob about the door.

WHITTLE: Stay, stay, Thomas. Tell them I am very busy and they must come tomorrow. Stay, stay; that is promising payment! No, no, no — tell 'em they must stay till I am married, and so they will be satisfied, and tricked into the bargain.

THOMAS: (aside) When you are tricked we shall all be satisfied. (Exit.)

WHITTLE: That of all dreadful things I should think of a woman, and that woman should be a widow, and that widow should be an Irish one! Quem deus vult perdere. Who have we here? Another of the family, I suppose. (Retires.)
            (Enter WIDOW as Lieutenant O'Neale, seemingly flustered, and putting up her sword, THOMAS following.)

THOMAS: I hope you are not hurt, captain.

WIDOW: Oh not at all, at all. 'Tis well they run away or I should have made them run faster; I shall teach them how to snigger, and look through glasses at their betters. These are your Maccaroons, as they call themselves. By my soul but I

Quem deus vult perdere (prius dementat): Whom God wishes to destroy (he first makes mad).

would have frightened their hair out of buckle if they would have stood still till I had overtaken them! These whipper-snappers look so much more like girls in breeches than those I see in petticoats that, fait and trot, it is a pity to hurt them. The fair sex in London here seem the most masculine of the two. – But to business: friend, where is your master?

THOMAS: There, captain. I hope he has not offended you.

WIDOW: If you are impartinent, sir, you will offend me. Lave the room.

THOMAS: I value my life too much not to do that. – (*aside to his master*) What a raw-boned tartar! I wish he had not been caught and sent here. (*Exit.*)

WHITTLE: Her brother, by all that's terrible! And as like him as two tigers! I sweat at the sight of him. I'm sorry Thomas is gone! He has been quarrelling already.

WIDOW: Is your name Whittol?

WHITTLE: My name is Whittle, not Whittol.

WIDOW: We shan't stand for trifles – and you were born and christened by the name of Thomas?

WHITTLE: So they told me, sir.

WIDOW: Then they told no lies, fait. So far, so good. (*Takes out a letter.*) Do you know that handwriting?

WHITTLE: As well as I know this good friend of mine, who helps me upon such occasions (*showing his right hand, and smiling*).

WIDOW: You had better not show your teeth, sir, till we come to the jokes. The handwriting is yours?

WHITTLE: Yes, sir; it is mine. (*Sighs.*)

WIDOW: Death and powder! What do you sigh for? Are you ashamed, or sorry, for your handy works?

WHITTLE: Partly one, partly t'other.

WIDOW: Will you be plased, sir, to rade it aloud, that you may know it again when you hare it.

WHITTLE: (*taking letter and reading*) 'Madam – '

WIDOW: Would you be plased to let us know what madam you mean? For women of quality, and women of no quality, and women of all qualities are so mixed together that you don't know one from t'other, and are all called *madams*. You should always rade the subscription before you open the letter.

WHITTLE: I beg your pardon, sir. – (*aside*) I don't like this ceremony. – 'To Mrs Brady, in Pall Mall.'

WIDOW: Now procade. Fire and powder but I would –

WHITTLE: Sir! What's the matter?

WIDOW: Nothing at all. Pray go on.

WHITTLE: (*Reads.*) 'Madam, as I prefer your happiness to the indulgence of my own passions – '

WIDOW: I will not prefer *your* happiness to the indulgence of *my* passions. Mr Whittol, rade on.

WHITTLE: (*reading*) 'I must confess that I am unworthy of your charms and virtues – '

WIDOW: Very unworthy indeed; rade on, sir.

WHITTLE: (*reading*) 'I have for some days had a severe struggle between my justice and my passion – '

WIDOW: I have had no struggle at all: my justice and my passion are agreed.

WHITTLE: (*continuing*) 'The former has prevailed, and I beg leave to resign you, with all your accomplishments, to some more deserving though not more admiring servant than your most miserable and devoted, THOMAS WHITTLE.'

WIDOW: And miserable and devoted you shall be. — To the postscript. Rade on.

WHITTLE: (*reading*) 'Postscript: Let me have your pity, but not your anger.'

WIDOW: In answer to this love epistle, you pitiful fellow, my sister presents you with her tinderest wishes and assures you that you have, as you desire, her pity, and she generously throws her contempt too into the bargain.

WHITTLE: I'm infinitely obliged to her.

WIDOW: I must beg lave in the name of all our family to present the same to you.

WHITTLE: I am ditto to all the family.

WIDOW: But as a brache of promise to any of our family was never suffered without a brache into somebody's body, I have fixed upon myself to be your operator; and I believe that you will find that I have as fine a hand at this work, and will give you as little pain, as any in the three kingdoms. (*Sits down and loosens her knee-bands.*)

WHITTLE: For heaven's sake, captain, what are you about?

WIDOW: I always loosen my garters for the advantage of lunging; it is for your sake as well as my own, for I will be twice through your body before you shall feel me once. (*She seems to practise.*)

WHITTLE: (*aside*) What a bloody fellow it is! I wish Thomas would come in.

WIDOW: Come, sir, prepare yourself. You are not the first by half a score that I have run through and through the heart before they knew what was the matter with them.

WHITTLE: But, captain, suppose I will marry your sister.

WIDOW: I have not the laste objection if you recover of your wounds. Callagon O'Connor lives very happy with my great aunt, Mrs Deborah O'Nale, in the county of Galloway, except a small astma he got by my running him through the lungs at the Currough; he would have forsaken her if I had not stopped his perfidy by a famous family styptic I have here. Oho! my little old boy, but you shall get it. (*Draws.*)

WHITTLE: What shall I do? — Well, sir, if I must, I must; I'll meet you tomorrow morning in Hyde Park, let the consequence be what it will.

WIDOW: For fear you might forget that favour, I must beg to be indulged with a little pushing now. I have set my heart upon it, and two birds in hand is worth one in the bushes, Mr Whittol. Come, sir.

WHITTLE: But I have not settled my matters.

WIDOW: Oh, we'll settle 'em in a trice, I warrant you. (*Puts herself in a position.*)

WHITTLE: But I don't understand the sword: I had rather fight with pistols.

WIDOW: I am very happy it is in my power to oblige you. There, sir, take your choice; I will plase you if I can. (*Offers pistols.*)

WHITTLE: Out of the pan into the fire! There's no putting him off. If I had chosen poison, I dare swear he had arsenic in his pocket. — Lookee, young gentleman, I am an old man, and you'll get no credit by killing me; but I have a nephew as young as yourself, and you'll get more honour by facing him.

WIDOW: Ay, and more pleasure too. I expect ample satisfaction from him after I have done your business. Prepare, sir.

WHITTLE: What the devil! Won't one serve your turn? I can't fight and I won't fight; I'll do anything rather than fight. I'll marry your sister — my nephew shall marry her — I'll give him all my fortune. What would the fellow have? Here, nephew! Thomas! Murder! Murder! (*He flies and she pursues.*)
       (*Enter* BATES *and* NEPHEW.)

NEPHEW: What's the matter, uncle?

WHITTLE: Murder, that's all. That ruffian there would kill me and eat me afterwards.

NEPHEW: I'll find a way to cool him. Come out, sir. I am as mad as yourself. I'll match you, I warrant you (*going out*).

WIDOW: I'll follow you all the world over (*going after him*).

WHITTLE: Stay, stay, nephew; you shan't fight; we shall be exposed all over the town, and you may lose your life, and I shall be cursed from morning to night. Do, nephew, make yourself and me happy; be the olive branch, and bring peace into my family. Return to the widow; I will give you my consent, and your fortune, and a fortune for the widow, five thousand pounds! Do persuade him, Mr Bates.

BATES: Do, sir; this is the very critical point of your life. I know you love her; 'tis the only method to restore us all to our senses.

NEPHEW: I must talk in private first with this hot young gentleman.

WIDOW: As private as you plase, sir.

WHITTLE: Take their weapons away, Mr Bates, and do you follow me to my study to witness my proposal; it is all ready, and only wants signing. Come along, come along. (*Exit.*)

BATES: Victoria! victoria! Give me your swords and pistols. And now do your worst, you spirited loving young couple. I could leap out of my skin! (*Exit.*)

THOMAS: (*peeping in*) Joy, joy to you, ye fond charming pair! The fox is caught, and the young lambs may skip and play. I leave you to your transports. (*Exit.*)

NEPHEW: Oh, my charming widow! What a day have we gone through!

WIDOW: I would go through ten times as much to deceive an old amorous rogue like your uncle, to purchase a young one like his nephew.

NEPHEW: I listened at the door all this last scene. My heart was agitated with ten thousand fears. Suppose my uncle had been stout, and drawn his sword?

WIDOW: I should have run away as he did. When two cowards meet, the struggle is who shall run first; and sure I can bate an old man at anything.

NEPHEW: Permit me thus to seal my happiness, (*Kisses her hand.*) and be assured that I am as sensible, as I think myself undeserving, of it.

WIDOW: I'll tell you what, Mr Whittol, were I not sure you deserved some pains, I would not have taken any pains for you; and don't imagine now, because I have gone a little too far for the man I love, that I shall go a little too far when I'm your wife. Indeed I shan't. I have done more than I should before I am your wife, because I was in despair; but I won't do as much as I may when I am your wife, though every Irish woman is fond of imitating her English betters.

NEPHEW: Thou divine, adorable woman! (*Kneels and kisses her hand.*)
        (*Enter* WHITTLE *and* BATES. WHITTLE *stares.*)
BATES: (*aside*) Confusion!
WHITTLE: (*turning to* BATES *aside*) Heyday! I'm afraid his head is not right yet!
    He was kneeling and kissing the captain's hand!
BATES: (*aside to* WHITTLE) Take no notice; all will come about.
WIDOW: I find, Mr Whittol, your family loves kissing better than fighting. He
    swears I am as like my sister as two pigeons. I could excuse his raptures; for
    I had rather fight the best friend I have than slobber and salute him *à la*
    françoise.
        (*Enter* SIR PATRICK O'NEALE.)
SIR PATRICK: I hope, Mr Whizzle, you'll excuse my coming back to give you an
    answer without having any to give. I hear a grate dale of news about myself,
    and came to know if it be true. They say my son is in London, when he tells
    me himself by letter here that he's in Limerick; and I have been with my
    daughter to tell her the news, but she would not stay at home to recave it, so
    I am come – *O gra ma chree my little din ousil craw*, what have we got here?
    A piece of mummery! Here is my son and daughter, fait! What, are you wear-
    ing the breeches, Pat, to see how they become you when you are Mrs Weezle?
WIDOW: I beg your pardon for that, sir! I wear them before marriage because I
    think they become a woman better than after.
WHITTLE: What, is not this your son?
SIR PATRICK: No, but it is my daughter, and that is the same thing.
WIDOW: And your niece, sir, which is still better than either.
WHITTLE: Mighty well! and I suppose you have not lost your wits, young man?
BATES: I sympathise with you, sir. We lost 'em together, and found 'em at the
    same time.
WHITTLE: Here's villainy! Mr Bates, give me the paper. Not a farthing shall they
    have till the law gives it 'em.
BATES: We'll cheat the law and give it them now. (*Gives* NEPHEW *the paper.*)
WHITTLE: He may take his own, but she shan't have a sixpence of the five thou-
    sand pounds I promised him.
BATES: Witness, good folks, he owns to the promise.
SIR PATRICK: Fait, I'll witness that, or anythink else in a good cause.
WHITTLE: What, am I choused again!
BATES: Why should not my friend be choused out of a little justice for the first
    time? Your hard usage has sharpened your nephew's wits; therefore beware;
    don't play with edge-tools. You'll only cut your fingers.
SIR PATRICK: And your trote too, which is all one; therefore, to make all azy,
    marry my daughter first and then quarrel with her afterwards; that will be in
    the natural course of things.
WHITTLE: Here! Thomas! Where are you? (*Enter* THOMAS.) Here are fine doings!
    I am deceived, tricked and cheated!

O gra ma chree . . . din ousil craw: mangled Gaelic for 'O love of my heart . . . honoured and
beloved person'.
choused: cheated.

THOMAS: I wish you joy, sir; the best thing could have happened to you; and as a faithful servant I have done my best to check you.

WHITTLE: To check me!

THOMAS: You were galloping full speed and downhill too, and if we had not laid hold of the bridle, being a bad jockey, you would have hung by the horns in the stirrup, to the great joy of the whole town.

WHITTLE: What, have *you* helped to trick me?

THOMAS: Into happiness. You have been foolish a long while: turn about and be wise. He has got the woman and his estate; give them your blessing, which is not worth much, and live like a Christian for the future.

WHITTLE: I will if I can, but I can't look at 'em; I can't bear the sound of my voice, nor the sight of my face. Look ye, I am distressed and distracted, and I can't come to yet. I will be reconciled if possible; but don't let me see or hear from you if you would have me forget and forgive you! I shall never lift up my head again! (*Exit.*)

WIDOW: I hope, Sir Patrick, that my preferring the nephew to the uncle will meet with your approbation. Though we have not so much money, we shall have more love; one mind and half a purse in marriage are much better than two minds and two purses. I did not come to England, nor keep good company, till it was too late to get rid of my country prejudices.

SIR PATRICK: You are out of my hands, Pat; so if you won't trouble me with your afflictions I shall sincerely rejoice at your felicity.

NEPHEW: It would be a great abatement of my present joy, could I believe that this lady should be assisted in her happiness or be supported in her afflictions by anyone but her lover and her husband.

SIR PATRICK: Fine notions are fine tings, but a fine estate gives everyting but ideas, and them too if you'll appale to those who help you to spend it. What say you, widow?

WIDOW: By your and their permission, I will tell them to this good company; and for fear my words should want ideas too, I will add an Irish tune to 'em, that may carry off a bad voice and bad matter.

Song

A widow bewitched with her passion,
Though Irish, is now quite ashamed
To think that she's so out of fashion
To marry and then to be tamed:
'Tis love the dear joy,
That old-fashioned boy,
Has got in my breast with his quiver;
The blind urchin he
Struck the *Cush la maw cree*,
And a husband secures me for ever!
Ye fair ones I hope will excuse me,
Though vulgar, pray do not abuse me;
I cannot become a fine lady;
O love has bewitched Widow Brady.

II

Ye critics, to murder so willing,
  Pray see all our errors with blindness;
For once change your method of killing,
  And kill a fond widow with kindness.
    If you look so severe
    In a fit of despair,
  Again I will draw forth my steel, sirs;
    You know I've the art
    To be twice through your heart
  Before I can make you to feel, sirs.
    Brother soldiers, I hope you'll protect me,
    Nor let cruel critics dissect me;
    To favour my cause be but ready,
    And grateful you'll find Widow Brady.

III

Ye leaders of dress and the fashions,
  Who gallop post-haste to your ruin,
Whose taste has destroyed all your passions,
  Pray, what do you think of my wooing?
    You call it damn low,
    Your heads and arms so, (*Mimics them.*)
  So listless, so loose and so lazy,
    But pray what can you
    That I cannot do?
  Oh fie! my dear craters, be azy.
    Ye patriots and courtiers so hearty
    To speech it and vote for your party,
    For once be both constant and steady
    And vote to support Widow Brady.

IV

To all that I see here before me,
  The bottom, the top and the middle,
For music we now must implore you –
  No wedding without pipe and fiddle!
    If all are in tune
    Pray let it be soon;
  My heart in my bosom is prancing!
    If your hands should unite
    To give us delight,
  O that's the best piping and dancing!
    Your plaudits to me are a treasure;
    Your smiles are a dow'r for a lady;
    O joy to you all in full measure,
    So wishes and prays Widow Brady.

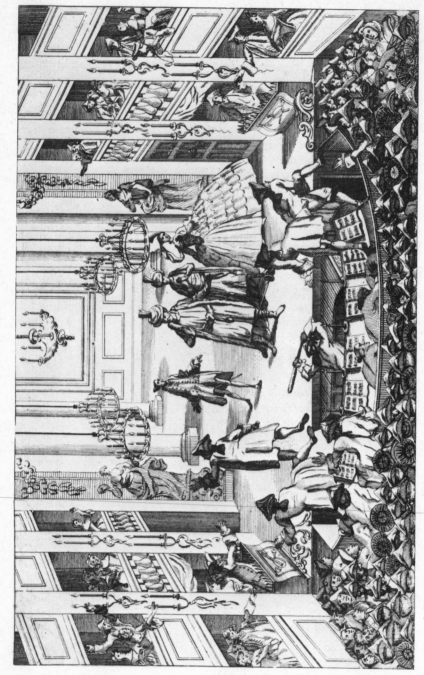

6. The stage at Covent Garden, 1763, during a riot which interrupted a performance of Arne's *Ataxerxes*. Engraving by L. Boitard. Notice stage boxes, stage doors, chandeliers and the scene

BON TON
or
HIGH LIFE ABOVE STAIRS

by David Garrick

First performed at Drury Lane on 18 March 1775,
with the following cast:

LORD MINIKIN	Mr Dodd
SIR JOHN TROTLEY	Mr King
COLONEL TIVY	Mr Brereton
JESSAMY	Mr Lamash
DAVY	Mr Parsons
MIGNON	Mr Burton
LADY MINIKIN	Miss Pope
LETITIA TITTUP	Mrs Abington
GYMP	Miss Platt

ACT I

SCENE 1.   *Enter* LADY MINIKIN *and* MISS TITTUP.

LADY MIN: It is not, my dear, that I have the least regard for my lord; I had no love for him before I married him, and you know, matrimony is no breeder of affection; but it hurts my pride, that he should neglect me, and run after other women.

MISS TITT: Ha, ha, ha, how can you be so hypocritical, Lady Minikin, as to pretend to uneasiness at such trifles? But pray have you made any new discoveries of my lord's gallantry?

LADY MIN: New discoveries! Why, I saw him myself yesterday morning in a hackney-coach, with a minx in a pink cardinal; you shall absolutely burn yours, Tittup, for I shall never bear to see one of that colour again.

MISS TITT: (*aside*) Sure she does not suspect me. – And where was your ladyship, pray, when you saw him?

LADY MIN: Taking the air with Colonel Tivy in his *vis-à-vis*.

MISS TITT: But, my dear Lady Minikin, how can you be so angry that my lord was hurting your pride, as you call it, in the hackney-coach, when you had him so much in your power in the *vis-à-vis*?

LADY MIN: What, with my lord's friend, and my friend's lover? (*Takes her by the hand.*) Oh fie, Tittup!

MISS TITT: Pooh, pooh, Love and Friendship are very fine names to be sure, but they are mere visiting acquaintance; we know their names indeed, talk of 'em sometimes, and let 'em knock at our doors, but we never let 'em in, you know (*looking roguishly at her*).

LADY MIN: I vow, Tittup, you are extremely polite.

MISS TITT: I am extremely indifferent in these affairs, thanks to my education. – We must marry, you know, because other people of fashion marry; but I should think very meanly of myself, if after I was married, I should feel the least concern at all about my husband.

LADY MIN: I hate to praise myself, and yet I may with truth aver that no woman of quality ever had, can have, or will have, so consummate a contempt for her lord, as I have for my most honourable and puissant Earl of Minikin, Viscount Perriwinkle, and Baron Titmouse. – Ha, ha, ha!

MISS TITT: But is it not strange, Lady Minikin, that merely his being your husband, should create such indifference; for certainly, in every other eye, his lordship has great accomplishments.

LADY MIN: Accomplishments! Thy head is certainly turned; if you know any of 'em, pray let's have 'em; they are a novelty, and will amuse me.

MISS TITT: Imprimis, he is a man of quality.

LADY MIN: Which, to be sure, includes all the cardinal virtues – poor girl! – go on!

MISS TITT: He is a very handsome man.

LADY MIN: He has a very bad constitution.

---

vis-à-vis: light carriage in which two (or four) passengers face each other.

MISS TITT: He has wit.

LADY MIN: He is a lord, and a little goes a great way.

MISS TITT: He has great good nature.

LADY MIN: No wonder — he's a fool.

MISS TITT: And then his fortune, you'll allow —

LADY MIN: Was a great one — but he games, and if fairly, he's undone; if not, he deserves to be hanged — and so, Exit my Lord Minikin. — And now, let your wise uncle, and my good cousin Sir John Trotley, Baronet, enter. Where is he, pray?

MISS TITT: In his own room, I suppose, reading pamphlets and newspapers, against the enormities of the times; if he stays here a week longer, notwithstanding my expectations from him, I shall certainly affront him.

LADY MIN: I am a great favourite, but it is impossible much longer to act up to his very righteous ideas of things. — Isn't it pleasant to hear him abuse everybody and everything, and yet always finishing with a — 'You'll excuse me, cousin'? — Ha, ha, ha!

MISS TITT: What do you think the Goth said to me yesterday? One of the knots of his tie hanging down his left shoulder, and his fringed cravat nicely twisted down his breast, and thrust through his gold button hole, which looked exactly like my little Barbet's head in his gold collar — 'Niece Tittup,' cries he, drawing himself up, 'I protest against this manner of conducting yourself, both at home and abroad'. — 'What are your objections, Sir John?' answered I, a little pertly. — 'Various and manifold' replied he. 'I have no time to enumerate particulars now, but I will venture to prophesy, if you keep whirling round in the vortex of Pantheons, Operas, Festinos, Coteries, Masquerades, and all the Devilades in this town, your head will be giddy, down you will fall, lose the name of Lucretia, and be called nothing but Tittup ever after — You'll excuse me, cousin!' — and so he left me.

LADY MIN: Oh, the barbarian!
        (*Enter* GYMP.)

GYMP: A card, your ladyship, from Mrs Pewitt.

LADY MIN: Poor Pewitt! — If she can be but seen at public places, with a woman of quality, she's the happiest of plebeians. (*Reads the card.*) 'Mrs Pewitt's respects to Lady Minikin, and Miss Tittup; hopes to have the pleasure of attending them, to Lady Filligree's ball this evening. — Lady Daisey sees masks.' — We'll certainly attend her. — Gymp, put some message cards upon my toilet; I'll send an answer immediately; and tell one of my footmen that he must make some visits for me today again, and send me a list of those he made yesterday: he must be sure to call at Lady Pettitoes, and if she should unluckily be at home, he must say that he came to inquire after her sprained ankle.

MISS TITT: Ay, ay, give our compliments to her sprained ankle.

LADY MIN: That woman's so fat, she'll never get well of it, and I am resolved not to call at her door myself, till I am sure of not finding her at home. — I am horridly low spirited today; do send your colonel to play at chess with me. Since he belonged to you, Titty, I have taken a kind of liking to him; I like everything that loves my Titty. (*Kisses her.*)

MISS TITT: I know you do, my dear lady. (*Kisses her.*)

LADY MIN: (*aside*) That sneer I don't like; if she suspects, I shall hate her. — Well, dear Titty, I'll go and write my cards, and dress for the masquerade, and if that won't raise my spirits, you must assist me to plague my lord a little. (*Exit.*)

MISS TITT: Yes, and I'll plague my lady a little, or I am much mistaken: my lord shall know every tittle that has passed. What a poor, blind, half-witted, self-conceited creature this dear friend and relation of mine is! And what a fine spirited gallant soldier my colonel is! My Lady Minikin likes him, he likes my fortune; my lord likes me, and I like my lord; however, not so much as he imagines, or to play the fool so rashly as he may expect; she must be very silly indeed, who can't flutter about the flame, without burning her wings. What a great revolution in this family, in the space of fifteen months! — We went out of England, a very awkward, regular, good English family! but half a year in France, and a winter passed in the warmer climate of Italy, have ripened our minds to every refinement of care, dissipation, and pleasure.

(*Enter* COLONEL TIVY.)

COL. TIV: May I hope, madam, that your humble servant had some share in your last reverie?

MISS TITT: How is it possible to have the least knowledge of Colonel Tivy and not make him the principal object of one's reflections.

COL. TIV: That man must have very little feeling and taste, who is not proud of a place in the thoughts of the finest woman in Europe.

MISS TITT: Oh fie, colonel! (*Curtsies and blushes.*)

COL. TIV: By my honour, madam, I mean what I say.

MISS TITT: By your honour, colonel! why will you pass off your counters to me? Don't I know that you fine gentlemen regard no honour but that which is given at the gaming table; and which indeed ought to be the only honour you should make free with.

COL. TIV: How can you, miss, treat me so cruelly? Have I not absolutely forsworn dice, mistress, everything, since I dared to offer myself to you?

MISS TITT: Yes, colonel, and when I dare to receive you, you may return to everything again, and not violate the laws of the present happy matrimonial establishment.

COL. TIV: Give me but your consent, madam, and your life to come —

MISS TITT: Do you get my consent, colonel, and I'll take care of my life to come.

COL. TIV: How shall I get your consent?

MISS TITT: By getting me in the humour.

COL. TIV: But how to get you in the humour?

MISS TITT: Oh, there are several ways; I am very good-natured.

COL. TIV: Are you in the humour now?

MISS TITT: Try me.

COL. TIV: How shall I?

MISS TITT: How shall I! — You a soldier, and not know the art military? — How shall I? — I'll tell you how. — When you have a subtle, treacherous, politic enemy to deal with, never stand shilly-shally, and lose your time in treaties and parleys, but cock your hat, draw your sword; — march, beat drum — dub,

dub, a-dub — present, fire, piff-pauff — 'tis done! They fly, they yield — Victoria! Victoria! — (*running off*)

COL. TIV: Stay, stay, my dear, dear angel! — (*bringing her back*)

MISS TITT: No, no, no, I have no time to be killed now; besides, Lady Minikin is in the vapours, and wants you at chess, and my lord is low spirited, and wants me at piquet; my uncle is in an ill humour and wants me to discard you, and go with him into the country.

COL. TIV: And will you, miss?

MISS TITT: Will I! — no, I never do as I am bid; but you ought — so go to my lady.

COL. TIV: Nay, but miss.

MISS TITT: Nay, but colonel, if you won't obey your commanding officer, you shall be broke, and then my maid won't accept of you; so march, colonel! — Look'ee, sir, I will command before marriage, and do what I please afterwards, or I have been well educated to very little purpose. (*Exit.*)

COL. TIV: What a mad devil it is! — Now, if I had the least affection for the girl, I should be damnably vexed at this! — But she has a fine fortune, and I must have her if I can. — Tol, lol, lol, — (*Exit singing.*)

(*Enter* SIR JOHN TROTLEY *and* DAVY.)

SIR JOHN: Hold your tongue, Davy; you talk like a fool.

DAVY: It is a fine place, your honour; and I could live here for ever!

SIR JOHN: More shame for you: — live here for ever! — what, among thieves and pick-pockets! — what a revolution since my time! The more I see, the more I've cause for lamentation; what a dreadful change has time brought about in twenty years! I should not have known the place again, nor the people; all the signs that made so noble an appearance, are all taken down — not a bob or tie-wig to be seen! All the degrees from the parade in St James's Park, to the stool and brush at the corner of every street, have their hair tied up — the mason laying bricks, the baker with his basket, the post-boy crying newspapers, and the doctor prescribing physic, have all their hair tied up; and that's the reason so many heads are tied up every month.

DAVY: I shall have my head tied up tomorrow — Mr Whisp will do it for me — your honour and I look like Philistines among 'em.

SIR JOHN: And I shall break your head if it is tied up; I hate innovation — all confusion and no distinction! — The streets now are as smooth as a turnpike-road! No rattling and exercise in the hackney-coaches; those who ride in 'em are all fast asleep; and they have strings in their hands, that the coachman must pull to waken 'em, when they are to be set down — what luxury and abomination!

DAVY: Is it so, your honour. 'Feckins, I liked it hugely.

SIR JOHN: But you must hate and detest London.

DAVY: How can I manage that, your honour, when there is everything to delight my eye, and cherish my heart.

SIR JOHN: 'Tis all deceit and delusion.

DAVY: Such crowding, coaching, carting, and squeezing, such a power of fine sights, fine shops full of fine things, and then such fine illuminations all of a row! and such fine dainty ladies in the streets, so civil and so graceless. — They talk of country girls — these here look more healthy and rosy by half.

SIR JOHN: Sirrah, they are prostitutes, and are civil to delude and destroy you:

they are painted Jezabels, and they who hearken to 'em, like Jezabel of old, will go to the dogs; if you dare to look at 'em, you will be tainted, and if you speak to 'em you are undone.

DAVY: Bless us, bless us! — How does your honour know all this! — Were they as bad in your time?

SIR JOHN: Not by half, Davy. — In my time, there was a sort of decency in the worst of women; but the harlots now watch like tigers for their prey; and drag you to their dens of infamy — see, Davy, how they have torn my neck-cloth. (*Shows his neckcloth.*)

DAVY: If you had gone civilly, your honour, they would not have hurt you.

SIR JOHN: Well, we'll get away as fast as we can.

DAVY: Not this month, I hope, for I have not had half my belly full yet.

SIR JOHN: I'll knock you down, Davy, if you grow profligate; you shan't go out again tonight, and tomorrow keep in my room, and stay till I can look over my things, and see they don't cheat you.

DAVY: (*sulkily*) Your honour then won't keep your word with me?

SIR JOHN: Why, what did I promise you?

DAVY: That I should take sixpen'oth of one of the theatres tonight, and a shilling place at the other tomorrow.

SIR JOHN: Well, well, so I did: is it a moral piece, Davy?

DAVY: Oh yes, and written by a clergyman; it is called the *Rival Canaanites, or the Tragedy of Braggadocia.*

SIR JOHN: Be a good lad, and I won't be worse than my word; there's money for you — (*Gives him some.*) but come straight home, for I shall want to go to bed.

DAVY: To be sure, your honour — as I am to go so soon, I'll make a night of it. (*Aside and exit.*)

SIR JOHN: This fellow would turn rake and maccaroni if he was to stay here a week longer — bless me, what dangers are in this town at every step! Oh, that I were once settled safe again at Trotley Place! — nothing but to save my country should bring me back again. My niece Lucretia is so be-fashioned and be-devilled that nothing, I fear, can save her; however, to ease my conscience, I must try; but what can be expected from the young women of these times, but sallow looks, wild schemes, saucy words, and loose morals! — They lie a-bed all day, sit up all night; if they are silent, they are gaming, and if they talk, 'tis either scandal or infidelity; and that they may look what they are, their heads are all feather, and round their necks are twisted, rattle-snake tippets — *O Tempora, O Mores!* (*Exit.*)

SCENE 2.   LORD MINIKIN *discovered in his powdering gown, with* JESSAMY *and* MIGNON.

LORD MIN: Prithee, Mignon, don't plague me any more; dost think that a noble-man's head has nothing to do. but be tortured all day under thy infernal fingers! Give me my clothes.

O Tempora, O Mores!: lament over new times, new morality.

MIGN: Ven you loss your monee, my lor, you no goot humour. The devil may
    dress your *cheveux* for me! (*Exit.*)
LORD MIN: That fellow's an impudent rascal, but he's a genius, so I must bear
    with him. Our beef and pudding enriches their blood so much, that the
    slaves, in a month, forget their misery and soup maigre. Oh, my head! – a
    chair, Jessamy! – I must absolutely change my wine-merchant: I can't
    taste his champagne, without disordering myself for a week! – Heigh-ho!
    – (*Sighs.*)
            (*Enter* MISS TITTUP.)
MISS TITT: What makes you sigh, my lord?
LORD MIN: Because you were so near me, child.
MISS TITT: Indeed! I should rather have thought my lady had been with you – by
    your looks, my lord. I am afraid Fortune jilted you last night.
LORD MIN: No, faith; our champagne was not good yesterday, and I am vapoured
    like our English November; but one glance of my Tittup can dispel vapours
    like – like –
MISS TITT: Like something very fine to be sure; but pray keep your simile for the
    next time; and hark'ee – a little prudence will not be amiss; Mr Jessamy will
    think you mad, and me worse (*half aside*).
JESS: (*entering*) Oh, pray don't mind me, madam.
LORD MIN: Gadso, Jessamy, look out my domino, and I'll ring the bell when I
    want you.
JESS: I shall, my lord; Miss thinks that everybody is blind in the house but herself.
    (*Aside and exit.*)
MISS TITT: Upon my word, my lord, you must be a little more prudent, or we shall
    become the town-talk.
LORD MIN: And so I will, my dear; and therefore to prevent surprise, I'll lock the
    door. (*Locks it.*)
MISS TITT: What do you mean, my lord?
LORD MIN: Prudence, child, prudence; I keep all my jewels under lock and key.
MISS TITT: You are not in possession yet, my lord: I can't stay two minutes: I
    only came to tell you that Lady Minikin saw us yesterday in the hackney-
    coach; she did not know me, I believe; she pretends to be greatly uneasy at
    your neglect of her; she certainly has some mischief in her head.
LORD MIN: No intentions, I hope, of being fond of me?
MISS TITT: No, no, make yourself easy; she hates you most unalterably.
LORD MIN: You have given me spirits again.
MISS TITT: Her pride is alarmed that you should prefer any of the sex to her.
LORD MIN: Her pride then has been alarmed ever since I had the honour of know-
    ing her.
MISS TITT: But, dear my lord, let us be merry and wise; should she ever be con-
    vinced that we have a *tendre* for each other, she certainly would proclaim it,
    and then –
LORD MIN: We should be envied, and she would be laughed at, my sweet cousin.
MISS TITT: Nay, I would have her mortified too – for though I love her ladyship
    sincerely, I cannot say but I love a little mischief as sincerely: but then if my
    uncle Trotley should know of our affairs, he is so old-fashioned, prudish, and

out of the way, he would either strike me out of his will, or insist upon my quitting the house.

LORD MIN: My good cousin is a queer mortal, that's certain; I wish we could get him handsomely into the country again — he has a fine fortune to leave behind him —

MISS TITT: But then he lives so regularly, and never makes use of a physician, that he may live these twenty years.

LORD MIN: What can we do with the barbarian?

MISS TITT: I don't know what's the matter with me, but I am really in fear of him; I suppose reading his formal books when I was in the country with him, and going so constantly to church, with my elbows stuck to my hips, and my toes turned in, has given me these foolish prejudices.

LORD MIN: Then you must affront him, or you'll never get the better of him.
> (*Knocking is heard at door.*)

SIR JOHN: (*without*) My lord, my lord, are you busy?
> (LORD MINIKIN *unlocks the door softly.*)

MISS TITT: Heav'ns! 'Tis that detestable brute, my uncle!

LORD MIN: That horrid dog, my cousin!

MISS TITT: (*softly*) What shall we do, my lord?

SIR JOHN: (*at the door*) Nay, my lord, my lord, I heard you; pray let me speak with you!

LORD MIN: Ho, Sir John, is it you? I beg your pardon. I'll put up my papers and open the door.

MISS TITT: Stay, stay, my lord, I would not meet him now for the world; if he sees me here alone with you, he'll rave like a madman; put me up the chimney — anywhere.

LORD MIN: (*aloud*) I'm coming, Sir John! Here, here, get behind my great chair; he shan't see you, and you may hear all; I'll be short and pleasant with him. (*Puts her behind the chair, and opens the door.*)
> (*Enter* SIR JOHN. *During this scene,* LORD MINIKIN *turns the chair, as* SIR JOHN *moves, to conceal* TITTUP.)

SIR JOHN: You'll excuse me, my lord, that I have broken in upon you! I heard you talking pretty loud; what, have you nobody with you? What were you about, cousin? (*looking about*)

LORD MIN: A particular affair, Sir John; I always lock myself up to study my speeches, and speak 'em aloud for the sake of the tone and action —

SIR JOHN: Ay, ay, 'tis the best way; I am sorry I disturbed you — you'll excuse me, cousin!

LORD MIN: I am rather obliged to you, Sir John — intense application to these things ruins my health; but one must do it for the sake of the nation.

SIR JOHN: May be so, and I hope the nation will be the better for't — you'll excuse me!

LORD MIN: Excuse you, Sir John, I love your frankness; but why won't you be franker still? We have always something for dinner, and you will never dine at home.

SIR JOHN: You must know, my lord, that I love to know what I eat — I hate to travel where I don't know my way; and since you have brought in foreign fashions and vagaries, everything and everybody are in masquerade; your men and manners too are as much frittered and fricasseed, as your beef and mutton; I love a plain dish, my lord.

MISS TITT: (*peeping*) I wish I was out of the room, or he at the bottom of the Thames.

SIR JOHN: But to the point — I came, my lord, to open my mind to you about my niece, Tittup; shall I do it freely?

MISS TITT: Now for it!

LORD MIN: The freer the better; Tittup's a fine girl, cousin, and deserves all the kindness you can show her.

(LORD MINIKIN *and* TITTUP *make signs at each other.*)

SIR JOHN: She must deserve it, though, before she shall have it; and I would have her begin with lengthening her petticoats, covering her shoulders, and wearing a cap upon her head.

MISS TITT: Oh, frightful!

LORD MIN: Don't you think a taper leg, and falling shoulders, and fine hair, delightful objects, Sir John?

SIR JOHN: And therefore ought to be concealed; 'tis their interest to conceal 'em; when you take from the men the pleasure of imagination, there will be a scarcity of husbands — and then taper legs, falling shoulders and fine hair may be had for nothing.

LORD MIN: Well said, Sir John; ha, ha! — Your niece shall wear a horseman's-coat, and jack-boots to please you.

SIR JOHN: You may sneer, my lord, but for all that, I think my niece in a bad way: she must leave me and the country, forsooth, to travel and see good company and fashions; I have seen 'em too, and wish from my heart that she is not much the worse for her journey — you'll excuse me!

LORD MIN: But why in a passion, Sir John? (*Nods and laughs at* MISS TITTUP, *who peeps from behind.*) Don't you think that my lady and I shall be able and willing to put her into the right road?

SIR JOHN: Zounds! my lord, you are out of it yourself. This comes of your travelling; all the town knows how you and my lady live together; and I must tell you — you'll excuse me! — that my niece suffers by the bargain. Prudence, my lord, is a very fine thing.

LORD MIN: So is a long neckcloth nicely twisted into a buttonhole, but I don't choose to wear one — you'll excuse me!

SIR JOHN: I wish that he who first changed long neckcloths, for such things as you wear, had the wearing of a twisted neckcloth that I would give him.

LORD MIN: Prithee, Baronet, don't be so horridly out of the way. Prudence is a very vulgar virtue, and so incompatible with our present ease and refinement, that a prudent man of fashion is now as great a miracle as a pale woman of quality; we got rid of our *mauvaise honte* at the time that we imported our neighbours' rouge, and their morals.

SIR JOHN: Did you ever hear the like! I am not surprised, my lord, that you think so lightly, and talk so vainly, who are so polite a husband; your lady, my cousin, is a fine woman, and brought you a fine fortune, and deserves better usage.

LORD MIN: Will you have her, Sir John? She is very much at your service.

SIR JOHN: Profligate! — What did you marry her for, my lord?

LORD MIN: Convenience! — Marriage is not nowadays an affair of inclination, but convenience; and they who marry for love, and such old-fashioned stuff, are to me as ridiculous as those that advertise for an agreeable companion in a post-chaise.

SIR JOHN: I have done, my lord. Miss Tittup shall either return with me into the country, or not a penny shall she have from Sir John Trotley, Baronet. (*Whistles and walks about.*)

MISS TITT: I am frightened out of my wits!

(LORD MINIKIN *sings and sits down.*)

SIR JOHN: Pray, my lord, what husband is this you have got for her?

LORD MIN: A friend of mine; a man of wit, and a fine gentleman.

SIR JOHN: May be so, and yet make a damned husband for all that. You'll excuse me! — What estate has he, pray?

LORD MIN: He's a colonel; his eldest brother, Sir Tan Tivy, will certainly break his neck, and then my friend will be a happy man.

SIR JOHN: Here's morals! — a happy man when his brother has broke his neck! — a happy man! Mercy on me!

LORD MIN: Why he'll have six thousand a year, Sir John —

SIR JOHN: I don't care what he'll have, nor I don't care what he is, nor who my niece marries; she is a fine lady and let her have a fine gentleman; I shan't hinder her; I'll away into the country tomorrow, and leave you to your fine doings; I have no relish for 'em, not I; I can't live among you, nor eat with you, nor game with you; I hate cards and dice, I will neither rob nor be robbed; I am contented with what I have, and am very happy, my lord, though my brother has not broke his neck — you'll excuse me! (*Exit.*)

LORD MIN: Ha, ha, ha! Come, fox, come out of your hole! Ha, ha, ha!

MISS TITT: Indeed, my lord, you have undone me; not a foot shall I have of Trotley Manor, that's positive! — but no matter, there's no danger of his breaking his neck; so I'll e'en make myself happy with what I have, and behave to him, for the future, as if he was a poor relation.

LORD MIN: (*kneeling, snatching her hand, and kissing it*) I must kneel and adore you for your spirit; my sweet, heavenly Lucretia!

(*Re-enter* SIR JOHN.)

SIR JOHN: One thing I had forgot. (*Starts.*)

MISS TITT: Ha! he's here again!

SIR JOHN: Why, what the devil; — heigh-ho! my niece, Lucretia, and my virtuous lord, studying speeches for the good of the nation! — Yes, yes, you have been making fine speeches, indeed, my lord; and your arguments have prevailed, I see. I beg your pardon, I did not mean to interrupt your studies — you'll excuse me, my lord!

LORD MIN: (*smiling, and mocking him*) You'll excuse me, Sir John!

SIR JOHN: Oh yes, my lord, but I'm afraid the devil won't excuse you at the proper

---

Sir Tan Tivy: farcical reference to hunting term *tantivy*, meaning full gallop.

time. — Miss Lucretia, how do you, child! You are to be married soon — I wish the gentleman joy, Miss Lucretia; he is a happy man to be sure, and will want nothing but the breaking of his brother's neck to be completely so.

MISS TITT: Upon my word, uncle, you are always putting bad constructions upon things; my lord has been soliciting me to marry his friend — and having that moment extorted a consent from me — he was thanking and wishing me joy — (*hesitating*) in his foolish manner.

SIR JOHN: Is that all! But how came you here, child? — Did you fly down the chimney, or in at the window? For I don't remember seeing you when I was here before.

MISS TITT: How can you talk so, Sir John? — You really confound me with your suspicions; and then you ask so many questions, and I have so many things to do, that — that — upon my word, if I don't make haste, I shan't get my dress ready for the ball; so I must run. — You'll excuse me, uncle! (*Exit running.*)

SIR JOHN: A fine hopeful young lady that, my lord.

LORD MIN: She's well-bred and has wit.

SIR JOHN: She has wit and breeding enough to laugh at her relations, and bestow favours on your lordship; but I must tell you plainly, my lord — you'll excuse me — that your marrying your lady, my cousin, to use her ill, and sending for my niece, your cousin, to debauch her —

LORD MIN: You're warm, Sir John, and don't know the world, and I never contend with ignorance and passion; live with me some time, and you'll be satisfied of my honour and good intentions to you and your family; in the meantime command my house. I must attend immediately Lady Filligree's masquerade, and I am sorry you won't make one with us. Here, Jessamy, give me my domino, and call a chair; and don't let my uncle want for any thing. You'll excuse me, Sir John, tol, lol, derol, — (*Exit singing.*)

SIR JOHN: The world's at an end! Here's fine work; here are precious doings! This lord is a pillar of the state too; no wonder that the building is in danger with such rotten supporters; — heigh-ho! — and then my poor Lady Minikin, what a friend and husband she is blessed with! — Let me consider! — Should I tell the good woman of these pranks, I may only make more mischief, and mayhap, go near to kill her, for she's as tender as she's virtuous — poor lady! I'll e'en go and comfort her directly, endeavour to draw her from the wickedness of this town into the country, where she shall have reading, fowling, and fishing, to keep up her spirits, and when I die, I will leave her that part of my fortune, with which I intended to reward the virtues of Miss Lucretia Tittup, with a plague to her! (*Exit.*)

SCENE 3.   LADY MINIKIN's *apartments.* LADY MINIKIN *and* COLONEL TIVY *discovered.*

LADY MIN: Don't urge it, colonel; I can't think of coming home from the masquerade this evening. Though I should pass for my niece, it would make an uproar among the servants; and perhaps from the mistake break off your match with Tittup.

COL. TIV: My dear Lady Minikin, you know my marriage with your niece is only a secondary consideration; my first and principal object is you — you, madam! — therefore, my dear lady, give me your promise to leave the ball with me; you must, Lady Minikin; a bold young fellow and a soldier as I am, ought not to be kept from plunder when the town has capitulated.

LADY MIN: But it has not capitulated, and perhaps never will; however, colonel, since you are so furious, I must come to terms, I think. — Keep your eyes upon me at the ball — I think I may expect that — and when I drop my handkerchief, 'tis your signal for pursuing; I shall get home as fast as I can, you may follow me as fast as you can; my lord and Tittup will be otherwise employed; Gymp will let us in the back way — no, no, my heart misgives me!

COL. TIV: Then I am miserable!

LADY MIN: Nay, rather than you should be miserable, colonel, I will indulge your martial spirit; meet me in the field; there's my gauntlet. (*Throws down her glove.*)

COL. TIV: (*seizing it*) Thus I accept your sweet challenge; and if I fail you, may I hereafter, both in love and war, be branded with the name of coward. (*Kneels and kisses her hand.*)

(*Enter* SIR JOHN, *opening the door.*)

SIR JOHN: May I presume, cousin.

LADY MIN: Ha! (*Squalls.*)

SIR JOHN: Mercy upon us, what are we at now? (*Looks astonished.*)

LADY MIN: How can you be so rude, Sir John, to come into a lady's room, without first knocking at the door? You have frightened me out of my wits!

SIR JOHN: I am sure you have frightened me out of mine!

COL. TIV: Such rudeness deserves death!

SIR JOHN: Death indeed! For I shall never recover myself again! All pigs of the same sty! All studying for the good of the nation!

LADY MIN: (*aside to the* COLONEL) We must soothe him, and not provoke him.

COL. TIV: (*aside to* LADY MINIKIN) I would cut his throat if you'd permit me.

SIR JOHN: The devil has got his hoof into the house, and has corrupted the whole family; I'll get out of it as fast as I can, lest he should lay hold of me too (*going*).

LADY MIN: Sir John, I must insist upon your not going away in a mistake.

SIR JOHN: No mistake, my lady, I am thoroughly convinced — mercy on me!

LADY MIN: I must beg you, Sir John, not to make any wrong constructions upon this accident; you must know, that the moment you were at the door — I had promised the colonel no longer to be his enemy in his designs upon Miss Tittup — this threw him into such a rapture — that upon my promising my interest with you — and wishing him joy — he fell upon his knees, and — and — (*laughing*) ha, ha, ha!

COL. TIV: Ha, ha, ha! Yes, yes, I fell upon my knees, and — and —

SIR JOHN: Ay, ay, fell upon your knees and — and — ha! ha! a very good joke, faith; and the best of it is, that they are wishing joy all over the house upon the same occasion: and my lord is wishing joy, and I wish him joy and you with all my heart.

LADY MIN: Upon my word, Sir John, your cruel suspicions affect me strongly; and though my resentment is curbed by my regard, my tears cannot be restrained; 'tis the only resource my innocence has left. (*Exit crying.*)

COL. TIV: I reverence you, sir, as a relation to that lady, but as her slanderer I
detest you: her tears must be dried, and my honour satisfied; you know what
I mean; take your choice; — time, place, sword or pistol; consider it calmly,
and determine as you please; I am a soldier, Sir John. (*Exit.*)

SIR JOHN: Very fine, truly! And so between the crocodile and the bully, my
throat is to be cut; they are guilty of all sorts of iniquity, and when they are
discovered, no humility and repentance — the ladies have resource to their
tongues or their tears, and the gallants to their swords. — That I may not be
drawn in by the one, or drawn upon by the other, I'll hurry into the country
while I retain my senses, and can sleep in a whole skin. (*Exit.*)

ACT II

SCENE 1.   *Enter* SIR JOHN *and* JESSAMY.

SIR JOHN: There is no bearing this! What a land are we in! Upon my word, Mr
Jessamy, you should look well to the house; there are certainly rogues about
it: for I did but cross the way just now to the pamphlet shop, to buy a touch
of the times, and they have taken my hanger from my side; ay, and had a
pluck at my watch too, but I heard of their tricks, and had it sewed to my
pocket.

JESS: Don't be alarmed, Sir John; 'tis a very common thing, and if you will walk
the streets without convoy, you will be picked up by privateers of all kinds;
ha, ha!

SIR JOHN: Not be alarmed when I am robbed! — Why, they might have cut my
throat with my own hanger; I shan't sleep a wink all night; so pray lend me
some weapon of defence, for I am sure if they attack me in the open street,
they'll be with me at night again.

JESS: I'll lend you my own sword, Sir John; but be assured there's no danger;
there's robbing and murder cried every night under my window; but it no
more disturbs me than the ticking of my watch at my bed's head.

SIR JOHN: Well, well, be that as it will, I must be upon my guard; what a dreadful
place this is! But 'tis all owing to the corruption of the times; the great folks
game, and the poor folks rob; no wonder that murder ensues; sad, sad, sad! —
Well, let me but get over this night, and I'll leave this den of thieves tomorrow.
How long will your lord and lady stay at this masking and mummery before
they come home?

JESS: 'Tis impossible to say the time, sir; that merely depends upon the spirits of
the company and the nature of the entertainment: for my own part, I generally make it myself till four or five in the morning.

SIR JOHN: Why, what the devil, do you make one at these masqueradings?

JESS: I seldom miss, sir; I may venture to say that nobody knows the trim and
small talk of the place better than I do; I was always reckoned an incomparable mask.

SIR JOHN: (*aside*) Thou art an incomparable coxcomb, I am sure.

JESS: An odd, ridiculous accident happened to me at a masquerade three years ago;
I was in tip-top spirits, and had drank a little too freely of the champagne, I
believe.

SIR JOHN: (*aside*) You'll be hanged, I believe.

JESS: Wit flew about. In short, I was in spirits; at last, from drinking and rattling, to vary the pleasure, we went to dancing: and who do you think I danced a minuet with? he! he! Pray guess, Sir John?

SIR JOHN: (*half aside*) Danced a minuet with.

JESS: My own lady, that's all; the eyes of the whole assembly were upon us. My lady dances well, and, I believe, I am pretty tolerable. After the dance, I was running into a little coquetry, and small talk with her.

SIR JOHN: With your lady? – (*aside*) Chaos is come again!

JESS: With my lady – but upon my turning my hand thus – (*conceitedly*) egad, she caught me; whispered me who I was. I would fain have laughed her out of it, but it would not do. 'No, no, Jessamy,' says she, 'I am not to be deceived: pray wear gloves for the future; for you may as well go bare-faced, as show that hand and diamond ring.'

SIR JOHN: (*aside*) What a sink of iniquity! Prostitution on all sides! from the lord to the pick-pocket. – Pray, Mr Jessamy, among your other virtues, I suppose you game a little, eh, Mr Jessamy?

JESS: A little whist or so; – but I am tied up from the dice; I must never touch a box again.

SIR JOHN: (*aside*) I wish you were tied up somewhere else; I sweat from top to toe! – Pray lend me your sword, Mr Jessamy; I shall go to my room; and let my lord and lady and my niece Tittup know that I beg they will excuse ceremonies, that I must be up and gone before they go to bed; and that I have a most profound respect and love for them, and – that I hope we shall never see one another again as long as we live.

JESS: I shall certainly obey your commands. (*aside*) What poor ignorant wretches these country gentlemen are! (*Exit.*)

SIR JOHN: If I stayed in this place another day, it would throw me into a fever! Oh I wish it was morning. – This comes of visiting my relations!

        (*Enter* DAVY, *drunk.*)

SIR JOHN: So, you wicked wretch you – where have you been, and what have you been doing?

DAVY: Merry-making, your honour. – London for ever!

SIR JOHN: Did not I order you to come directly from the play, and not be idling and raking about?

DAVY: Servants don't do what they are bid in London.

SIR JOHN: And did not I order you not to make a jackanapes of yourself, and tie your hair up like a monkey?

DAVY: And therefore I did it. No pleasing the ladies without this. My lord's servants call you an old out-of-fashioned codger, and have taught me what's what.

SIR JOHN: Here's an imp of the devil! He is undone, and will poison the whole country. – Sirrah, get everything ready, I'll be going directly.

DAVY: To bed, sir! – I want to go to bed myself, sir.

SIR JOHN: Why how now – you are drunk too, sirrah.

DAVY: I am a little, your honour, because I have been drinking.

SIR JOHN: That is not all – you have been in bad company, sirrah!

DAVY: Indeed, your honour's mistaken, I never kept such good company in all my life.

SIR JOHN: The fellow does not understand me. — Where have you been, you drunkard?

DAVY: Drinking, to be sure, if I am a drunkard; and if you had been drinking too, as I have been, you would not be in such a passion with a body — it makes one so good-natured —

SIR JOHN: This is another addition to my misfortunes! I shall have this fellow carry into the country as many vices as will corrupt the whole parish.

DAVY: I'll take what I can, to be sure, your worship.

SIR JOHN: Get away, you beast you, and sleep off the debauchery you have contracted this fortnight, or I shall leave you behind, as a proper person to make one of his lordship's family.

DAVY: So much the better — give me more wages, less work, and the key of the alecellar, and I am your servant; if not, provide yourself with another. (*Struts about.*)

SIR JOHN: Here's a reprobate! This is the completion of my misery! But hark'ee, villain — go to bed — and sleep off your iniquity, and then pack up the things, or I'll pack you off to Newgate, and transport you for life. (*Exit.*)

DAVY: That for you, old codger. (*Snaps his fingers.*) I know the law better than to be frightened with moonshine! I wish that I was to live here all my days! This is life indeed! A servant lives up to his eyes in clover; they have wages, and board-wages, and nothing to do, but to grow fat and saucy. They are as happy as their master, they play for ever at cards, swear like emperors, drink like fishes, and go a-wenching with as much ease and tranquillity, as if they were going to a sermon! Oh! 'tis a fine life! (*Exit reeling.*)

SCENE 2.   *A chamber in* LORD MINIKIN's *house. Enter* LORD MINIKIN, *and* MISS TITTUP, *in masquerade dresses, lighted by* JESSAMY.

LORD MIN: Set down the candles, Jessamy, and should your lady come home let me know. Be sure you are not out of the way.

JESS: I have lived too long with your lordship, to need the caution. Who the devil have we got now? But that's my lord's business, and not mine. (*Exit.*)

MISS TITT: (*pulling off her mask*) Upon my word, my lord, this coming home so soon from the masquerade is very imprudent, and will certainly be observed. I am most inconceivably frightened, I can assure you. My uncle Trotley has a light in his room; the accident this morning will certainly keep him upon the watch. Pray, my lord, let us defer our meetings till he goes into the country. I find that my English heart, though it has ventured so far, grows fearful and awkward to practise the freedoms of warmer climates. (LORD MINIKIN *takes her by the hand.*) If you will not desist, my lord — we are separated forever — the sight of the precipice turns my head. I have been giddy with it too long, and must turn from it while I can. — Pray be quiet, my lord. I will meet you tomorrow.

LORD MIN: Tomorrow! 'Tis an age in my situation. — Let the weak, bashful, coyish whiner be intimidated with these faint alarms, but let the bold experienced lover kindle at the danger, and like the eagle in the midst of storms thus pounce upon his prey. (*Takes hold of her.*)

MISS TITT: Dear Mr Eagle, be merciful. Pray let the poor pigeon fly for this once.

LORD MIN: If I do, my Dove, may I be cursed to have my wife as fond of me, as I am now of thee. (*Offers to kiss her.*)

JESS: (*without, knocking at the door*) My lord, my lord! —

MISS TITT: (*Screams.*) Ha!

LORD MIN: Who's there?

JESS: (*peeping*) 'Tis I, my lord. May I come in?

LORD MIN: Damn the fellow! What's the matter?

JESS: Nay, not much, my lord — only my lady's come home.

MISS TITT: Then I'm undone. What shall I do? — I'll run into my own room.

LORD MIN: Then she may meet you going to hers.

JESS: There's a dark, deep closet, my lord. Miss may hide herself there.

MISS TITT: For heaven's sake put me into it, and when her ladyship's safe, let me know, my lord. — What an escape have I had!

LORD MIN: The moment her evil spirit is laid, I'll let my angel out. (*Puts her into the closet.*) Lock the door on the inside. — Come softly to my room, Jessamy —

JESS: If a board creaks, your lordship shall never give me a laced waistcoat again. (*Exeunt.*)

> (*Enter* GYMP *lighting in* LADY MINIKIN *and* COLONEL TIVY, *in masquerade dresses.*)

GYMP: Pray, my lady, go no farther with the colonel; I know you mean nothing but innocence, but I'm sure there will be bloodshed, for my lord is certainly in the house — I'll take my affadavy that I heard —

COL. TIV: It can't be, I tell you; we left him this moment at the masquerade — I spoke to him before I came out.

LADY MIN: He's too busy and too well employed to think of home — but don't tremble so, Gymp. There is no harm, I assure you. The colonel is to marry my niece, and it is proper to settle some matters relating to it — they are left to us.

GYMP: Yes, yes, madam, to be sure it is proper that you talk together. I know you mean nothing but innocence, but indeed there will be bloodshed.

COL. TIV: The girl's a fool. I have no sword by my side.

GYMP: But my lord has, and you may kill one another with that — I know you mean nothing but innocence, but I certainly heard him go up the backstairs into his room talking with Jessamy.

LADY MIN: 'Tis impossible but the girl must have fancied this. — Can't you ask Whisp, or Mignon, if their master is come in?

GYMP: Lord, my lady, they are always drunk before this, and asleep in the kitchen.

LADY MIN: This frightened fool has made me as ridiculous as herself. Hark! — colonel, I'll swear there is something upon the stairs; now I am in the field I find I am a coward.

GYMP: There will certainly be bloodshed.

COL. TIV: I'll slip down with Gymp this back way then (*going*).

GYMP: Oh dear, my lady, there is somebody coming up them too.

COL. TIV: Zounds! I've got between two fires!

LADY MIN: Run into the closet.

COL. TIV: (*Runs to the closet.*) There's no retreat — the door is locked!

LADY MIN: Behind the chimney-board, Gymp.

COL. TIV: I shall certainly be taken prisoner. (*Goes behind the board.*) You'll let me know when the enemy's decamped.

LADY MIN: Leave that to me. — Do you, Gymp, go down the backstairs, and leave me to face my lord. I think I can match him at hypocrisy. (*Sits down.*)
>   (*Enter* LORD MINIKIN.)

LORD MIN: What, is your ladyship so soon returned from Lady Filligree's?

LADY MIN: I am sure, my lord, I ought to be more surprised at your being here so soon when I saw you so well entertained in a *tête-à-tête* with a lady in crimson. Such sights, my lord, will always drive me from my most favourite amusements.

LORD MIN: You find, at least, that the lady, whoever she was, could not engage me to stay, when I found your ladyship had left the ball.

LADY MIN: Your lordship's sneering upon my unhappy temper may be a proof of your wit, but is none of your humanity, and this behaviour is as great an insult upon me as even your falsehood itself. (*Pretends to weep.*)

LORD MIN: Nay, my dear Lady Minikin; if you are resolved to play tragedy, I shall roar away too, and pull out my cambric handkerchief.

LADY MIN: I think, my lord, we had better retire to our apartments; my weakness, and your brutality will only expose us to our servants. — Where is Tittup, pray?

LORD MIN: I left her with the colonel. A masquerade to young folks, upon the point of matrimony, is as delightful as it is disgusting to those who are happily married, and are wise enough to love home, and the company of their wives. (*Takes hold of her hand.*)

LADY MIN: (*aside*) False man! — I had as lief a toad touched me.

LORD MIN: (*aside*) She gives me the *frisson* — I must propose to stay, or I shall never get rid of her. — I am quite aguish tonight, — he — he — do, my dear, let us make a little fire here, and have a family *tête-à-tête*, by way of novelty. (*Rings a bell.*)
>   (*Enter* JESSAMY.)

LORD MIN: Let 'em take away that chimney-board, and light a fire here immediately.

LADY MIN: (*aside*) What shall I do? — Here, Jessamy, there is no occasion — I am going to my own chamber, and my lord won't stay here by himself.
>   (*Exit* JESSAMY.)

LORD MIN: How cruel it is, Lady Minikin, to deprive me of the pleasure of a domestic duetto. — (*aside*) A good escape, faith!

LADY MIN: I have too much regard for Lord Minikin to agree to anything that would afford him so little pleasure. I shall retire to my own apartments.

LORD MIN: Well, if your ladyship will be cruel, I must still, like the miser, starve and sigh, though possessed of the greatest treasure — (*Bows.*) I wish your ladyship a good night — (*He takes one candle, and* LADY MINIKIN *the other.*) May I presume — (*Salutes her.*)

LADY MIN: Your lordship is too obliging. — (*aside*) Nasty man!

LORD MIN: (*aside*) Disagreeable woman!

(*They wipe their lips, and exeunt ceremoniously.*)

MISS TITT: (*peeping out of the closet*) All's silent now, and quite dark. What has been doing here I cannot guess. I long to be relieved. I wish my lord was come — but I hear a noise! (*She shuts the door.*)

COL. TIVY: (*peeping over the chimney-board*) I wonder my lady does not come. — I would not have Miss Tittup know of this — 'twould be ten thousand pounds out of my way, and I can't afford to give so much for a little gallantry.

MISS TITT: (*Comes forward.*) What would my colonel say to find his bride, that is to be, in this critical situation?

(*Enter* LORD MINIKIN, *at one door in the dark.*)

LORD MIN: Now to relieve my prisoner. (*Comes forward.*)

(*Enter* LADY MINIKIN, *at the other door.*)

LADY MIN: My poor colonel will be as miserable as if he were besieged in garrison; I must release him (*going towards the chimney*).

LORD MIN: Hist — hist! —

MISS TITT, LADY MIN *and* COL. TIV: Here! here! —

LORD MIN: This way.

LADY MIN: Softly.

(*They all grope about till* LORD MINIKIN *has got* LADY MINIKIN, *and the* COLONEL, MISS TITTUP.)

SIR JOHN: (*Speaks without.*) Light this way, I say; I am sure there are thieves; get a blunderbuss.

JESS: Indeed you dreamed it; there is nobody but the family.

(*All stand and stare. Enter* SIR JOHN, *in his cap, and with hanger drawn, with* JESSAMY.)

SIR JOHN: Give me the candle; I'll ferret 'em out I warrant. Bring a blunderbuss, I say. They have been skipping about that gallery in the dark this half hour; there must be mischief. — I have watched 'em into this room — ho, ho, are you there? If you stir, you are dead men — (*They retire.*) — and (*seeing the ladies*) women too! — egad — ha! What's this? The same party again! and two couple they are of as choice mortals as ever were hatched in this righteous town. — You'll excuse me, cousins! (*They all look confounded.*)

LORD MIN: In the name of wonder, how comes all this about?

SIR JOHN: Well, but hark'ee my dear cousins, have you not got wrong partners? Here has been some mistake in the dark; I am mighty glad that I have brought you a candle, to set all to rights again — you'll excuse me, gentlemen and ladies!

(*Enter* GYMP, *with a candle.*)

GYMP: What, in the name of mercy, is the matter?

SIR JOHN: Why the old matter, and the old game, Mrs Gymp, and I'll match my cousins here at it, against all the world, and I say done first.

LORD MIN: What is the meaning, Sir John, of all this tumult and consternation? May not Lady Minikin and I, and the colonel and your niece, be seen in my house together without your raising the family, and making this uproar and confusion?

SIR JOHN: Come, come, good folks, I see you are all confounded. I'll settle this matter in a moment. — As for you, colonel — though you have not deserved plain dealing from me, I will now be serious. You imagine this young lady has an independent fortune, besides expectations from me. — 'Tis a mistake; she has no expectations from me. If she marry you, and I don't consent to her marriage, she will have no fortune at all.

COL. TIV: Plain dealing is a jewel, and to show you, Sir John, that I can pay you in kind, I am most sincerely obliged to you for your intelligence, and I am, ladies, your most obedient humble servant. I shall see you, my lord, at the club tomorrow? (*Exit* COLONEL TIVY.)

LORD MIN: *Sans doute, mon cher Colonel* — I'll meet you there without fail.

SIR JOHN: My lord, you'll have something else to do.

LORD MIN: Indeed! What is that, good Sir John?

SIR JOHN: You must meet your lawyers and creditors tomorrow, and be told, what you have always turned a deaf ear to, that the dissipation of your fortune and morals must be followed by years of parsimony and repentance. As you are fond of going abroad, you may indulge that inclination without having it in your power to indulge any other.

LORD MIN: (*aside*) The bumpkin is no fool, and is damned satirical.

SIR JOHN: This kind of quarantine for pestilential minds will bring you to your senses, and make you renounce foreign vices and follies, and return with joy to your country and property again. Read that, my lord, and know your fate. (*Gives a paper.*)

LORD MIN: What an abomination this is! That a man of fashion, and a nobleman, shall be obliged to submit to the laws of his country.

SIR JOHN: Thank heaven, my lord, we are in that country! — You are silent, ladies. If repentance has subdued your tongues, I shall have hopes of you — a little country air might perhaps do well. As you are distressed, I am at your service. What say you, my lady?

LADY MIN: However appearances have condemned me, give me leave to disavow the substance of those appearances. My mind has been tainted, but not profligate. Your kindness and example may restore me to my former natural English constitution.

SIR JOHN: Will you resign your lady to me, my lord, for a time?

LORD MIN: For ever, dear Sir John, without a murmur.

SIR JOHN: Well, miss, and what say you?

MISS TITT: Guilty, uncle (*curtsying*).

SIR JOHN: Guilty! The devil you are! Of what?

MISS TITT: Of consenting to marry one whom my heart could not approve, and coquetting with another, which friendship, duty, honour, morals, and every-thing but fashion, ought to have forbidden.

SIR JOHN: Thus then, with the wife of one under this arm, and the mistress of another, under this, I sally forth a Knight Errant, to rescue distressed damsels from those monsters, foreign vices and *Bon Ton*, as they call it; and I trust that every English hand and heart here, will assist me in so desperate an under-taking. — *You'll excuse me, sirs?*

7. Garrick reciting his Ode to Shakespeare, engraving by John Lodge. This was a re-enacting on the stage at Drury Lane, 1769, of a celebration in the Shakespeare Jubilee at Stratford upon Avon earlier in that year

THE DRAMATIC WORKS OF DAVID GARRICK

MAIN PLAYS

Lethe. Produced Drury Lane, 15 April 1740. One-act satire. Published 1749.

The Lying Valet. Produced Goodman's Fields, 30 November 1741. Two-act farce. Published 1742.

Miss in Her Teens. Produced Covent Garden, 17 January 1747. Two-act farce. Published 1747.

The Guardian. Produced Drury Lane, 3 February 1759. Two-act comedy. Published 1759.

The Clandestine Marriage (with Colman). Produced Drury Lane, 20 February 1766. Five-act comedy. Published 1766.

The Irish Widow. Produced Drury Lane, 23 October 1772. Two-act farce. Published 1772.

Bon Ton or *High Life Above Stairs.* Produced Drury Lane, 18 March 1775. Two-act comedy. Published 1775.

Dramatic Works of David Garrick. Published 1768, 1774 and 1798.

INTERLUDES, PANTOMIMES, MUSICALS AND SATIRES

Lilliput. Produced Drury Lane, 3 December 1756. Satire from *Gulliver.* Published 1757.

The Male Coquette. Produced Drury Lane, 24 March 1757. Two-act farce. Published 1757.

Harlequin's Invasion. Produced Drury Lane, 31 December 1759. Pantomime. Published in *Three Plays by David Garrick,* ed. Stein, New York 1926.

The Enchanter or *Love and Magic.* Produced Drury Lane, 13 December 1760. Musical entertainment. Published 1760.

The Farmer's Return from London. Produced Drury Lane, 20 March 1762. Interlude. Published 1762.

Neck or Nothing. Produced Drury Lane, 18 November 1766. Two-act farce. Published 1766.

Cymon. Produced Drury Lane, 2 January 1767. Five-act musical romance with spectacle. Published 1767.

Linco's Travels. Produced Drury Lane, 6 April 1767. Short interlude with music. Published in *Poetical Works of David Garrick,* 1785.

A Peep Behind the Curtain. Produced Drury Lane, 23 October 1767. Theatrical satire. Published 1767.

The Jubilee. Produced Drury Lane, 14 October 1769. Interlude. Published in *Three Plays by David Garrick,* ed. Stein, New York 1926.

A Christmas Tale. Produced Drury Lane, 27 December 1773. Musical entertainment. Published 1774.

The Meeting of the Company. Produced Drury Lane, 17 September 1774. Theatrical satire. Published in *Three Plays by David Garrick*, ed. Stein, New York 1926.

The Theatrical Candidates. Produced Drury Lane, 23 September 1775. Theatrical satire. Published with *May-Day* 1775.

May-Day or *The Little Gipsy*. Produced Drury Lane, 28 October 1775. One-act musical. Published with *The Theatrical Candidates*, 1775.

ALTERATIONS AND ADAPTATIONS

(Garrick revived Elizabethan plays long neglected or forgotten, restored Shakespeare's words to versions traditionally played with extensive alterations, but also wrote passages of his own and ruthlessly shortened originals to suit his audience.)

Romeo and Juliet (from Shakespeare) 1748.

Every Man in His Humour (from Jonson) 1751.

The Chances (from Fletcher) 1754.

Florizel and Perdita (from Shakespeare's *The Winter's Tale*) 1755.

Antony and Cleopatra (from Shakespeare) 1755.

The Fairies (musical from Shakespeare's *A Midsummer Night's Dream*) 1756.

The Fatal Marriage (from Southerne) 1757.

Cymbeline (from Shakespeare) 1763.

A Midsummer Night's Dream (from Shakespeare) with Colman 1763.

King Lear (from Shakespeare) 1764.

The Country Girl (from Wycherley's *The Country Wife*) 1766.

King Arthur (opera from Dryden) 1770.

Hamlet (from Shakespeare) 1772.

THE DRAMATIC WORKS OF
GEORGE COLMAN THE ELDER

MAIN PLAYS

Polly Honeycombe. Produced Drury Lane, 5 December 1760. One-act comedy. Published 1760.

The Jealous Wife. Produced Drury Lane, 12 February 1761. Five-act comedy. Published 1761.

The Musical Lady. Produced Drury Lane, 6 March 1762. Two-act comedy. Published 1762.

The Deuce is in Him. Produced Drury Lane, 4 November 1763. Two-act comedy. Published 1763.

The Clandestine Marriage (with Garrick). Produced Drury Lane, 20 February 1766. Published 1766.

The Oxonian in Town. Produced Covent Garden, 7 November 1767. Two-act comedy. Published 1770.

The Portrait. Produced Covent Garden, 22 November 1770. Burletta. Published 1770.

The Man of Business. Produced Covent Garden, 29 January 1774. Five-act comedy. Published 1774.

The Spleen or *Islington Spa.* Produced Drury Lane, 24 February 1776. Two-act comedy. Published 1776.

The Suicide. Produced Haymarket, 11 July 1778. Four-act comedy. Not published.

The Separate Maintenance. Produced Haymarket, 31 August 1779. Four-act comedy. Not published.

The Dramatic Works of George Colman (four vols) published 1777.

OCCASIONAL PIECES, PRELUDES AND PANTOMIMES

Man and Wife or *The Shakespeare Jubilee.* Produced Covent Garden, 9 October 1769. Three-act comedy with pantomime. Published 1770.

An Occasional Prelude. Produced Covent Garden, 21 September 1772. Published 1776.

New Brooms (with Garrick). Produced Drury Lane, 21 September 1776. Occasional prelude. Published 1776.

The Manager in Distress. Produced Haymarket, 30 May 1780. Prelude. Published 1780.

The Genius of Nonsense. Produced Haymarket, 2 September 1780. Satirical extravaganza. Published (songs only) 1781.

Harlequin Teague or *The Giant's Causeway* (with O'Keefe). Produced Haymarket, 17 August 1782. Published (songs only) 1782.

The Election of the Managers. Produced Haymarket, 2 June 1784. Prelude. Not published.

Ut Pictura Poesis or *The Enraged Musicians*. Produced Haymarket, 18 May 1789. Musical entertainment founded on Hogarth. Published 1789.

ADAPTATIONS, ALTERATIONS, TRANSLATIONS AND COLLECTED EDITIONS

Philaster (from Beaumont & Fletcher). Produced Drury Lane, 8 October 1763. Published 1763.

A Fairy Tale (from Shakespeare). Produced Drury Lane, 26 November 1763. Published 1763.

The Comedies of Terence translated into blank verse. Not for stage presentation. Published 1765.

The English Merchant (trans. and adapted from Voltaire). Produced Drury Lane, 21 February 1767. Published 1767.

The History of King Lear (from Shakespeare). Produced Covent Garden, 20 February 1768. Published 1768.

The Fairy Prince (from Jonson's *Oberon*). Produced Covent Garden, 12 February 1771

Comus (from Milton). Produced Covent Garden, 16 October 1772. Published 1772.

Achilles in Petticoats (from Gay's *Achilles*). Produced Covent Garden, 16 December 1773. Published 1774.

Epicoene or *The Silent Woman* (from Jonson). Produced Drury Lane, 13 January 1776. Published 1776.

Polly (from Gay). Produced Haymarket, 19 June 1777. Published 1777.

The Sheep Shearing (from Shakespeare's *Winter's Tale*). Produced Haymarket, 18 July 1777. Published 1777.

The Spanish Barber (from Beaumarchais). Produced Haymarket, 30 August 1777. Not published.

The Works of Beaumont and Fletcher (10 vols. with preface by Colman). Published 1778.

Bonduca (from Beaumont and Fletcher). Produced Haymarket, 30 July 1778. Published 1778.

English Plays by Samuel Foote (6 posthumous plays adapted by Colman, presented at the Haymarket, and published 1778).

The Beggar's Opera Reversed (from Gay, with sexes transposed). Produced Haymarket, 8 August 1781. Not published.

The Fatal Curiosity (from Lillo). Produced Haymarket, 29 August 1782. Published 1783.

Tit for Tat or *The Mutual Deception* (from Marivaux via Atkinson). Produced Haymarket, 29 August 1786. Published 1788.

BIBLIOGRAPHY

Burnim, Kalman A., *David Garrick, Director.* University of Pittsburgh, 1961

Davies, Thomas, *Memoirs of the Life of David Garrick, Esq.* London, 1780

Dunbar, Janet, *Peg Woffington and her World.* London: Heinemann, 1968

Fitzgerald, Percy, *Life of Catherine Clive.* London, 1888

Hampden, J. (ed.), *The Beggar's Opera and Other 18th-Century Plays.* London: Dent, 1928. (Contains *The Clandestine Marriage*)

Nash, Mary, *Life and Times of Susannah Cibber.* London: Hutchinson, 1977

Nettleton, G.H. and Case, A.E. (eds.), *British Dramatists from Dryden to Sheridan,* 1939, revised by G.W. Stone Jr, New York, 1969. (Contains *The Clandestine Marriage, The Jealous Wife* and *The Lying Valet*)

Nicoll, Allardyce, *The Garrick Stage.* Manchester University Press, 1980

Oman, Carola, *David Garrick.* London: Hodder & Stoughton, 1958

Page, Eugene R., *George Colman the Elder.* Columbia University Press, 1935

Peake, R.B. (ed.), *Memoirs of the Colman Family.* London, 1841

Pedicord, H.W., *The Theatrical Public in the Time of Garrick.* Southern Illinois University Press, 1966

Pedicord, H.W. and Bergmann, F.L. (eds.), *The Plays of David Garrick.* Southern Illinois University Press, 1979

Price, Cecil, *Theatre in the Age of Garrick.* Oxford: Basil Blackwell, 1973

Richards, Kenneth and Thomson, Peter (eds.), *The Eighteenth Century English Stage.* London: Methuen, 1972

Stein, Elizabeth, *David Garrick, Dramatist.* Modern Language Association of America, 1938

Stone, G.W. and Kahrl, G.M. (eds.), *The Letters of David Garrick* (3 vols.). Cambridge, Mass., 1963

Vaughan, A., *Born to Please. Hannah Pritchard, Actress.* London: Society for Theatre Research, 1979

Victor, Benjamin, *History of the Theatres of London and Dublin.* London, 1761